God:
The Ultimate Search Engine

Jen Ward

Copyright © 2019 Jen Ward and Jenuine Healing®

All rights reserved. No part of this book may be reproduced, stored in a retrieval system, or transmitted in any form by any means without written permission of the author.

ISBN-13: 978-0-9994954-8-3

ISBN-10: 0-9994954-8-8

Jen Ward

CONTENTS

	Introduction	1
1	Overcoming the Dark Ages	3
2	A Man-Made God	111
3	The Shift to the Fifth Dimension	137
4	Awakening	197
5	Free Yourself and Humanity	255
6	Source	317
7	Glossary of Terms	357
8	About the Author	361
9	Other Books by Jen Ward	363

Jen Ward

INTRODUCTION

Tapping into Your God-Self

The concept of God has to be universally upgraded from being a man in the clouds. This deference to a lofty old white man is reflected in our outmoded governing body of bloated, entitled, old white men.

How about thinking of God as the intangible part of yourself that you are only limited in knowing because of the limitations of your physical apparatus. God is the invisible aspect of yourself that knows all, sees all and experiences all.

Some people who call themselves empaths, or who tap into profound truths, have incredible compassion and are blurring the lines between their physical self and their own omniscience as spiritual beings. They get a sense of their own God-self calling to them beyond the veil of the physical realm.

Accepting yourself as a living, breathing aspect of God affords you great peripheral benefits. If you know yourself to be an expression of God, then it just makes sense that everyone else is an expression of God as well.

Instead of needing to flock to a building to kneel at the altar of God, know that you meet God a million times a day. You are in sacred communion every time you assist another being and make their sense of self feel more fulfilled. At first, it is done in grand gestures to stroke your own ego, but when you get to the point where you are consumed with loving God through empowering God in all forms, then you most likely will have a sense of your own empowerment.

The paradox in this understanding is that those who deem themselves the most devout are the ones who damage the God qualities in others the most. Besting others is a demonstrative act of the physicality of self but not necessary from the God side. Also, judgment and adherence to religious mandates crush the spirit in others. Many of the most sacred texts have been edited through the years by entitled men. They support and perpetuate an understanding of God that was forged in fear during the Dark Ages. These are the mandates that actually prevent people from knowing their God-self. There are embedded threats in any religion or spiritual group that prevent them from overstepping their boundaries by questioning the mandates laid out.

How long are humans going to keep falling for it? If the tenets of their faith of choice were so empowering, then we would see love, kindness and truth everywhere. There would be less of a drive to better others. What is the difference if the God in them or the God in you is empowered? God is God and we are all God stuff, so assisting others is a form of worship.

That is why it feels so good to help others. Helping others is us brushing up against our greatness. Besting others outside of friendly competition is going in the opposite direction. Needing to be the best is feeding the ego. The true self is the aspect of you that has been trampled on all sides yet is still compelled to love.

1. OVERCOMING THE DARK AGES

The Moment

The quivering line between horizon and ocean

The magnetic play between stillness and motion

The oil of the sweat of a labor of love

The knee-jerk relief when escaping a shove

Ten million moments conjoined in an hour

The disarming grace of a play without power

The biting cry of a fallen bird's call

Recovering your dignity after a fall

The rhythm created when writing a poem

The sanctity felt when journeying home.

The Alchemy of Our Lives

Kindness, resolve and a sense of peace are reflections of who we are as spiritual beings. Our work and home lives are the points of entry that showcase our spiritual state to all who know us. Converting the chaos that characterizes the physical realm into joy, love, abundance and freedom for all is the spiritual alchemy that is spinning straw into gold. How we use our gifts to uplift and enlighten others is where the rubber meets the road.

God's Awakening

The more empowered we realize that we are, the closer to God we are. The more we realize how our thoughts and feelings affect everyone, the closer we are to God. Because don't God's thoughts and feelings affect everyone? To feel unworthy and small is to be farther away from God because God is omnipotent and omnipresent.

We were told that we were unworthy by those who used God to control us. If they were superior to us, it was only in their belief that they were. It was not by the grace of God. But our hearts tell us that we are loved and worthy. Are we going to listen to the booming voice of man or the sweet caressing voice of God?

The more we stop fidgeting in our own minds with the faults of others, the more we awaken to God's love. The more we see God in everyone, the more God presents Itself to us. The more we pour love into every expression of life, the more we act as ambassadors of God. The more we refuse to separate ourselves from the omniscience of God's love, the more we immerse the world in the all-permeating love and grace of God's presence. By being loving and kind in the world, we are acting as the breath of God.

Your Contract with God

God never said you have to do this or that. Man said that and put that on God. Then we use God as a crutch to not be as empowered as we possibly can be. God has no intention to limit us, compartmentalize us, choose some over others or subjugate us. That is all done by man acting as a mouthpiece for God.

You don't need a mouthpiece for God. You have the capabilities to tune into God through your own communication system. What has interfered with that is listening for God with outer senses instead of the more intangible ones. This has left you feeling that God is understood and perhaps loved by others more than you. That is the lie.

It has been very difficult to convey to people who are hell-bent stubborn, how easy it is to connect to God. It is too simple for them. They choose to believe the hype and give up their empowerment to anyone who says that they know God. The lesson was never to follow these people blindly.

The lesson was, and always has been, to gain your own understanding and relationship with the divine from the resources strewn about your own life. These include gratitude, simple kindness, listening to the inner promptings of your own spirit and having the courage to act upon them to initiate great understanding.

I would not even be writing this if it were not for the consistent practicing of those things, beyond all reason or common sense. Who wants to be common?

Alpha and Omega

God wants what you want--the higher good for all. You are the eyes and ears and heart of God in this world as much as you allow yourself to be. God does not want you to cower in a corner of yourself and give It credit for all that you are. God wants you to claim the empowerment to know that you work hand and heart to create Its presence here and everywhere.

It wants everyone to know that we are not separate from It. That is part of the insanity. We are atoms of God and every atom of our beingness is an atom of God. That is what is meant by the alpha and omega. It is man who has separated us from the source of all. God is our essence and that essence is love.

Be Where Alpha and Omega Meet

I facilitated a private, remote session for a dynamic healer. We have done extensive work together and her sessions have been a means of discovering powerful taps to share with everyone. Before her session, I was tuning into her energy and it went to particles smaller than molecules.

It showed how, even though we released all her issues on a cellular level, the particles of her cells were still in chaos from issues. The taps I gave her were to extract all the issues from every particle of her beingness. But even deeper than that, it seemed that on a metaphysical level, we were dipping into the depth of the microcosm to connect with the macrocosm in a surreal way and cleansing the macrocosm of all through her microcosm.

It felt like we had found the place that the alpha and omega connect and were cleansing that with our work. It felt like Jesus's statement, "I am the alpha and the omega." I had a realization then that it only took one soul to cleanse all of humanity. In a male dominated world, it would only be done through a man's own awareness. But in a female-centric world, a female would uplift humanity by empowering or unleashing the alpha and omega in all others. That is what these taps do.

(Say each statement three times out loud while tapping on the top of your head at the crown chakra and say it a fourth time while tapping on your chest.)

"I extract all hate from all the miniscule particles of my beingness; in all moments."

"I recalibrate all the miniscule particles of my beingness to divine love; in all moments."

"I extract all sadness and depression from all the miniscule particles of my beingness; in all moments."

"I recalibrate all the miniscule particles of my beingness to Joy; in all moments."

"I extract all poverty and lack from all the miniscule particles of my beingness; in all moments."

"I recalibrate all the miniscule particles of my beingness to divine infinite abundance; in all moments."

"I extract all slavery and imprisonment from all the miniscule particles of my beingness; in all moments."

"I recalibrate all the miniscule particles of my beingness to the ultimate freedom; in all moments."

"I extract all pain from all the miniscule particles of my beingness; in all moments."

"I extract all suffering and disease from all the miniscule particles of my beingness; in all moments."

"I recalibrate all the miniscule particles of my beingness to optimal health; in all moments."

"I extract all failure from all the miniscule particles of my beingness; in all moments."

"I recalibrate all the miniscule particles of my beingness to ultimate success; in all moments."

"I extract all insecurity from all the miniscule particles of my beingness; in all moments."

"I recalibrate all the miniscule particles of my beingness to empowerment; in all moments."

"I extract all rejection, abandonment and isolation from all the miniscule particles of my beingness; in all moments."

"I recalibrate all the miniscule particles of my beingness to exponential interconnectedness; in all moments."

"I extract all of hell from all the miniscule particles of my beingness; in all moments."

"I recalibrate all the miniscule particles of my beingness to nirvana; in all moments."

"I extract all of the concept of God from all the miniscule particles of my beingness; in all moments."

"I recalibrate all the miniscule particles of my beingness to the light and sound of awakening; in all moments."

"I extract all conformity from all the miniscule particles of my beingness; in all moments."

"I recalibrate all the miniscule particles of my beingness to unabashed creativity; in all moments."

"I extract all war and violence from all the miniscule particles of my beingness; in all moments."

"I recalibrate all the miniscule particles of my beingness to unequivocal peace; in all moments."

"I extract all death and decay from all the miniscule particles of my beingness; in all moments."

"I recalibrate all the miniscule particles of my beingness to everlasting life; in all moments."

"I extract all fractures and fragmentation from all the miniscule particles of my beingness; in all moments."

"I recalibrate all the miniscule particles of my beingness to wholeness; in all moments."

"I extract all ugliness from all the miniscule particles of my beingness; in all moments."

"I recalibrate all the miniscule particles of my beingness to breathtaking beauty; in all moments."

"I extract all apathy from all the miniscule particles of my beingness; in all moments."

"I recalibrate all the miniscule particles of my beingness to exuberant enthusiasm; in all moments."

"I extract all chaos and discontent from all the miniscule particles of my beingness; in all moments."

"I recalibrate all the miniscule particles of my beingness to contentment; in all moments."

"I extract all floundering and doubt from all the miniscule particles of my beingness; in all moments."

"I recalibrate all the miniscule particles of my beingness to spirituality; in all moments."

"I recalibrate all the miniscule particles of my beingness to spiritual family; in all moments."

"I extract all ignorance from all the miniscule particles of my beingness; in all moments"

"I recalibrate all the miniscule particles of my beingness to intellect; in all moments."

"I extract all programming and conditioning from all the miniscule particles of my beingness; in all moments."

"I recalibrate all the miniscule particles of my beingness to the ability to discern; in all moments."

"I extract all karmic conditioning from all the miniscule particles of my beingness; in all moments."

"I recalibrate all the miniscule particles of my beingness to spiritual enlightenment and freedom; in all moments."

Stop Carrying the Weight of the World on Your Shoulders

(Say each statement three times out loud while continuously tapping on the top of your head at the crown chakra and say it a fourth time while tapping on your chest.)

"I release carrying the weight of the world on my shoulders; in all moments."

"I release the belief I do it alone; in all moments."

"I remove all engrams of being worked to exhaustion; in all moments."

"I release reliving primal memories of being worked to exhaustion; in all moments."

"I release reliving primal memories of being martyred; in all moments."

"I release continuing to martyr myself; in all moments."

"I release trying to micromanage the Universe; in all moments."

"I release basing my self-worth on the ability to do it all; in all moments."

"I release confusing being overwhelmed with unworthiness; in all moments."

"I release the belief that I let God down; in all moments."

"I release myself from the cycle of benevolence and resentment; in all moments."

"I release judging others as incompetent; in all moments."

"I release hating those that I love; in all moments."

"I release being trapped in schisms of confusion; in all moments."

"I shift my paradigm to surrender and acceptance; in all moments."

"I replenish my weary essence in surrender and acceptance; in all moments."

"I am centered and empowered in surrender and acceptance; in all moments."

The Spiritual Law of Love

There are spiritual laws that run the Universe. They are as exacting as the law of gravity. Gravity doesn't just work sometimes. It works all the time. The law of attraction is a real spiritual law--not just for gaining things--but it is exacting as gravity in attracting our reality to us.

There are other spiritual laws as well. The law of reversed efforts says that the harder you try, the more difficult things will be because of the law of reversed efforts. You see this one play out in achieving goals and in dating when someone tries too hard and it is a turn off.

The law of unity says that two parts added together in agreement make up more than the sum of their parts. One plus one doesn't equal two; it equals something exponential. A recipe is a great example of this. An egg, milk, flour and sugar become something greater when you mix them together. They become cake.

The law of karma is about energy flow. Everything is made of energy. The law of karma simply balances energies. It is people who put the attribute of revenge on it. It is not like that at all.

There is a belief--a fear if you will--that people shouldn't heal others because they will take on their karma. This is what I have been chided with by so many "aware" people. And yet I have the awareness to help people.

So what I have been brought to realize is that the law of karma or the balancing of energy only happens if the two things are at the same vantage point--meaning that the law of love is at a different vantage point than the other spiritual laws. It is almost like love, pure love, raises one's vantage point above reproach of the other spiritual laws. I do not take on the issues of anyone that I work with because I don't put myself at their vantage point.

There are conscious ways I do this. I stay detached, never getting emotional about their issues. I stay alert to always keeping my personal realm out of the dynamics by never talking about myself or sharing personal information. I never need, want or ask anything emotionally from the client. The exchange is one-sided. That is why payment is so important, to maintain this professional distance yet have a fair energetic exchange between the two. This is a way to prevent a karmic backwash from giving more than what is received. If I "felt" invalidated, it would be a form of coming out of the law of love, in this case self-love.

I stay in the law of love by never seeking outside advice or wavering from truth. This is about tuning in with such a depth of understanding that no one can tell me otherwise. That is unless I am instructed from within to listen to them and regard their input. Truth can come through another, but usually not through facts and definitely not through opinion.

These are parts of the disciplines that I have acquired to stay in the law of love. They started out in life as defenses and may seem like defensiveness to those looking with exterior eyes. But they are a deep, consistent practice of tuning in and transcending the other spiritual laws through the law of love as much as possible.

Fear, doubt, worry, disease and even dread want to be Love too. They just need the compassion to get there. The trick for love is to assist without being pulled down to their level by sympathy and manipulation.

How to Enter the Pure Chambers of God

Every time I use the bathroom, the two kittens come in and want to play. One day, I took a tiny square of tissue and rolled it up into a ball right in front of them. They were mesmerized that I could do this. To them it was the alchemy of all times. I could feel their adulation and respect. That isn't easy to gain from the cat species.

Every single time I use the bathroom, the boy kitten will come in and wait for me to throw him a ball or two. I will say, "Are you ready?" Then he will blink or get more focused. He will catch so many of them between his paws that it is impressive. I awaken in the middle of the night and see him sitting at the open doorway half asleep too, but he is there ready to catch. The game is his joy.

To onlookers it could look like a ridiculous indulgence. I have all these wads of little tissues collecting in my living room. It makes the room look messy perhaps. But every time he is sitting there waiting for me, I am reminded about when something is important to me. I feel that joy he has for the game and it would bring me pain not to play it with him.

Sure he would be fine if we didn't play. He would entertain himself in another way. It is I who am honored to have this very real connection with him. He is allowing me into his world as much as it may look to others that I am indulging him.

This is what compassion looks and feels like: To truly care for someone's happiness and quality of life as well as your own. I honor all beings in playing catch with my boy. I challenge the systemic, concrete belief in human superiority that is choking humanity. That is why society demonizes the tree hugger, the cat lady, and all those who care about the oceans and planet. We are not paying homage to human superiority.

No, we are not weak and pathetic and we are not such a minority. We honor the sacredness of all beings. To me, this is much more noble than stroking the ego of a needy God. Love and truth are really the only things that one can bring to the altar of Source. Demonstrative displays of reverence are hypocritical if they diminish any of God's creatures in any way.

Compassion, in a sense, is teleporting into the other person's vantage point and feeling and experiencing exactly what they are, as they are.

Honoring the other being as a valued member of the house of God is the purest form of worship. Nothing but this carries the true nectar of kindness. Love will make it past the vestibule of the mind and empty reason into the pure chambers of God.

Releasing Deep-Seated Unworthiness

In many of my clients, there is one cause or another for deep-seated unworthiness. It doesn't just start in gym class by not getting picked at kickball. The issues are triggered when we are not included, teased or overlooked. It is much deeper in some than in others. That is why one person can laugh off a comment where another one feels excruciating offense. People have come by their reactions honestly.

Different cultures have different ways of subjugating their people. Some of them come up in my private sessions. Following is a list of taps that may undo some of the ingrained unworthiness of past times.

(Say each statement three times while tapping on your head and say it a fourth time while tapping on your chest.)

"I release being an untouchable; in all moments."

"I release being damned; in all moments."

"I release being enslaved; in all moments."

"I release being tortured; in all moments."

"I release the belief that I am a sinner; in all moments."

"I release the trauma of being sacrificed; in all moments."

"I release having my feet bound; in all moments."

"I release letting my people down; in all moments."

"I release being ostracized; in all moments."

"I release being an abomination; in all moments."

"I release being left for dead; in all moments."

"I release the belief that I am unholy; in all moments."

"I release the belief that God hates me; in all moments."

"I release the belief that I let God down; in all moments."

"I release the belief that I am unworthy; in all moments."

"I shift my paradigm for unworthiness to Joy, Love, Abundance, Freedom, Life and Wholeness; in all moments."

In doing all the taps, get a sense of which ones are harder to do and which ones bring up more emotion. Use that as a clue to discovering the initial causes to some things that affect the present day. Doing so can help you achieve more of a sense of freedom.

Divine Providence

The world thrives on the kindness that we all are able to exude. When we speak about what a horrible place this is, we make it a self-fulfilling prophecy. It just became a little less nice to that person you just mentioned that to. Since man has killed off so many inhabitants that exude goodness, it is up to us who are aware to take up the slack and consciously pour love, gratitude and positive vibes back into the ground.

People think I am unrealistic. I am very realistic. People who disconnect from their responsibility to give back to earth are like middle management, meaning they see half of the picture and believe they are privy to the whole scope. Half of the picture is seeing what can be taken. The higher visionaries understand that what needs to be taken, needs to be replenished, and more, to sustain balance.

Believe it or not, there are some people who are happy to run this world to the ground. They believe that by the time it is depleted, we will have discovered another planet to conquer or a way to sustain ourselves in a toxic world. This is the belief system that we interrupt with our kind intentions in the world. It doesn't matter how warm and fuzzy they make their fracking commercials and how they sidestep the word fracking. This is the intention that they have. Pay attention to what you are watching. The more heartfelt the commercial, the more poison or destruction they are trying to feed you. Love is endless but it isn't perpetuated by eating food that is laden with toxins and carcinogens.

It is our responsibility to put kindness back into the world. It is a sort of enzyme or a vitamin to life to do so. It may not be taught anymore, so some may have to dig deep to do this. For some, it may mean simply turning off the negative streams of the news and commercials in their life or to stop using gossip, complaints and health issues as topics of conversation. Another thing someone can do is to keep asking themselves as they go about their day, "Am I taking right now or am I giving?"

We have been trained to be takers and depend on establishments to give to us. This has made us weak and dependent as a society. The way to counter this is to change the energetic flow of this dynamic. We do so by giving in every possible situation. It can range from just being kind, saying something uplifting, allowing someone else to go first, checking in on a neighbor or doing something totally out of your comfort zone.

The more you give, the more giving will feel empowering not only for you but for others. I never realized I was a healer. I just started out listening to people on the phone because they had no one else to talk to. I went to massage therapy school and realized that I could move energy with my loving intention. I combined the two and now I help people release devastating issues that they have not been able to relieve anywhere else. I went from having no self-esteem to helping others by sharing whatever experience I can. It was done simply with divine providence and my desperate desire to contribute.

Most people don't realize how dynamic and empowered they are. Most people are just starting to wake up and look around as if awakening from a deep, fitful slumber--perhaps a nightmare. But now is the time to wipe the sand from our eyes, shake off the sleep and awaken to the dynamic potential that we are. We are the best of the best of us. We have examples of what one determined person can do. We have evidence of what one determined group can do. It's time to roll up our sleeves, unlatch our hearts, retrain our minds, shatter all glass ceilings and shake each other into action.

Plant a tree, grow a garden, feed the starving, take in a stray, invent a better way of doing things, become self-sustaining, take others into consideration, show up positive, let a stranger go first, interrupt the gossip, take the higher ground, question authority, ask why, ask why not, dream big, let things go, see the other point of view, forgo grandstanding, forgo taking sides, see the good in all, draw it out, take up a hobby, live your dream, live your purpose and encourage others to live theirs.

Be the Leader, Teacher, Helper, Healer, and Lover of life that you are slated to be. We are the co-facilitators and saviors to our own fate. Use this moment as a turning point to shift into the new paradigm. See each other the way that I see you: Joyful, Loving, Abundant, Healthy, Whole and Free! Most of all, see us all Empowered.

Releasing All Ignoble Intentions

Here are powerful taps. They are releasing all ignoble intentions. ISIL, dictators and all power plays are all ignoble intentions. Do these taps to do some good for humanity.

(Say each statement three times out loud while tapping on the top of your head at the crown chakra and say it a fourth time while tapping on your chest at the heart chakra. Say each word deliberately.)

"I declare myself a surrogate for humanity in doing these taps; in all moments."

"I access the macrocosm through my microcosm; in all moments."

"I dip into my own well of enlightenment; in all moments."

"I release bowing out of the fabric of life; in all moments."

"I release being the dropped stitch in the fabric of life; in all moments."

"I remove all vivaxes between myself and being the dropped stitch; in all moments."

"I remove all tentacles between myself and being the dropped stitch; in all moments."

"I release dropping the stitch by compartmentalizing myself; in all moments."

"I remove all engrams that being the dropped stitch has put on me; in all moments."

"I remove all programming and conditioning that being the dropped stitch has put on me, in all moments."

"I pull out the stitching of all my ignoble intentions, in all moments."

"I send all energy matrices into the light and sound that immerse me in ignoble intention; in all moments."

"I send all energy matrices into the light and sound that cause me to drive ignoble intentions; in all moments."

"I remove all vivaxes between myself and all ignoble intentions; in all moments."

"I remove all tentacles between myself and all ignoble intentions; in all moments."

"I remove all engrams that all ignoble intentions have put on me; in all moments."

"I remove all programming and conditioning that all ignoble intentions have put on me; in all moments."

"I release being the driving force behind all ignoble intentions; in all moments."

"I release allowing my love to be converted to fear to fuel ignoble intentions; in all moments."

"I recant all vows and agreements between myself and all ignoble intentions; in all moments."

"I remove all curses between myself and all ignoble intentions; in all moments."

"I remove all blessings between myself and all ignoble intentions; in all moments."

"I send all energy matrices into the light and sound that support ignoble intentions; in all moments."

"I sever all strings, cords and wires between myself and all ignoble intentions; in all moments."

"I dissolve all karmic ties between myself and all ignoble intentions; in all moments."

"I remove all the pain, burden and limitations that all ignoble intentions have put on me; in all moments."

"I remove all the pain, burden and limitations that all ignoble intentions have caused me to put on others; in all moments."

"I remove all the suffering and illusion of separateness that all ignoble intentions have put on me; in all moments."

"I remove all the suffering and illusion of separateness that all ignoble intentions have caused me to put on others; in all moments."

"I take back all the good that all ignoble intentions have taken from me; in all moments."

"I give back to all others all the good that all ignoble intentions have caused me to take from them; in all moments."

"I release resonating with any or all ignoble intentions; in all moments."

"I release emanating with any or all ignoble intentions; in all moments."

"I extract all ignoble intentions from my sound frequency and the universal sound frequency; in all moments."

"I extract all ignoble intentions from my light emanation and the universal light emanation; in all moments."

"I shift my paradigm from all ignoble intentions to universal goodwill; in all moments."

"I shift the world's paradigm from all ignoble intentions to goodwill for all; in all moments."

"I transcend all ignoble intentions; in all moments."

"I empower the world to universally transcend all ignoble intentions; in all moments."

"I and the world are centered and empowered in divine love; in all moments."

"I and the world take our rightful place in the universal tapestry; in all moments."

God Or a Prop?

In past times, life was brutal. People did not have much to hold onto. They clung to a concept of God that was similar to them, so they could endure their life and hope for a better hereafter where they would indulge in preferential treatment. That is why they personified such a petty God that needed stroking, obedience and worship. The world is much more savvy now.

We no longer need such limiting tactics to cling to. We are now more able to expand our stretch of imagination to realize a God that is so advanced beyond our petty squabbles that it is not necessary to name It, identity with It or even worship It. We simply advance towards being closer to It by loving all in our path. Love is the single commonality we have with God that we can all improve upon.

Anything that attempts to stroke the ego of God simply diminishes It to the limitations of man. You can tell who is actually closer to God by their ability and capacity to love. It has nothing to do with culture, breeding, finances or heritage. It has everything to do with love.

Natural State...

Dynamic and amazing souls, striving and having their experiences, swimming in a perpetual state of love...

But that is not what I see in all souls, just as you would not see a beautiful ocean dwelling creature taking in the microscopic food.

That is all daily issues are--plankton for the soul allowing it to thrive. They have little need for attention in the ultimate expression of swimming in love. Please don't allow them to be a distraction from your own beautiful continuation. They are part of the environment. Think of them as insignificant components of the scenery that add their own charm to the backdrop of life.

By seeing them as small and insignificant, you assign little value to them mentally. You make them small. You have always done the assigning. Even in your feelings of unworthiness and invalidation, you were the one that allotted the value. In this way, you are empowered. You have always been empowered.

Game Changing Marathon

Release calling up issues out of habit. (Say each statement three times while continuously tapping on your head and say it a fourth time while tapping on your chest.)

"I declare myself a surrogate for humanity in doing these taps; in all moments."

"I deactivate the muscle memory of trauma; in all moments."

"I deactivate the muscle memory of anguish; in all moments."

"I deactivate the muscle memory of sadness; in all moments."

"I deactivate the muscle memory of depression; in all moments."

"I deactivate the muscle memory of loss; in all moments."

"I deactivate the muscle memory of fear; in all moments."

"I deactivate the muscle memory of hate; in all moments."

"I deactivate the muscle memory of pain; in all moments."

"I deactivate the muscle memory of lack; in all moments."

"I deactivate the muscle memory of need; in all moments."

"I deactivate the muscle memory of want; in all moments."

"I deactivate the muscle memory of poverty; in all moments."

"I deactivate the muscle memory of imprisonment; in all moments."

"I deactivate the muscle memory of slavery; in all moments."

"I deactivate the muscle memory of dis-ease; in all moments."

"I deactivate the muscle memory of sickness; in all moments."

"I deactivate the muscle memory of failure; in all moments."

"I deactivate the muscle memory of being violated; in all moments."

"I deactivate the muscle memory of being rejected; in all moments."

"I deactivate the muscle memory of being abandoned; in all moments."

"I deactivate the muscle memory of being isolated; in all moments."

"I deactivate the muscle memory of being attacked; in all moments."

"I deactivate the muscle memory of being apathetic; in all moments."

"I deactivate the muscle memory of being indifferent; in all moments."

"I deactivate the muscle memory of being numb; in all moments."

"I deactivate the muscle memory of being raped; in all moments."

"I deactivate the muscle memory of being paralyzed; in all moments."

"I deactivate the muscle memory of fighting; in all moments."

"I deactivate the muscle memory of being defensive; in all moments."

"I deactivate the muscle memory of being killed; in all moments."

"I deactivate the muscle memory of being in hell; in all moments."

"I deactivate the muscle memory of being destroyed; in all moments."

"I deactivate the muscle memory of being in-firmed; in all moments."

"I deactivate the muscle memory of being an asshole; in all moments."

"I deactivate the muscle memory of being ugly; in all moments."

"I deactivate the muscle memory of being deformed; in all moments."

"I deactivate the muscle memory of being mutilated; in all moments."

"I deactivate the muscle memory of being retarded; in all moments."

"I deactivate the muscle memory of being tortured; in all moments."

"I deactivate the muscle memory of being an abomination; in all moments."

"I deactivate the muscle memory of being an untouchable; in all moments."

"I deactivate the muscle memory of being discouraged; in all moments."

"I deactivate the muscle memory of being unworthy; in all memories."

"I deactivate the muscle memory of being subservient; in all moments."

"I deactivate the muscle memory of being angry; in all moments."

"I deactivate the muscle memory of suffering; in all moments."

"I deactivate the muscle memory of conformity; in all moments."

"I deactivate the muscle memory of being a heathen; in all moments."

"I deactivate the muscle memory of being a sinner; in all moments."

"I deactivate the muscle memory of being ignorant; in all moments."

"I deactivate the muscle memory of being insecure; in all moments."

"I deactivate the muscle memory of being lonely; in all moments."

"I deactivate the muscle memory of feeling lost; in all moments."

"I deactivate the muscle memory of being arrogant; in all moments."

"I deactivate the muscle memory of feeling hopeless; in all moments."

"I deactivate the muscle memory of being helpless; in all moments."

"I deactivate the muscle memory of all programming and conditioning; in all moments."

"I am centered and empowered in exponential joy, love, abundance, and freedom; in all moments."

"I resonate, emanate, and am interconnected with all life in exponential joy, love, abundance, and freedom; in all moments."

"I deactivate the muscle memory of the limitations of being human; in all moments."

Activating Your Muscle Memory

After Peyton Manning's injury--that was a possible end to his career--he was training with a beloved, longtime coach he respected. He had been out of commission for a while and the speculation was that his career was over. But the coach was very wise. What he said is the seed for this powerful exercise.

He told Peyton that no one was going to be able to tell him how to get to the top of his game again but him. He held the blueprint of how to be the greatest quarterback in his muscle memory. The coach pushed him to throw the ball repeatedly. He told him by going through the motions, he would activate the muscle memory of how to be great again. Peyton went on to win another super bowl ring.

You hold the muscle memory of being happy, loved, healthy, nurtured, safe, etc. Here is an exercise to activate the achievement of your highest potential. Do these taps and then go about your life. As with Peyton learning to throw again, you need to move to activate the muscle memory. Try picking up old hobbies, reactivating passions you left by the wayside, digging into the earth and life, and being present as much as possible with your surroundings and the people you love. Your highest success lies in the awakening of your own presence in each moment. Yes, it is that simple.

(Say each statement three times while tapping on your head and say it a fourth time while tapping on your chest.)

"I release micromanaging the universe; in all moments."

"I declare myself a surrogate for humanity in doing these taps; in all moments."

"I activate the muscle memory of my greatest joy; in all moments."

"I activate the muscle memory of being in love; in all moments."

"I activate the muscle memory of being abundant; in all moments."

"I activate the muscle memory of being free; in all moments."

"I activate the muscle memory of being healthy; in all moments."

"I activate the muscle memory of being young; in all moments."

"I activate the muscle memory of being successful; in all moments."

"I activate the muscle memory of being safe; in all moments."

"I activate the muscle memory of knowing companionship; in all moments."

"I activate the muscle memory of being connected; in all moments."

"I activate the muscle memory of being nurtured; in all moments."

"I activate the muscle memory of being creative; in all moments."

"I activate the muscle memory of being at peace; in all moments."

"I activate the muscle memory of surging with life; in all moments."

"I activate the muscle memory of being adventurous; in all moments."

"I activate the muscle memory of being fearless; in all moments."

"I activate the muscle memory of being complete; in all moments."

"I activate the muscle memory of being beautiful; in all moments."

"I activate the muscle memory of being enlightened; in all moments."

"I activate the muscle memory of being empowered; in all moments."

"I activate the muscle memory of achieving my highest potential; in all moments."

"I am centered, empowered, and immersed in the fluidity of life; in all moments."

More Powerful Taps

(Say each statement three times out loud while continuously tapping on the top of your head at the crown chakra and say it a fourth time while tapping on your chest at the heart chakra.)

"I declare myself a surrogate for the world in doing these taps; in all moments."

"I release being energetically raped; in all moments."

"I release burning out of control; in all moments."

"I release being stripped of all resources; in all moments."

"I release being devoid of love; in all moments."

"I release struggling to maintain my balance; in all moments."

"I release letting all my inhabitants down; in all moments."

"I release being poisoned; in all moments."

"I release being plagued by power and dis-ease; in all moments."

"I release breaking out in rashes of war; in all moments."

"I release being drained of my life force; in all moments."

"I release being humiliated and abused; in all moments."

"I release being a scapegoat; in all moments."

"I release allowing my energy to be pissed away; in all moments."

"I take back all the energy that has been taken from me; in all moments."

"I repair all the layers of my auric field; in all moments."

"I release being enslaved; in all moments."

"I remove all curses and blessings that have been put on me; in all moments."

"I recant all vows and agreements between myself and being diminished; in all moments."

"I remove all vivaxes between myself and being diminished; in all moments."

"I remove all tentacles between myself and being diminished; in all moments."

"I remove the claws of control from my beingness; in all

moments."

"I send all energy matrices into the light that diminish me; in all moments."

"I sever all strings and cords between myself and being diminished; in all moments."

"I align all my bodies; in all moments."

"I dissolve all karmic ties between myself and being diminished; in all moments."

"I withdraw all my energy from being diminished; in all moments."

"I remove all the pain, burden, limitations, and illusion of separateness that being diminished has put on me; in all moments."

"I transcend being diminished; in all moments."

"I extract all of being diminished from both my sound frequency and light emanation; in all moments."

"I infuse joy, love, abundance into both my sound frequency and light emanation; in all moments."

"I infuse freedom, peace, and wholeness into my sound frequency and light emanation; in all moments."

"I strip all illusion off of being diminished; in all moments."

"I remove all masks, walls, and armor from all those who diminish; in all moments."

"I put out all fires with divine love; in all moments."

"I drench myself with divine love; in all moments."

"I am centered, empowered, and saturated in divine love; in all moments."

"I hold my stance in divine love; in all moments."

"I repair and fortify my wei chi; in all moments."

"I release hiding my empowerment; in all moments."

"I perpetuate my empowerment; in all moments."

"I maintain the charge of empowerment and divine love through my beingness; in all moments."

Eradicating War

We are enjoying a ceasefire. I would like to think it is more than a time for Israel to reload supplies that we are giving them. So much of the hardware that kills has been initiated by the United States. But so many are uncomfortable speaking about war because it sets a target site on them. I don't want to be a target but since I feel so much of the conflict in the world within my own body, I feel compelled to try and resolve it.

It is a great opportunity for the world to see war from a distant vantage point. If people stay detached, they will see both sides are good people and innocence everywhere is suffering. People who get mad at this statement are being drawn into war. It really is as simple as seeing the good in people. If individuals don't fuel the conflict, it will naturally dry up like a limited supply of arsenals. Opinions, passion, finger pointing, great intellectual debate, actually generate the interest and support that fuel the conflict. That is why representatives of both are on news channels now.

We could all study up, take sides, argue points, and use our wits and talents to make one side right and one side wrong. Some people reading this right now want to let me have it for my naive approach. But has it been tried? To withdraw all support for either side being vindicated and to pour love, healing, and peaceful intentions into the whole region.

I am fortunate enough to *not* know the details. I chose not to know. Yes, both sides want their position known and are rallying support for their side on the news shows. To me, this is similar to two fighting children wanting to tell mom what the other did. Mom, in her infinite wisdom, takes no side and loves both children equally. She knows there are issues, but trusts that there is enough love to work things out. Why can't we do the same?

Please don't try to educate me on the merits of either side. I will just see that as a justification for killing. With all our evolution of knowledge, to still be destroying what others hold sacred, destroys an aspect of ourselves. We are all connected. When a child on the other side of the world loses their teddy bear, it matters to me. When terror is inflicted on others, it affects us all. When mass murder over ideas is still sanctioned as a solution, we all show up as barbarians. Nothing is worth taking life. No God worthy of being worshiped condones murder.

(Say each statement three times out loud while tapping on your head. Say it a fourth time while tapping on your chest.)

"I declare myself a surrogate for the macrocosm; in all moments."

"We release condoning war; in all moments."

"We release supplying energy to war; in all moments."

"We withdraw all our energy from war; in all moments."

"We release killing innocence; in all moments."

"We release choosing power over love; in all moments."

"We release defining God in petty terms; in all moments."

"We release choosing ideals over people; in all moments."

"We release the arrogance of man; in all moments."

"We think for ourselves; in all moments."

"We release being victims of war; in all moments."

"We release being an advocate of war; in all moments."

"We release the belief that God is vindictive; in all moments."

"We release enjoying the excitement of war; in all moments."

"We release being bored with peace; in all moments."

"We release having a disregard for the reverence of life; in all moments."

"We recant all vows and agreements between ourselves and war; in all moments."

"We remove all curses between ourselves and war; in all moments."

"We dissolve all karmic ties between ourselves and war; in all moments."

"We remove all the pain, burden, limitations and engrams that war has put on us; in all moments."

"We remove all the pain, burden, limitations and engrams that we have put on everyone due to war; in all moments."

"We take back all the Joy, Love, Abundance, Freedom, Health, Success, Security, Companionship, Peace, Life, Wholeness, Beauty, Enthusiasm, Confidence, Spirituality and Enlightenment that war has taken from us; in all moments."

"We give back all the Joy, Love, Abundance, Freedom, Health, Success, Security, Companionship, Peace, Life, Wholeness, Beauty, Enthusiasm, Confidence, Spirituality and Enlightenment that war has taken from everyone; in all moments."

"We release resonating with war; in all moments."

"We release emanating with war; in all moments."

"We remove all war from our sound frequency; in all moments."

"We remove all war from our light body; in all moments."

"We shift our paradigm from war to Joy, Love, Abundance, Freedom, Health, Success, Security, Companionship, Peace, Life, Wholeness, Beauty, Enthusiasm, Confidence, Spirituality and Enlightenment; in all moments."

"We eradicate war as an option and a concept; in all moments."

"We transcend war; in all moments."

"We are centered and empowered in divine love for everyone; in all moments."

We all feel so helpless. But what if it was the *exact opposite*? What if just one of us could harness an intention so loving that it could end world fighting? What if just one of us could draw in such a surging, vast amount of divine love that--like a tidal wave--it could singe out all the embers of war? What if we have been enslaving ourselves to a complacency that is an illusion? What if we are all the proverbial elephant that has not yet realized that the chain that holds him tied to the post is his belief and not the actual chain?

Some believe that peace will never happen on earth. They believe this is a warring world and have accepted that. I have been taught to challenge every belief, no matter the source. Truth itself is always evolving. In challenging everything that we have been told, we continue to evolve ourselves.

Saving the World Saviors

What if you could go back in time and space and heal the pain of those who died for the advancement of humanity? That is exactly the intention of this exercise. Please feel the love and gratitude of those you have turned to for comfort in your time of need. This is a powerful act of kindness and a way to say thank you to your favorite world savior.

(Say each statement three times while tapping on your head and say it again a fourth time while tapping on your chest.)

"We declare ourselves surrogates for all true world saviors in doing these taps; in all moments."

"We pierce illusion in doing these taps; in all moments."

"We raise consciousness in doing these taps; in all moments."

"We release being demonized for sharing truth; in all moments."

"We release being tortured for sharing truth; in all moments."

"We release being killed for sharing truth; in all moments."

"We release being desecrated; in all moments."

"We free chickens everywhere; in all moments."

"We release being raped of our truth; in all moments."

"We release being used to propagate power; in all moments."

"We release being used to propagate slavery; in all moments."

"We release being used to mutilate truth; in all moments."

"We remove all engrams of being tortured; in all moments."

"We remove all engrams of being betrayed; in all moments."

"We remove all engrams of being crucified; in all moments."

"We heal all our bodies; in all moments."

"We release the aversion to serve humanity; in all moments."

"We repair and fortify the wei chi of all our bodies; in all moments."

"We release being torn asunder; in all moments."

"We release being ensconced in being torn asunder; in all moments."

"We release being paralyzed in being torn asunder; in all moments."

"We remove all vivaxes between ourselves and being torn asunder; in all moments."

"We remove all tentacles between ourselves and being torn asunder; in all moments."

"We remove the claws of being torn asunder from our beingness; in all moments."

"We remove all engrams of being torn asunder; in all moments."

"We remove all programming and conditioning that being torn asunder has put on us; in all moments."

"We send all energy matrices into the light and sound that have torn us asunder; in all moments."

"We command all complex energy matrices that have torn us asunder to be escorted into the light and sound; in all moments."

"We strip all illusion off of all those who have torn us asunder; in all moments."

"We remove all masks, walls, and armor from all those who have torn us asunder; in all moments."

"We send all energy matrices into the light and sound that have impersonated us; in all moments."

"We command all complex energy matrices that have impersonated us to be escorted into the light and sound; in all moments."

"We send all energy matrices into the light and sound that misrepresent truth; in all moments."

"We command all complex energy matrices that misrepresent truth to be escorted into the light and sound; in all moments."

"We send all energy matrices into the light and sound that propagate power in the lower worlds; in all moments."

"We command all complex energy matrices that propagate power in the lower worlds to be escorted into the light and sound; in all moments."

"We send all energy matrices into the light and sound that elicit fear in the lower worlds; in all moments."

"We command all complex energy matrices that elicit fear in the lower worlds to be escorted into the light and sound; in all moments."

"We nullify all contracts between ourselves and being torn asunder; in all moments."

"We withdraw all our energy from being torn asunder; in all moments."

"We recant all vows and agreements to be torn asunder; in all moments."

"We release being sacrificed to being torn asunder; in all moments."

"We remove all curses that being torn asunder has put on us; in all moments."

"We remove all blessings to being torn asunder; in all moments."

"We release resigning to being torn asunder; in all moments."

"We release the belief that being torn asunder is inevitable; in all moments."

"We release resolving to being torn asunder; in all moments."

"We sever all strings, cords, and shackles to being torn asunder; in all moments."

"We dissolve all karmic ties between ourselves and being torn asunder; in all moments."

"We remove all the devastation that being torn asunder has put on us; in all moments."

"We remove all the devastation that being torn asunder has put on the lower worlds; in all moments."

"We take back ALL that being torn asunder has taken from us; in all moments."

"We release resonating with being torn asunder; in all moments."

"We release emanating with being torn asunder; in all moments."

"We extract all of being torn asunder from our sound frequency and the universal sound frequency; in all moments."

"We extract all of being torn asunder from our light emanation and the universal light emanation; in all moments."

"We extract all of being torn asunder from our whole beingness and all of the lower worlds; in all moments."

"We shift our paradigm from being torn asunder, to being whole in love and truth; in all moments."

"We transcend being torn asunder; in all moments."

"We are centered, empowered, and imbued in being whole in love and truth; in all moments."

"We resonate, emanate, and are interconnected with all souls in being whole in love and truth; in all moments."

Living in Zen

Don't need to stay

Don't feel like going

Original ideas

Perpetually flowing

No judgment here

No points to belabor

Every moment of Peace

Is one to be savored

Nothing to prove

No one to belittle

The world is aligned

By staying in the middle

Each soul met

Is great amongst men

Honor their presence

By Living in Zen.

Remove the Stronghold of the Past

(Say each statement three times while tapping on your head and say it a fourth time while tapping on your chest.)

"We declare ourselves surrogates for humanity in doing these taps; in all moments."

"We release being fixated on the past; in all moments."

"We release trying to reinstate the past; in all moments."

"We pull up roots from the past; in all moments."

"We remove all vivaxes with the past; in all moments."

"We release being imbedded in the past; in all moments."

"We pluck ourselves out of the past; in all moments."

"We remove all tentacles between ourselves and the past; in all moments."

"We remove the claws of the past from our beingness; in all moments."

"We remove all programming and conditioning that the past has put on us; in all moments."

"We remove all engrams of the past; in all moments."

"We strip all illusion off the past; in all moments."

"We strip all illusion off of our attempts to reinstate the past; in all moments."

"We withdraw all our energy from the past; in all moments."

"We collapse and dissolve all portals to the past; in all moments."

"We eliminate the first cause in reinstating the past; in all moments."

"We send all energy matrices into the light that keep us connected to the past; in all moments."

"We send all energy matrices into the sound that keep us connected to the past; in all moments."

"We command all complex energy matrices that keep us connected to the past to be escorted into the light and sound; in all moments."

"We nullify all contracts with the past; in all moments."

"We recant all vows and agreements between ourselves and the past; in all moments."

"We remove all curses between ourselves and the past; in all moments."

"We remove all blessings between ourselves and the past; in all moments."

"We remove all shackles of the past; in all moments."

"We sever all strings and cords between ourselves and the past; in all moments."

"We dissolve all karmic ties between ourselves and the past; in all moments."

"We remove all the burden of the past; in all moments."

"We take back all that the past deprives us of; in all moments."

"We release resonating with the past; in all moments."

"We release emanating with the past; in all moments."

"We extract all of the past from the individual and universal sound frequencies; in all moments."

"We extract all of the past from the individual and universal light emanation; in all moments."

"We shift our paradigm from the past to the moment; in all moments."

"We transcend the past; in all moments."

"We are centered and empowered in the moment; in all moments."

"We resonate, emanate and are interconnected with all life in the moment; in all moments."

Remove the Stranglehold of Major Groups on Humanity

These taps can be used with any major group that affects humanity. It can be a religion, a political group, or any group structure that affects the multitudes. Do them with as many different sects as possible by inserting the name of the group in the blanks below.

"We declare ourselves surrogates for humanity in doing these taps; in all moments."

"We declare ourselves surrogates for all of life in doing these taps; in all moments."

"We declare ourselves surrogates for truth seekers everywhere in doing these taps; in all moments."

"We release being limited by _____; in all moments."

"We release being lied to by _____; in all moments."

"We remove all blind loyalty to _____; in all moments."

"We release being enslaved by _____; in all moments."

"We release being enslaved to _____; in all moments."

"We release being cursed by _____; in all moments."

"We release the fear of repercussions of leaving _____; in all moments."

"We release confusing _____ for the highest truth; in all moments."

"We remove all vivaxes between ourselves and _____; in all moments."

"We release giving our proxy to _____; in all moments."

"We release pinning all our hopes on _____; in all moments."

"We untangle all our energy from _____; in all moments."

"We extract all of _____ from our beingness; in all moments."

"We remove all tentacles between ourselves and _____; in all moments."

"We remove the claws of _____ from our beingness; in all moments."

"We strip all illusion off of _____; in all moments."

"We remove all masks, walls and armor from _____; in all moments."

"We remove all masks, walls and armor of _____ from our beingness; in all moments."

"We shatter all glass ceilings that _____ has put on us; in all moments."

"We shatter all illusion of superiority that _____ has put on us; in all moments."

"We withdraw all our energy from _____; in all moments."

"We release being deceived by _____; in all moments."

"We eliminate the first cause in regards to _____; in all moments."

"We eliminate the first cause in moving off the path of love; in all moments."

"We eliminate the first cause in moving away from truth; in all moments."

"We eliminate the first cause in being programmed and conditioned; in all moments."

"We eliminate the first cause in ignoring the ancient ones; in all

moments."

"We exonerate _____; in all moments."

"We remove all programming and conditioning that _____ has put on us; in all moments."

"We remove all engrams of _____ from our beingness; in all moments."

"We nullify all contracts with _____; in all moments."

"We send all energy matrices of _____ into the light; in all moments."

"We send all energy matrices of _____ into the sound; in all moments."

"We command all complex energy matrices of _____, to be escorted into the light and sound; in all moments."

"We recant all vows and agreements between ourselves and _____; in all moments."

"We release romanticizing _____; in all moments."

"We release using _____ to hide from truth; in all moments."

"We remove all curses between ourselves and _____; in all moments."

"We remove all curses that we have put on all others due to _____; in all moments."

"We release influencing others for _____; in all moments."

"We remove all blessings between ourselves and _____; in all moments."

"We remove all blessings that we have put on all others for the sake of _____; in all moments."

"We sever all strings, cords and wires between ourselves and _____; in all moments."

"We sever all strings, cords and wires between ourselves and all others due to _____; in all moments."

"We dissolve all karmic ties between ourselves and _____; in all moments."

"We dissolve all karmic ties between ourselves and all others due to _____; in all moments."

"We remove all the pain, burden and limitations that _____ has put on us; in all moments."

"We remove all the pain, burden and limitations that we have put on all others due to _____; in all moments."

"We remove all the fear, futility and unworthiness that _____ has put on us; in all moments."

"We remove all indoctrination, slavery and illusion of separateness that _____ has put on us; in all moments."

"We remove all the fear, futility and unworthiness that we have put on all others due to _____; in all moments."

"We remove all indoctrination, slavery and illusion of separateness that we have put on all others due to _____; in all moments."

"We take back ALL that _____ has taken from us; in all moments."

"We give back to all others ALL that we have taken from them due to, or on behalf of, _____; in all moments."

"We extract all of _____ from our beingness; in all moments."

"We extract all of _____ from the universal embodiment of humanity; in all moments."

"We extract all of _____ from the 32 layers of our auric field and all 32 layers of the universal auric field; in all moments."

"We extract all of _____ from our sound frequency and the universal sound frequency; in all moments."

"We extract all of _____ from our light emanation and the universal light emanation; in all moments."

"We shift our paradigm from _____ to exponential love and truth; in all moments."

"We shift the universal paradigm from _____ to exponential love and truth; in all moments."

"We individually and universally transcend _____; in all moments."

"We are individually and universally centered and empowered in exponential love and truth; in all moments."

"We individually and universally resonate, emanate and are interconnected with all life in exponential love and truth; in all moments."

Evidence of Love's Existence

I was starving and exhausted beyond compare. In my mind, even though I wasn't allowed to think (he would know), I ran a thought loop through my head that defied my captor's attempts to break me. His programming was that I was disgusting, reviled, and hated by all that was pure and sacred and all the angels thought that I deserved to suffer in a miserable eternal existence of pain.

He laughed and scoffed at my humiliation, and the more that I suffered, the happier he was. He would invent ways to draw out my anguish. He would eat in front of me and mock me as he forced me to work in over 100-degree heat until I was exhausted and emaciated. He told me that God hated me, that I had defiled all that was good to such a degree that God wanted to see me suffer and was pleased at my misery. Not because God was unkind, but because I was such a disgusting waste of existence.

There was really nothing from my history that obviously contradicted his statements. I had a large family that didn't seem to embrace me; I had made no great strides in the community to show great evidence of the contrary. I had no family of my own. He took my dog from me and convinced me that my dog, that I had rescued, really hated me. He made me serve the dog as a king because it was an extension of him.

My brain nearly gave up the ability to think rationally. It had exhausted the possibilities to counter his programming, but there was one statement from my spiritual teachings that kept me alive: Soul exists because God loves it. I existed so God must love me. It was the one irrefutable argument I had in my mental and physical fog. It defied all his efforts to break me. I existed. God must love me. I was lovable. Others exist so God must love others. So now I am connected to all through this realization. I am connected to all through the Love. That is all that remained of who I was. I AM the evidence of Love's existence.

Stoking True Compassion

When there was a new ceasefire in a major war and the people were being fed, it wasn't even trending. Society has been conditioned not to care. Individuals need to awaken compassion in themselves. It needs to happen. It is part of the transcendence process. It doesn't mean to get all militant in your opinions. It just means that you must become aware and relate to the suffering that is happening in the world. It is touching your life in some way. Distance does not prevent suffering from bleeding into the collective, and it is not possible to remove yourself from the collective. So the suffering that is happening on the other side of the world should be more relevant, perhaps as relevant as the anguish of your own dear ones.

When you think of something in the world that is disturbing, see it as a deflated balloon because the situation is deflated from lack of love. Visualize blowing kindness and love into those who need it. There is no advantage to taking sides or a political stand. This just feeds the beast. Just "blow" your loving intention into all those who are not being loved. It can be in a certain area, demographic or situation.

You can send your loving intentions to all those who are starving to death at the hands of their government, all those who are suffering at the hands of a tormentor, all those who are imprisoned as a result of systemic need, all little boys shot and killed for playing with toy guns and all those who are suffering at the hands of their own actions.

If you keep your opinion and judgment out of it and just feed love into those who need love, you will be doing more good than riding upon a billion bandwagons. The bandwagons feed society. Your love nurtures the individuals. This is a form of good you can do in the world. It isn't a matter of *looking* caring and compassionate to others. It is a matter of stoking true compassion into the world.

Expound

(Say each statement three times while tapping on your head and say it a fourth time while tapping on your chest.)

"I am relinquished from the grip of the negative forces; in all

moments."

"I relinquish volleying around out of fear; in all moments."

"My journey is centered, empowered and infused with light, love and celestial music; in all moments."

Anger

I recently had a private session with a woman who was drawn to angry people. As much as she abhorred the behavior, there was something about the anger that she was drawn to. During her session, Santa Claus came through. From that image, I realized that she was confusing anger for strength, authority and completeness. She felt weak because she didn't indulge in anger.

Her past life in a puritanical religion revealed itself during her session. She saw God as an angry God. In this lifetime, devoting herself to knowing God, she got the wires mixed up through past programming that God was angry. Since she outgrew anger in herself long ago, the only way she felt she could get closer to God was by having relationships with angry people.

We untangled the misconceptions that were preventing her from having a personal relationship with joy, love, abundance, freedom and wholeness, which are all attributes of God.

Here are some of the taps that we used. They may help you as well.

(Say each statement three times while tapping the head and say it a fourth time while tapping the chest.)

"I release confusing anger for strength; in all moments."

"I release the belief that I am weak; in all moments."

"I release the fear of anger; in all moments."

"I release revering anger; in all moments."

"I release the belief that God is angry; in all moments."

"I release using angry people to compensate; in all moments."

"I release confusing anger for Love; in all moments."

It Really Is That Simple

Blind loyalty builds up resentment. Male energy has dominated all the possible engrams in distorting the importance of those who serve humanity. As much as those in true service reject such adulation, it is still an engram etched in this world. It is a glass ceiling on humanity. It is an unhealthy dynamic for individual growth.

For as soon as you elevate someone, you have just lowered your own stance. Those in true service to humanity do not wish to see individuals debase themselves. Any practice that expects this does not honor the true nature of God.

Service is all about elevating the one assisted. People try to elevate me but I am just fine where I am. I am grateful for the respect because it is the same respect that I give. I wish everyone else to merely elevate themselves. That is all that needs to happen for truth and love to prevail. Everyone must simply elevate themselves in service to life in some way. It is really that simple.

Stop Confusing Spirituality with Suffering

In past lives, we have been martyred for own sacred devotion. It has many times left us with an aversion to our spirituality in order to avoid the suffering. Here is to releasing the connection between spirituality and suffering.

(Say each statement three times while continuously tapping on your head and say it a fourth time while tapping on your chest.)

"I release confusing spirituality with suffering; in all moments."

"I remove all vivaxes between spirituality and suffering; in all moments."

"I remove all engrams of suffering for my spirituality; in all moments."

"I untangle all suffering from my spirituality; in all moments."

"I extract all suffering from my spirituality; in all moments."

"I release all fear of suffering for being spiritual; in all moments."

"I expound on my spirituality; in all moments."

"I flourish in my spirituality; in all moments."

"I awaken to a new dawn of my exponential empowerment; in all moments."

Dipping a Toe into Life Versus Diving in

We all are told that being positive is healthier but then there is a disconnect as to why.

The body response that comes from the experience of the mundane is different from the experience of being excited. The body releases different hormones for excitement. The mind becomes alert; there is an expectancy that is sustained and a general enthusiasm when one is looking forward to something. There are all these hormones that play into the body being enthusiastic.

Pregnant women are not the only people who are affected by hormones. Everyone is. We are just used to the ones that we fire, so they don't shift our moods and body as drastically as a pregnant woman's hormones shift. But they can be drastically changed by our intention to do so. In the zoo, they design the displays for natural predators to be next to their natural prey. It extends the life of both. They both get a sense of the danger and excitement and it shifts their chemical make-up.

In the same way, it is important to do things that we feel are dangerous. To take a risk is to flood your body with exhilarating chemicals that give it an edge. But what we do as humans is to pound out every adventure to the fine mulch of a problem. We ruminate and overthink it and extract all organic thrill from it. Questions like how, why, when and the worst of all--what if--extract all the joy out of the adventure of living.

The key to joy is to look for the risk and do it anyway. Look at the fears and break through them. So many people are living in the shadow of an invisible fear. They are afraid to be different, afraid to be on the wrong side of an issue, afraid to speak their truth. They are even afraid of the techniques I post to uncover their own truth. A little fear is healthy. It is a way the heart and gut sensors signal something is not right. But when someone is afraid to do anything, it is like they are living in a bowl of lime jello and unable to move. They are being encumbered by the fear.

When an opportunity comes up and there is resistance, ask the internal question, "What am I afraid of?" Answer it honestly. Break down that answer to another layer by continuing to ask, "What am I afraid of?" If you do this technique honestly, it will always come down to the fear of not being loved. So simply pour incredible love into yourself and go create an adventure for yourself.

The Universe has kept you alive and whole in your present condition. It has never let you down or you would not be here. But you are here, thriving and thinking and processing life. Since it has never let you down yet, there is no need to doubt it. There is no reason to think that you will not continue to thrive and there is really little evidence to support that you did it without the help of the Universe. So why not trust it and go out and challenge life.

Create an adventure. Go conquer love. Create a new business. Challenge the way people perceive you. Challenge the way you perceive yourself. Live like a king, think like a crazy person, dream like a poet, act like a child and make no apologies or give no explanation of who you are. The one rule is to respect all others and to respect yourself just as much. Have fun with life. We only have forever.

Powerful Taps to Free All of Negative Influence

The negative energies have been removed from being entrenched in our worldly affairs. These taps are to assist in moving out the residual effects sooner. It is time that we claim our empowerment and stop worrying about seeming paranoid. With the state that the world has gotten into, no one should worry about seeming crazy for thinking more is going on than what we are privy to at the surface. The people who think things are running in accordance with God's law are actually more delusional.

(Say each statement three times while tapping on your head and say it a fourth time while tapping on your chest.)

"We declare ourselves surrogates for humanity in doing these taps; in all moments."

"We release being manipulated by anyone in cahoots with the cabal; in all moments."

"We strip all illusion off of the cabal; in all moments."

"We strip all illusion off of those in cahoots with the cabal; in all moments."

"We release being influenced by the cabal; in all moments."

"We released being influenced by anyone in cahoots with the cabal; in all moments."

"We release deferring to anyone who is in cahoots with the cabal; in all moments."

"We release admiring anyone who is in cahoots with the cabal; in all moments."

"We withdraw all our energy from everyone in cahoots with the cabal; in all moments."

"We remove all masks, walls, and armor from everyone who is in cahoots with the cabal; in all moments."

"We nullify all contracts with anyone and everyone who is in cahoots with the cabal; in all moments."

"We remove all vivaxes between ourselves and anyone or everyone in cahoots with the cabal; in all moments."

"We remove all tentacles between ourselves and anyone or everyone in cahoots with the cabal; in all moments."

"We remove all tentacles between ourselves and everyone in cahoots with the cabal; in all moments."

"We remove all tentacles between ourselves and anyone in cahoots with the cabal; in all moments."

"We remove all vivaxes between ourselves and everyone in cahoots with the cabal; in all moments."

"We remove all programming and conditioning that anyone in cahoots with the cabal has put on us; in all moments."

"We remove all programming and conditioning that anyone in cahoots with the cabal has put on us; in all moments."

"We remove all engrams that anyone who is in cahoots with the cabal has put on us; in all moments."

"We send all energy matrices into the light and sound that cause us to associate with anyone in the cabal; in all moments."

"We command all complex energy matrices that cause us to associate with anyone in the cabal to be escorted into the light and sound; in all moments."

"We send all energy matrices into the light and sound that taint our spiritual connection; in all moments."

"We command all complex energy matrices that taint our spiritual connection to be escorted into the light and sound; in all moments."

"We recant all vows and agreements between ourselves and everyone in cahoots with the cabal; in all moments."

"We remove all curses between ourselves and anyone in cahoots with cabal; in all moments."

"We remove all blessings between ourselves and anyone in cahoots with the cabal; in all moments."

"We free all souls that are inadvertently coerced by the cabal; in all moments."

"We purify all souls of the cabal; in all moments."

"We free all souls from all influence of the cabal; in all moments"

"We sever all strings and cord between ourselves and everyone who is in cahoots with the cabal; in all moments."

"We dissolve all karmic ties between ourselves and everyone who is in cahoots with the cabal; in all moments."

"We remove all the pain, burden, and limitations that anyone who is in cahoots with the cabal has put on us; in all moments."

"We remove all fear, futility, and unworthiness that anyone who is cahoots with the cabal has put on us; in all moments."

"We remove all the apathy, fear, and illusion of separateness that anyone who is in cahoots with the cabal has put on us; in all moments."

"We release being influenced by the cabal; in all moments."

"We remove ALL that we have put on all others due to the influence of the cabal; in all moments."

"We take back ALL that all those who are in cahoots with the cabal have taken from us; in all moments."

"We give back to all others all that we have taken from them due to the influence of the cabal; in all moments."

"We collapse and dissolve all portals to those who are in cahoots with the cabal; in all moments."

"We release resonating with anyone who is in cahoots with the cabal; in all moments."

"We release emanating with anyone who is in cahoots with the cabal; in all moments."

"We extract ALL of all those who are in cahoots with the cabal from our sound frequency; in all moments."

"We extract ALL of all those who are in cahoots with the cabal from our light emanation; in all moments."

"We extract ALL of all those who are in cahoots with cabal from all 32 layers of our auric field; in all moments."

"We extract ALL of all those who are in cahoots with the cabal from our whole beingness; in all moments."

"We shift our paradigm from all those who are in cahoots with the cabal to free and sovereign souls; in all moments."

"We transcend all those who are in cahoots with the cabal; in all moments."

"We are centered and empowered in being free and sovereign souls; in all moments."

"We resonate, emanate, and are interconnected with all life in being free and sovereign souls; in all moments."

Faith Defined

Faith is tapping into our own resilience and realizing that whatever we are experiencing is nothing compared to the incredible sanctity and spiritual acquiescence of simply existing. Because realizing we exist is also a realizing that we are love.

Love is all there really is. Everything else is an illusion to assist ourselves in realizing ourselves as pure love. That is what self-realization is. Faith is trusting that we will experience the sanctity of being love without the feeling of separation that illusion creates.

Releasing Ignorance to Live One's Highest Purpose

So many people have a problem with what I do. They criticize, ostracize, judge and even ridicule me. It is funny; in this world it seems okay to lie, cheat, bully, manipulate, exploit, diminish and steal from others but if you share your unconventional gifts and serve to raise the consciousness with loving intention, it is deemed unacceptable.

Maybe they don't realize that the gifts I share and encourage in others were practiced in ancient cultures but were diminished and eventually extinguished by those who wished to have complete control. Maybe they are conditioned by the control and don't realize that I am not the one with the agenda. There really was no reason for me to survive imprisonment except to assist others. There really was no purpose in me going through that year of sensory deprivation and torture except to hone any talents I have and use them to help free the hearts and minds of others. Maybe these people don't realize that the gifts that they have are just as unique and they will be discovered when they break away from the herd mentality.

People themselves aren't ignorant but there is an underlying current of ignorance that creates an apathy in society. It is the cousin of power. It prevents individuals from realizing their own worth, from being able to formulate an original point of view, and it prevents them from striving at all costs to dream their dreams and share their gifts.

I encourage all to do these taps as a surrogate for society:

(Say each statement three times while tapping on your head and say it a fourth time while tapping on your chest.)

"I release subscribing to ignorance; in all moments."

"I release being deceived by ignorance; in all moments."

"I release being duped by ignorance; in all moments."

"I release being blind to ignorance; in all moments."

"I release being immersed in ignorance; in all moments."

"I withdraw all my energy and support from ignorance; in all moments."

"I release being a conduit for ignorance; in all moments."

"I remove all the pain, burden, apathy and limitations that ignorance has put on me; in all moments."

"I remove all the pain, burden, apathy and limitations I have put on all others as a conduit for ignorance; in all moments."

"I take back all the Joy, Love, Abundance, Freedom, Success, Health, Life, Wholeness and Enlightenment that ignorance has taken from me; in all moments."

"I give back all the Joy, Love, Abundance, Freedom, Success, Health, Life, Wholeness and Enlightenment that I have taken from all others as a conduit for ignorance; in all moments."

"I shift my paradigm from ignorance to enlightenment; in all moments."

"I make space in this world to share my gifts and to live my highest purpose; in all moments."

"I remove all obstacles to sharing my gifts and living my highest purpose; in all moments."

"I stretch my capacity and hone my capabilities to share my gifts and live my highest purpose; in all moments."

"I am centered and abundant in sharing my gifts and living my highest purpose; in all moments."

Perspective

Your worst…day may be a…day in the park to someone else.

Your worst…meal may be a…banquet to someone else.

Your worst…living condition may be a…palace to someone else.

Your…deepest disappointment may be a…dream come true to someone else.

Your worst…date may be a…love of their life to someone else.

Your…haziest stupor may be a…moment of clarity to someone else.

Your…throw away attempt may be the…highest accomplishment

to someone else.

Your…failing body may be…renewed health to someone else.

Your…fat pants may be…skinny pants to someone else.

Your…bad luck could be…catching a break to someone else.

Your lack of gratitude may be an insult to 90% of the planet.

Break Through All Resistance

(Say each statement three times out loud while tapping on the top of your head at the crown chakra and say it a fourth time while tapping on your chest.)

"I release being paralyzed in resistance; in all moments."

"I release relinquishing my momentum for resistance; in all moments."

"I release succumbing to resistance; in all moments."

"I release confusing resistance for defeat; in all moments."

"I release allowing resistance to defeat me; in all moments."

"I release confusing resistance for exhaustion; in all moments."

"I release allowing resistance to exhaust me; in all moments."

"I release being overwhelmed by resistance; in all moments."

"I release allowing resistance to overwhelm me; in all moments."

"I release processing resistance as being overwhelmed; in all moments."

"I release rolling over for resistance; in all moments."

"I remove all vivaxes between myself and resistance; in all moments."

"I remove the claws of resistance from my beingness; in all moments."

"I remove all tentacles between myself and resistance; in all moments."

"I remove all engrams that are triggered by resistance; in all moments."

"I send all energy matrices into the light and sound that cause resistance within me; in all moments."

"I break through all resistance; in all moments."

"I collapse and dissolve all resistance; in all moments."

"I shift my paradigm from resistance to enthusiasm and empowerment; in all moments."

"I transcend all resistance; in all moments."

"I am centered and empowered in enthusiasm and empowerment; in all moments."

Please Don't Enlighten Me

There is no point rallying for social change until every human feels valued and heard. My humble opinions may not change society, but I believe things that aren't accepted in today's climate. Here are some of my random beliefs. Maybe others will feel empowered to share theirs if they see how out of the box someone else thinks. So here are my "ridiculous" notions. I am curious, but not interested, in how many people will feel compelled to enlighten me.

- It is insanity that chemical medication is accepted as the norm but alternative practices are considered wacko.

- Prisons are filled with talented people whose strengths and talents do not conform to a narrow band of what society deems beneficial.
- The welfare system doesn't work, not because people don't need the assistance. It is because they need the assistance because there are no avenues for so many to learn and share their skills and talents.
- It is not only government that needs overhauling but all of society. Society is failing because its structure is based on archaic beliefs.
- Anything or anyone that hurts, diminishes, judges, manipulates, excludes, kills, is not an authority on God.
- There is no such thing as a lack of energy. It is an unnatural manipulation of the masses. We are all living, breathing expressions and interactions of energy and energy are a byproduct of everything. We are just refusing to harness it.
- We are not going to make society healthy by rallying around disease and making it a social event. The main purpose, though inadvertent and unbeknownst to the sincere individuals, is to make disease socially acceptable and the norm.
- God does not need to be stroked and worshiped like an egotistical male. God is Love, an expression of Love, Love in action, Love personified. Anything that is loving, pure, natural, kind, accepting, free, aware, unafraid, alive, is God personified.
- People aren't more important than other forms of life. Plant life and animals communicate in a nonverbal language and all can hear if they develop the perceptions to do so.
- The world and all its inhabitants wouldn't have to be governed if respect of the individual was the major priority and golden rule of the land.

Walking with the Spiritual Masters

Some people are ready to transcend this lifetime and to know themselves beyond what they perceive themselves to be at this moment. But they have wrapped themselves up in the relationships and experiences around them to prevent themselves from being damaged by the starkness of truth.

Some crave truth like breath or food to a starving body. For those few dynamic souls, being bubble-wrapped in the niceties of life no longer suffices to placate their need to know.

If you are one who has outgrown your current agreement with this life, you may have the courage to do these taps. They may change you in subtle or not so subtle ways.

(Say each statement three times while tapping on your head, and say a fourth time while tapping on your chest.)

"I recant all vows and agreements between myself and Everyone and Everything; in all moments."

"I remove all curses between myself and Everyone and Everything; in all moments."

"I dissolve all karmic ties between myself and Everyone and Everything; in all moments."

"I remove all the pain, burden and limitations that Everyone and Everything have put on me; in all moments."

"I remove all the pain, burden and limitations that I have put on Everyone and Everything; in all moments."

"I take back all the Joy, Love, Abundance, Freedom and Wholeness that Everyone and Everything have taken from me; in all moments."

"I give back all the Joy, Love, Abundance, Freedom and Wholeness that I have taken from Everyone and Everything; in all moments."

"I shift my paradigm from Everyone and Everything to Joy, Love, Abundance, Freedom and Wholeness; in all moments."

"I walk amongst the Spiritual Masters; in all moments."

Removing Secondhand Engrams

Everything that we do out of habit is an engram. We don't even think about doing it. It is just something that we have been taught and it helps us acclimate in a societal group. We do the same things, we believe the same things and we even think the same things.

We are so defined by all the habitual behaviors, beliefs, and actions we do that we don't define them or even question them. Since our mind is a 3-D printer and manifests everything that we program it to create, perhaps we are using too many variables to limit the manifestation of our self-creation.

Each of these engrams that have been programmed into us, and that we operate under, uses fear as a way to delve them into our energy field. The fear is like the ring a glass makes when it is put on a wood surface. It leaves a mark in the wood. Fear is what singes these engrams into our soul. Gaining mastership (the thing I assist with) is rubbing all these water stains out.

Think about it. Don't touch fire. It will burn you. Don't speak your truth. People will judge you. Don't be different. People will be mean to you. Don't stand out. You will be rejected and abandoned. These are all secondhand engrams. You may have come by them honestly in this lifetime or the past, but they have been reinforced by the groups you belong to: society, religions, government, family, friends, etc.

(Say each statement three times while tapping on your head and say it a fourth time while tapping on your chest.)

"I remove all secondhand engrams; in all moments."

"I release accepting secondhand engrams; in all moments."

"I release handing out secondhand engrams; in all moments."

"I release being warped by secondhand engrams; in all moments."

"I release leading with my reactions; in all moments."

"I release limiting others by generalizing them; in all moments."

"I remove all generalizations that I have put on all others; in all moments."

"I amp up my intentions; in all moments."

"I release allowing my intentions to reflect other people's fears; in all moments."

"I release all pettiness; in all moments."

Put Away All Childish Things

There is a passage from the Bible that discusses "putting away childish things" when one grows up. (I Corinthians, 13:11)

Here are some childish things to put away:

- Diminishing women
- Demonizing others for their personal preferences
- Genocide of any kind: trees, animals and even humans
- Using the forefathers' sincere efforts to maintain freedom to now hold us all captive
- Choosing money and power over the sanctity of life

- Killing anything for amusement
- Desecrating the potential of anyone
- Using God to demoralize others
- Male superiority
- Bullying anyone who doesn't agree with you
- Perpetuating negative morality
- Deciding for others what their morality should be
- Cutting down magnificent trees to plug up the void in pathetic humans
- Looking outside of one's self for Joy, Love, Abundance, Freedom and Wholeness.
- Worshiping monetary wealth
- Degrading others who seem different

(Say each statement three times out loud while continuously tapping on the top of your head at the crown chakra and say it a fourth time while tapping on your chest at the heart chakra.)

"I declare myself a surrogate for humanity; in all moments."

"I release diminishing women; in all moments."

"I release demonizing others for their personal preferences; in all moments."

"I release genocide of any kind--trees, animals and even humans; in all moments."

"I release using the forefathers' sincere efforts to maintain freedom to now hold us all captive; in all moments."

"I release choosing money and power over the sanctity of life; in all moments."

"I release killing anything for amusement; in all moments."

"I release desecrating the potential of anyone; in all moments."

"I release using God to demoralize others; in all moments."

"I release male superiority; in all moments."

"I release bullying anyone who doesn't agree with me; in all moments."

"I release perpetuating negative morality; in all moments."

"I release deciding for others what their morality should be; in all moments."

"I release cutting down magnificent trees to plug up the void in pathetic humans; in all moments."

"I release looking outside of myself for Joy, Love, Abundance, Freedom and Wholeness; in all moments."

"I release worshiping monetary wealth; in all moments."

"I release degrading others who seem different; in all moments."

"I release procreating out of habit or false duty; in all moments."

"I reject all diminishing practices; in all moments."

GRACE

G give kindness to all

R respect the sanctity of all souls

A attune to what is the highest good in every situation

C consider the vantage point of all others

E empathize with everyone

Grace is artistry and a skill like all others.

It can be cultivated, nurtured and taught.

What we do in each act of Grace is empower the integrity of humanity.

From each act of Grace:

Illumination of spirit is revealed,

Heaviness lifts,

Hearts unburden,

Silent pleas are answered,

Resolve unfurls its wings,

Insights take their first breath,

Paths are cleared,

Innocence is nurtured,

Kindness is empowered,

Hope restores,

Resolve is instilled,

Quietude is respected,

Peace expands,

A way is secured.

What you do in Grace is:

Eliminate the primal urge to initiate hostile acts,

Forgo the path of petty indifference,

Repair all divide,

Create resiliency in the intricate woven fabric of life,

Reclaim wonder for all those in your wake,

Teach lost souls a way to be found,

Demonstrate a dying art to fervent generations,

Enlighten the murky hallways of tradition.

Your acts of Grace:

Bring relief to those who are desperate in their own plight,

Satiate those starving to know kindness,

Address the deprived in whatever way they have been depreciated,

Illuminate dark corners of the world,

Wipe the brow of faces you may never see,

Hush the muted cries of indifference,

Ripple out into a sea of kindred spirits,

Sing to the sweetest aspect of every point of light,

Attune the heart of goodness with the voice of reason,

Uplift all souls to their own quickening to enlightenment

Anchor your stance as a mighty force for mass enlightenment.

This is what you choose to do or not do, every moment.

You have this much power.

You always have.

1/29/16

Powerful Taps to Release the Fear of Enlightenment

(Say each statement three times while tapping on your head and say it a fourth time while tapping on your chest.)

"I release the belief that I am alone; in all moments."

"I release the belief that I am insignificant; in all moments."

"I release the belief that I don't matter; in all moments."

"I release the belief that I am not being heard; in all moments."

"I release believing the lie that I am alone; in all moments."

"I release glazing over from all that I've seen; in all moments."

"I release confusing surgery as an assault; in all moments."

"I release confusing the surgeon with the enemy; in all moments."

"I release being blinded to truth; in all moments."

"I release being pinned down in fear; in all moments."

"I release being stuck in defense mode; in all moments."

"I release being stuck in primal mode; in all moments."

"I release deferring to primal mode; in all moments."

"I release the genetic propensity to revert to primal mode; in all moments."

"I release the trauma of being stabbed in the eye; in all moments."

"I remove all engrams in the eyes; in all moments."

"I heal my causal eyes; in all moments."

"I repair my vision; in all moments."

"I declare myself a surrogate for humanity in doing these taps; in all moments."

"I release being trapped in primal mode; in all moments."

"I release the fear of transcending; in all moments."

"I release confusing transcending with death; in all moments."

"I release fighting amongst my peers; in all moments."

"I remove myself from infighting; in all moments."

"I open my spiritual eye; in all moments."

"I awaken my subtle senses; in all moments."

"I repair all the energy systems in my beingness; in all moments."

"I recharge all the energy systems in my beingness; in all moments."

"I synchronize all the energy systems in my beingness to work in harmony; in all moments."

"I remove all the outmoded filters from my beingness; in all moments."

"I release filtering out the joy; in all moments."

"I release filtering out the love; in all moments."

"I release filtering out the abundance; in all moments."

"I release filtering out the freedom; in all moments."

"I release filtering out health; in all moments."

"I release filtering out success; in all moments."

"I release filtering out wholeness; in all moments."

"I release filtering out enlightenment; in all moments."

"I recalibrate my whole energy system to embrace joy; in all moments."

"I recalibrate my whole energy system to embrace love; in all moments."

"I recalibrate my whole energy system to embrace abundance; in all moments."

"I recalibrate my whole energy system to embrace freedom; in all moments."

"I recalibrate my whole energy system to embrace health; in all moments."

"I recalibrate my whole energy system to embrace success; in all moments."

"I recalibrate my whole energy system to embrace wholeness; in all moments."

"I recalibrate my whole energy system to embrace enlightenment; in all moments."

"I release the disconnect between the microcosm and the macrocosm; in all moments."

"I shift my paradigm from primal mode to spiritual being; in all moments."

"I shift the universal paradigm from primal mode to spiritual being; in all moments."

"I shift my paradigm from primal mode to enlightenment; in all moments."

"I shift the universal paradigm from primal mode to enlightenment; in all moments."

"I am centered and empowered in enlightenment; in all moments."

"I am universally centered and empowered in enlightenment; in all moments."

"I resonate, emanate, and am interconnected with all life in enlightenment; in all moments."

"I resonate, emanate, and am interconnected with all life in universal enlightenment; in all moments."

Taking Up Causes

I had a session with someone who had many lifetimes taking up causes. The core scenario that played again and again was of someone else in power that my client was devoted to helping. So he used much of his lifeblood in many lifetimes to promote a cause that he didn't wholeheartedly believe in. The way it played out in this lifetime was a great sense of apathy. My client wanted to find a cause to support but couldn't find one he was willing to commit his energy to. His quest was actually for approval and self-love.

The truth that came out for my client was that he was better off not taking on a global cause in this life because in his case, he would be doing it to try to fix past life transgressions that still triggered guilt in him. I am wondering if this is also the case for others. Maybe for some people, trying to fix the world is a form of self-denial. It may keep their focus outward instead of working on inner issues, like releasing shame, guilt, a sense of disconnectedness and unworthiness.

Maybe the work that people do on uplifting themselves is a great way to uplift humanity. Maybe it raises the internal bar for us all and is the noblest thing one can do.

Here is a tap for people to try to shift focus back onto themselves.

(Say this three times while tapping on your head and say it a fourth time while tapping on your chest.)

"I release using social issues as a form of self-denial; in all moments."

Absolutes

When we are children, we think our parents are the authority on all of life. This is a child's absolute. It keeps them comforted in their role as a child. It is a difficult transition sometimes for the growth of the child but they must outgrow deferring to their parents to be healthy and continue to thrive. This includes thinking on their own, making their own decisions and taking the next step into self-responsibility.

A child can continue to have a healthy respect and admiration for their parents but must always forge on into adulthood.

This analogy directly correlates with our spiritual beliefs. Most people are like children in their relationship with God. They defer to what they have been told and do exactly what has been dictated to them as the ultimate truth from a third party. Yet, like a teenager, the promptings from within will let them know when they need more responsibility in their relationship with God. It doesn't mean they have to leave their spiritual "home" but maybe it is time to take on a little bit more responsibility around the house.

A way to do this is to simply challenge everything you know in a respectful way. What are the absolutes in your faith and in your life? What is their benefit or their hindrance? There may be a need for absolutes to contain the group. But are they necessary when one learns to develop a more mature relationship with God?

Think of the absolutes in a faith that you have no affinity for. Look at their purpose. Then look at the absolutes in your own and see how they may now be putting a glass ceiling on your own spiritual growth.

One common absolute is to not read the doctrines of another faith lest you be damned. This may be very important for an immature soul to keep them from wandering into some intangible harm. But what about the older souls that have learned discernment? The absolutes become a curfew on you.

God in Its infinite awareness doesn't need to be adulated or worshiped. God doesn't care about the faith that you chose. These are matters for men, not God. Does God really want us to kill in Its name or defer to someone else outside of direct connection with It?

Maybe God has been speaking directly to each soul--heart to heart--their whole existence. Maybe man overlays his voice on the soundtrack of love that God provides. Maybe it has never been about killing or praising in "His" name. Maybe it has always been about loving in the sanctity of your own depth and listening to that inner calling.

Maybe God is infinite Love and Patience and awaits each soul to outgrow the confines of all the outer commandments. Maybe he is lovingly ushering us into an adult relationship with Love itself. Maybe it is one where we all are an authority on our unique relationship with It. Maybe we merely respectfully stay in the confines of our faith to show others how to go past outer limitations of doctrine.

Maybe we can perpetuate more divinity by venturing into the heart of acceptance instead of staying pooled in a mass of "should" and "can't." I challenge all to challenge their own absolutes. It is easy to see how others are limited by theirs. It takes more courage to peek on the other side of our own and step on the fresh soil of enlightenment. I look forward to seeing you on the other side.

Take the Initiative

In monasteries, there was a hierarchy based on an obedience and performance level. These initiations were given out by merit. But if you think about it, an initiation represents taking more of an initiative. Those who want to be empowered can take their own initiative instead of needing someone to give them an initiation to progress. It is a way to be more empowered.

Every time you take the initiative, you are expanding your world exponentially. In past times, it was enough to just live an ordinary life in the linear realms. But the linear reality here on earth has proven to be a stagnant existence with little possibility for growth. Every aspect of it seems tainted. Here is a way to energetically expound beyond the limitations of this world as we have been perceiving it.

(Say each statement three times while tapping on your head and say it a fourth time while tapping on your chest.)

"I release manipulating others; in all moments."

"I make space in this world to take the initiative; in all moments."

"I remove all blockages to taking the initiative; in all moments."

"I stretch my capacity to take the initiative; in all moments."

"I make space in his world to seed a pure intention; in all moments."

"I remove all blockages to seeding a pure intention; in all moments."

"I stretch my capacity to seed a pure intention; in all moments."

"I break up all linear illusion to live dynamically and exponentially; in all moments."

"I make space in this world to live dynamically and exponentially; in all moments."

"I remove all blockages to living dynamically and exponentially; in all moments."

"I stretch my capacity to live dynamically and exponentially; in all moments."

God Does Not Hear Linearly

God does not hear linearly. People are so narrow-banded in their awareness that they perceive God to be so narrow as well. God hears each heartbeat, breath, desire and intention. God hears each hope, dream and cry in the night; God is not fixated on "his" own issues, waiting for "his" time to speak, laden with problems, gossip or ready with a sarcastic quip. God is eager to assist each soul as it advances deeper into "his" heart.

The Free Range of God

It is a powerful manipulative ploy to put a label on anyone. How does this sound, "Tree Hater"? It sticks, right? Those who are tree huggers don't want people to stay tree haters. That is the difference between love and power. Power uses labels to paralyze others into inaction. Love wishes the best for everyone and so does not put labels on others.

That is why those of love seem weak to those immersed in power. Love will not stoop to such methods. Pay attention when someone stamps a label on someone. It is so they can dismiss them into a group and not think of them as whole beings with passions and feelings. Isn't that what is done to cattle before they are slaughtered? I prefer to roam the range of God freely. I hold this intention for all others.

God Doesn't Hate You

It's no secret to many that organized religion has caused many to feel less connected to God than the opposite intention. Nothing on earth is perfect. A religion may have the best intention but there may be a disconnect sometimes between sacred doctrine and knowing the heart and intention of each member of the flock.

In past lives, many of us have been ostracized, excommunicated, martyred, soldiers in holy wars, and just plain disillusioned. These experiences are so ingrained that they may interfere with feelings of worthiness in the present and our relationship with God.

Here are some taps that may assist with deep feelings of unworthiness and separation from Love. If you have a resistance to doing them, that could be a cue that they may be helpful in releasing some deep seated emotion and beliefs.

(Say each statement three times while continuously tapping on the head; say it a fourth time while tapping the chest.)

"I release the belief that God hates me; in all moments."

"I release the belief that I am damned; in all moments."

"I release the belief that I am unworthy of God's Love; in all moments."

"I release the trauma of being martyred; in all moments."

"I release the guilt of cursing God; in all moments."

"I release the belief that I am separate from God; in all moments."

"I Am centered in God's Love; in all moments."

Individuality

A grain of sand on the shore that catches the Light

That one grounded bird that learns to take flight

The unencumbered soul that stretches to be free

That voice in dissension that learns to agree

The infant who remembers what it's like to be old

A flame that never forgets what it's like to be cold

Defeating lost hope by saying, "I can"

Experience being comfortable whether woman or man

Creating a symphony one note at a time

Knowing peace during chaos, albeit sublime

The sliver of knowledge that turns into a wedge

Being pushed past all reason and jumping over the ledge

There's no separation between the foam and the sea

Illusion's the only distinction between you and what's me.

11/10/13

Thank You

Jesus said himself that the things he did others could do and more. His mission was to empower the individual, not to enslave them to worshiping him. That was a twisting of his intention. Just like we see the public manipulated in the present election, they have been manipulated and controlled through this one belief system.

We demonize someone for having a God complex. I say by all means have a God complex. It means that you are feeling your own empowerment. The skew is when one believes that they are the only one who is the fabric of God. We are all empowered. To diminish those who are tapping into their own potential and empowerment is a desecration of God.

If you truly want to honor the life of Jesus, you will forgo all the brainwashing and conditioning that has turned us into spiritual sheep. You will heed Jesus' heart and intention for you and all others. Look past all that you have been taught about what his true message is, embrace the spirit of his words and embody them.

Truth and love resonate at similar frequencies. So you can't really resonate with love if you are in denial about truth and holding onto an antiquated belief system, especially if it has an agenda built into it. Jesus supports my work and is grateful that I clear up misunderstandings and the abuse of his good intentions.

Offense Against God

Anyone who glorifies God and then thinks, says or does anything unkind towards anyone else is a hypocrite. The face of God does not exist in the ethereal sky in intangible realms. The face of God is personified in everyone that we meet. Any act towards others is a direct offense against God.

Those who say they love God most are the ones who:

- Want to keep God out at the borders
- Think they are better than God
- Chop God down randomly for their own purposes
- Go to war against God
- Hate God
- Turn away from the plight of God
- Hunt God down for sport
- Ignore God

- Mock God
- Invalidate God loving God
- Curse God
- Abuse God.

Anything that we do as an offense to each other, we are literally doing to God.

Get Out of Your Head

My client had a dream experience of being in a school of higher learning. It looked like a classroom in a dream but she realized that she was actually there in the higher realms learning spiritual lessons. In the classroom was someone from her Facebook page who posts negative posts and is very opinionated. He is one of these people who will argue on principle and believe they are always right. They have all the answers memorized from a script that they have run in their head for forever.

This person was just sitting in the class with the rest of the students. The teacher (spirit guide) turned from the lesson on the board and addressed the young man. He was very direct in asking him to turn down his sound. My client understands that we are not solid matter but a frequency of sound woven into an emanation of light. The spirit guide told the young man that his sound was distracting to those around him who were trying to learn.

And so it is in this world. Those who are too immersed in facts and "this reality," or their own understanding of reality, distract those around them who are trying to grasp higher truths for themselves.

(Say each statement three times out loud while tapping on the top of your head at the crown chakra and say it a fourth time while tapping on your chest.)

"I declare myself a surrogate for all those stuck in the mental realms; in all moments."

"We release being stuck in the mental realms; in all moments."

"We declare ourselves surrogates for all those who wish to transcend; in all moments."

"We remove all the limitations that the mental realms have put on us; in all moments."

"We remove all vivaxes between ourselves and the mental realms; in all moments."

"We remove all tentacles between ourselves and the mental realms; in all moments."

"We remove the glass ceiling that the mental realms have put on us; in all moments."

"We remove all thought forms of control from our beingness; in all moments."

"We release seeking others' approval; in all moments."

"We release going off our path to gain others' approval; in all moments."

"We choose freedom over fear; in all moments."

"We release refusing to share my gifts; in all moments."

"We release the belief that my gifts aren't worthy of making a contribution; in all moments."

"We release spitting away my gifts; in all moments."

"We release weighing ourselves down with thought forms; in all moments."

"We release choosing war over sharing my gifts; in all moments."

"We release feeding my own issues; in all moments."

"We take ourselves off of energetic mute; in all moments."

"We shift our paradigm from mental slavery to spiritual freedom; in all moments."

"We shift our paradigm from being stuck in thought forms to spiritual freedom; in all moments."

"We transcend all thought forms; in all moments."

"We are centered and empowered in spiritual freedom; in all moments."

"We resonate and emanate spiritual freedom for all; in all moments."

Go Beyond the Mind

(Say each statement three times out loud while tapping on the top of your head at the crown chakra and say it a fourth time while tapping on your chest at the heart chakra.)

"I release deferring to the ego; in all moments."

"I release being at the mercy of the ego; in all moments."

"I release being enslaved to the ego; in all moments."

"I release being lied to by the ego; in all moments."

"I release protecting the ego at all costs; in all moments."

"I release worshiping the mind; in all moments."

"I release the fear losing the mind; in all moments."

"I release confusing overcoming the ego with death; in all moments."

"I release the fear of not existing; in all moments."

"I release confusing myself for the ego; in all moments."

"I release blurring the difference between myself and the ego; in all moments."

"I release feeding the ego; in all moments."

"I release the belief that I am the ego; in all moments."

"I recant all vows and agreements between myself and the ego; in all moments."

"I remove all curses between myself and the ego; in all moments."

"I sever all strings and cords between myself and the ego; in all moments."

"I dissolve all karmic ties between myself and the ego; in all moments."

"I remove all the pain, burden, limitations, lies and engrams that the ego has put on me; in all moments."

"I remove all the pain, burden, limitations, lies and engrams that I have put on all others due to the ego; in all moments."

"I remove all the responsibility and importance that I have put on the ego; in all moments."

"I withdraw all my energy from the ego; in all moments."

"I strip all illusion off myself in regards to the ego; in all moments."

"I remove all the masks, walls and armor that the ego has put on me; in all moments."

"I remove all masks, walls and armor that I have put on the ego; in all moments."

"I release building up the ego; in all moments."

"I release the fear of being raw and exposed; in all moments."

"I release the belief that I am nothing without the ego; in all moments."

"I release being defensive and petty; in all moments."

"I repair and fortify my spiritual wei chi; in all moments."

"I take back all the Joy, Love, Abundance, Freedom, Health, Success, Security, Companionship, Creativity, Peace, Life, Wholeness, Beauty, Enthusiasm, Contentment, Spirituality, Enlightenment and Confidence that the ego has taken from me; in all moments."

"I give back all the Joy, Love, Abundance, Freedom, Health, Success, Security, Companionship, Creativity, Peace, Life, Wholeness, Beauty, Enthusiasm, Contentment, Spirituality, Enlightenment and Confidence that I have taken from all others due to the ego; in all moments."

"I shatter all glass ceilings that the ego has put on me; in all moments."

"I release resonating with the ego; in all moments."

"I extract all of the ego from my sound frequency; in all moments."

"I extract all of the ego from my light body; in all moments."

"I shift my paradigm from the ego to Joy, Love, Abundance, Freedom, Health, Success, Security, Companionship, Creativity, Peace, Life, Wholeness, Beauty, Enthusiasm, Contentment, Spirituality, Enlightenment and Confidence; in all moments."

"I transcend the ego; in all moments."

"I am centered and empowered in the vulnerability and strength of my transcended self; in all moments."

"I embrace the translucent freedom of myself as personified love; in all moments."

"I surrender to myself as personified love; in all moments."

"I am centered and empowered as personified love; in all moments."

"I resonate and emanate divine love; in all moments."

"I see love in all forms; in all moments."

"I accept the fluid omniscience, omnipresence, and omnipotence of divine love in all forms and ways; in all moments."

"I see myself as divine love in all; in all moments."

"I embrace the love of myself in all and embrace all within myself; in all moments."

The Confusion About Heaven

The concept of heaven was formulated when the majority of people were illiterate. There was no other way to help them comprehend that heaven existed in a finer vibratory rate than the coarse vibration of solid matter. There was no way to help them understand that coarse matter is made up of dense molecules, that there is space between each molecule and that accumulated space between all molecules is where heaven is.

If they couldn't understand that, they surely couldn't fathom that we are all immersed in heaven right now because not only are we made up of coarse matter but we are also the spaces between the molecules of all coarse matter. So, in fact, we are in heaven and hell right now. It depends on whether we focus on the dense matter or whether we focus on the spaces between the molecules of the dense matter.

The way to stay dense is to gossip, complain, judge and worry. The way to slip through the cracks of coarse matter and find ourselves in heaven is through gratitude, kindness and love. It is a conscious choice. Humanity is ready for this understanding and does not have to be fixed in the allegory of heaven being in the sky any more.

The Angel of Death

Did you ever have a real tough boss that you were terrified of but when you got more mature you began to like? Maybe a mutual respect grew between you. Anyone reading this is able to develop that type of relationship with the Angel of Death.

In past times, people were real superstitious and created much fear around death. Maybe they created this faceless terrifying being out of their fear. I had one client who was terrified to cross over because she was afraid of seeing the Angel of Death. I have had clients terrified of glimpsing the Angel of Death because it meant that he would be visiting.

(Say each statement three times out loud while tapping on the top of your head at the crown chakra and say it a fourth time while tapping on your chest at the heart chakra. Say each word deliberately.)

"I release the belief that the Angel of Death is evil; in all moments."

"I release my fear of the Angel of Death; in all moments."

"I release the fear of death; in all moments."

"I release the belief that death is coming for me; in all moments."

"I release expecting a visit from the Angel of Death; in all

moments."

"I recant all vows and agreements between myself and the Angel of Death; in all moments."

"I remove all curses between myself and the Angel of Death; in all moments."

"I dissolve all karmic ties between myself and the Angel of Death; in all moments."

"I remove all the pain, burden and limitations that the Angel of Death has put on me; in all moments."

"I take back all the Joy, Love, Abundance, Freedom, Health, Success, Life and Wholeness that the Angel of Death has taken from me; in all moments."

"I withdraw all my energy from the Angel of Death; in all moments."

"I shift my paradigm from the Angel of Death to Love, Light and Healing; in all moments."

"I transcend the Angel of Death; in all moments."

"I release resonating with the Angel of Death; in all moments."

"I release emanating with the Angel of Death in all moments."

"I remove all of the Angel of Death from my sound frequency; in all moments."

"I remove all of the Angel of Death from my light body; in all moments."

"I am centered and empowered in Love, Light and Healing; in all moments."

Things to Know When a Loved One Is Ready to Cross Over

Getting ready to cross is a very personal time. Talking about someone's health issue, bodily functions or story is a desecration to their person. People do this at first to convey information, but then to get attention from it, and then out of a repetitive habit. It really is nobody's business. People want to know details but almost all of wanting to know is lascivious in some way. It is a very private time.

Some people resent those who are quiet during this time. That is their coping mechanism. They may have a better understanding of the process than one who is trying to keep busy all the time. If someone is quiet, please respect that. It is their sacred prerogative.

Talking about the person crossing in the third person is an overt violation of their personhood. Many people take great pride in doing this. It is like they are proud of having a role of domination over this dynamic person who was once larger than life. Talking to the doctors or others in front of them about them is passive aggressive. It is like saying, "I am important now and you are not anymore." At the least, it is disrespectful.

Talking about the person as if they are well and not experiencing something profound is a form of denial. It is a coping mechanism for those not emotionally ready to accept a shift in their world of losing this presence. It is invalidating though to the person who is fighting for their life. Please don't tell them, they are "just fine and going to beat this," when it is common knowledge that they aren't. This is isolating for the individual preparing to cross who wants to just feel close to their loved ones at that time.

No need to fill space up with mindless chatter. Some patients may want to hear about mundane things but others may want to enjoy the silence. Silence is not a bad thing. When someone is working on crossing over, silence is very pleasant and it helps them tune into the vibration that they are acclimating to.

All the drama is self-indulgent. Removing ourselves from the physical body is a very natural process. We have done it infinite times. Be grateful for the transition time of illness that allows your loved one to do this on their terms with the ability to say goodbye. Crossing over is a simple matter of slipping out of the physical body and adjusting to the new vibration of the astral plane. We are evolved enough to tune into this vibration as a species but control factions have prevented it. Those who use their imagination and are creative may more easily tune into the vibration of the astral plane. Those who are rigid and conform may have a harder time with someone crossing.

The process of crossing over is really simple and pleasant. It is more traumatic to be born than it is to leave the physical realm.

Death is a naïve notion inflicted on man to control his behavior in society. It works. There is a direct correlation between a group's belief system and how adamant they are in controlling others. We do not die. We attain our awareness and keep accruing the ability for love and compassion lifetime after lifetime. All of life is an exercise in stretching our capacity to love.

Using a person's illness to get attention is very low on the survival scale. People who do this stand out as having little understanding or compassion for the one who is actually going through the process of crossing over. Talking about someone who is ill just to indulge yourself is a violation of spiritual law and desecrates the person you talk about.

When it is someone's time to cross and they have accepted it, the best thing you can do is show your gratitude for knowing them and give them permission to cross. Many times the people in the physical are holding the one who is ready to cross back from their journey. It is very difficult for one crossing when people do this. We do this to our pets too. It is self-indulgent to pray for them to stay or have prayer circles to get them well after the point they are gearing to cross. This is such a personal thing and the person may not have the strength to say it out loud because they don't want to upset their loved ones. But it is self-indulgent to keep them here. It is a violation of their sacred essence. It is also a huge violation to start a prayer circle for them. Many people who do this are merely gleaning attention from their spiritual group for themselves.

Don't put your concepts of the process of crossing onto the individual. Imagery and belief systems are very personal and can be limiting to a person who has different reference points. You may think it is the most beautiful imagery to say that, "God will meet you at the door," but they may have different imagery and think of God as vengeful. It may conjure up imageries of past life crossings of the angel of death looming nearby. It may induce fear in them that is counterproductive. Allow people to have their experience in crossing and don't put the limitations of your belief system on them unless they ask.

Crossing over is very natural. The person stays in tune with the body for about three days and there can be a great connection made with them at this time. Being fixated in despair can block this subtle communication, which is frustrating to the one who has crossed because they are eager for you to know how great they are doing and to reassure you that everything is fine.

When you go to sleep, you are able to slip out of the physical body and visit your loved one in their new life that can, many times, look similar to their life on earth. There will be much more freedom. You have a great time visiting with them and when you wake up, because of your limiting belief systems, don't remember that you have just had a great time with your loved one. They get exasperated in seeing you sad when you wake up. Sometimes you have a good laugh with them about how silly the beliefs are here on earth, but then you wake up and forget.

The person who has crossed is able to manipulate electricity or induce a song to play to mean something to you. They want you to know they are fine. They still are working to comfort you. There will be a sign from nature, the wind, or one of their familiar phrases will come out of the mouth of a stranger. But this takes effort for them. It would be so much easier for our loved ones who have crossed if an initial understanding of the process was in place. It would make it easier for them to connect and offer comfort if death wasn't immersed in so much mystery.

Talking about what led to your loved one's death locks them into the traumatic experience. It pulls on them from the other side and distracts them from their joy in the moment. This is true with our pets as well. That is why Native Americans never talk about those who have crossed over. They know it is an insult to them. They understood that our loved ones come back to us in the bodies of our babies. That is why they respect their children so much. They knew and recognized them as their forefathers.

Your loved ones will also come back to the family if there are strong bonds to do that. You can look for them in the eyes of your children, nieces and nephews, and even grandchildren.

When someone has taken their own life, they immediately realize that they have made a mistake. They are taken through a process of understanding that is horrific compared to what they were trying to escape on earth. Immediately, they will pull on friends and family members that they left behind. That is why there is such a balm of despair over the home of someone who has committed suicide. They are trying to relieve their anguish by inflicting it on those who love them. Many times, they will compel others take their life to keep them company. If someone takes their own life, you have to cut off all connection and sympathy to them. It is self-survival. You can't help them. It is tough love and they need to take their "medicine." Having sympathy or guilt for them can be used to psychically manipulate you and can destroy the happiness of whole families. It is best to focus your attention on the ones who are here with you in that case. It really is self-survival because hardly anyone is equipped to deal with such an energy as one who has ended their own physical life.

When you cross over, you don't magically attain superpowers and transform into a cosmic angel. You can give little insights to someone who loves you but you do not become omniscient merely by crossing over. It is a lateral move. One woman thought her drug-dealing brother who committed suicide was now her guardian angel. He merely used her to satiate his cravings for drugs, alcohol and cigarettes. She thought it was funny she took up smoking after he died. Once she understood why, she could wean herself off of them.

Your pets love you but are so "in the moment." When they go outside and you get very upset, it induces the belief in them that they have crossed over and are in another life. They may leave you behind when that happens. It is important that you depict calm and loving thoughts to your pets especially when they are lost or going through a procedure. When it is time for them to cross, the most loving thing you can do is stay in a loving state with them and not talk about or relive their trauma. This can be a form of hell for them because every time you talk about them getting hit by the car, they are forced to relive it. By keeping your thoughts pleasant and loving, you are demonstrating the greatest love possible. Drama and sadness do not register well on our pets. It doesn't actually register well on people either.

Overcoming the Limitations of the Mind

I facilitated a session with a very aware person, but there was a part of her that was getting stuck. The visual I received was a wire birdcage. It would allow in all the experiences of sunlight, interactions and experiences. But the little bird inside wasn't free. This was an analogy of the woman and her relationship with the mind. She was trapped within it like so many of us. She did not even realize that because of her vantage point within the cage, she seemed to have so much freedom.

In many lifetimes, the mind was considered the highest truth. In lifetimes when ignorance was so prevalent, intelligence was coveted like wealth. That is one reason so many people glorify intelligence and debate. In lifetimes of depravity, such intelligence would be considered a form of wealth or even of celebrity status. God is even considered by many to be the Universal mind, but the mind is one of the last stops in the journey of unfolding. The mind is a cage to soul.

The sessions I facilitate are so beneficial because we work on such a deep level. I am able to pull the client out of all their bodies, even the mind, and assist them in looking at themselves objectively. The mind tries to prevent this. You can't fix something using the very thing that has created the distortion. This is what people are doing when they try to fix themselves by using the mind. It just creates mind loops and larger distortions.

Here are taps to disable the debilitating effects of an overprotective mind. When the mind is being addressed, it will sometimes cause the person to feel like they are dying. It is the ego clutching on the sides of the person with nails dug in. It is best to stay in a nonreactive state. The ego loves drama. By taking away its shtick, you are unlatching each bony finger of the possessive mind, one by one. It may feel scary. But that is the biggest ploy of the ego. You are empowered when you don't give in to the fear and forgo the drama. You are you at your most dynamic self.

(Say each statement three times out loud while tapping on your head and say it a fourth time while tapping repeatedly on your chest.)

"I release being caged in the mind; in all moments."

"I release being caged by the mind; in all moments."

"I release being enslaved to the mind; in all moments."

"I release being diminished by the mind; in all moments."

"I release all the hopeless eddies of the mind; in all moments."

"I release being trapped in an illusion of the mind; in all moments."

"I free myself from the myriad of the mind; in all moments."

"I remove all the illusions of the mind; in all moments."

"I release using the mind to satiate the craving for love; in all moments."

"I release using the mind to accrue power; in all moments."

"I release creating drama to feel important; in all moments."

"I release creating illness to validate myself; in all moments."

"I release creating problems to prove that I exist; in all moments."

"I release the layers of ego that engulf the mind; in all moments."

"I release the mind's control from all 32 layers of my auric field; in all moments."

"I separate the wise mind from the destructive mind; in all moments."

"I empower the wise mind to dissolve the destructive mind; in all moments."

"I separate the wise mind from the selfish mind; in all moments."

"I empower the wise mind to dissolve the selfish mind; in all moments."

"I separate the wise mind from the fearful mind; in all moments."

"I empower the wise mind to dissolve the fearful mind; in all moments."

"I separate the wise mind from the ignorant mind; in all moments."

"I empower the helpful mind to dissolve the ignorant mind; in all moments."

"I separate the wise mind from the combative mind; in all moments."

"I empower the wise mind to dissolve the combative mind; in all moments."

"I recant all vows and agreements between myself and the mind; in all moments."

"I remove all curses between myself and the mind; in all moments."

"I release the fear of losing my mind; in all moments."

"I release the belief that the mind is God; in all moments."

"I release confusing the mind with the highest state; in all moments."

"I release the fear of surpassing the mind; in all moments."

"I recant the vow to not transcend; in all moments."

"I release worshiping the mind; in all moments."

"I release giving all my power to the mind; in all moments."

"I withdraw all my energy from the mind; in all moments."

"I sever all strings and cords between myself and the mind; in all moments."

"I dissolve all karmic ties between myself and the mind; in all

moments."

"I remove all the pain, burden, limitations and engrams that the mind has put on me; in all moments."

"I remove all the pain, burden, limitations and engrams that I have put on all others due to the mind; in all moments."

"I take back all the joy, love, abundance, freedom, life and wholeness that the mind has taken from me; in all moments."

"I give back all the joy, love, abundance, freedom, life and wholeness that I have taken from all others due to the mind; in all moments."

"I release resonating with the mind; in all moments."

"I release emanating with the mind; in all moments."

"I remove all of the mind from my sound frequency; in all moments."

"I remove all of the mind from my light body; in all moments."

"I shift my paradigm from the mind to joy, love, abundance, freedom, life and wholeness; in all moments."

"I transcend the mind; in all moments."

"I align all my bodies; in all moments."

"I am centered and empowered in joy, love, abundance, freedom, life and wholeness; in all moments."

How to Manifest Your Greatest Purpose

People underestimate the power of a pure loving intention fueled by conviction. It is a means of dipping into that infinite place where the stars are born. It is utilizing the same process of forming planets to command all the dust and the particles in your realm to gravitate in your orbit of greatness.

We are meant to create. It is blueprinted into our DNA. It has taken era after era of being beaten down and diminished as a means to subjugate us, for us to cower at the thought. These are our primal memories and the reason that we shy away from our own abilities. But buried underneath all the fear of being called out, humiliated, rejected, scorned and false humility, is the deep knowing and understanding of our greatness. It is the secret we hold deeply within ourselves and fear uttering out loud.

But here is the truth. You are great. You know you are. Your frustration is in not having a means to express it and have it validated. Here is the key. It is very simple. Combine these two things and you will unravel your greatness: Do what you love and do it as a service to others. In this way, you will be serving your greatest purpose.

We were never meant to spend our days lamenting about a relationship, worrying about what we look like, feeling like paupers and chasing after paper money. We are descendants of kings and genius. Galileo, Copernicus, da Vinci, Gandhi and King all have the same make up as our own. We are meant to convert all our pain, anguish, disappointments and wounds into kindness and compassion for those who don't quite have the good fortune of our awareness yet.

Prove this theory to yourself. Take that noble sacred intention that you hold dearly and set it free into motion. Work towards that dream and goal without the need for outer validation. Fuel it with that deep conviction that you have something worthy to contribute. Empower it with your greatness, conviction and goodness. Send it out in the world to land sweetly in the lives of others, as it will, and inspire them in the way that it will.

Instead of sucking up energy with false modesty and humility, pour your love and conviction out into mass consciousness as easily as your breath and allow all others to partake of its fragrance. Disengage the need to claim it as your own. It will live on long past your clay self. It will succor and nurture innocents forever and beyond if you merely have the courage to convert everything you are to love and pour it into the ether.

Has Anyone Told You Lately How Awesome You Are?

You have survived incredible feats just to be here. You have conquered demons, slayed dragons, beaten the odds, rolled with the punches, sidestepped landmines, grabbed the glass ring, given it your all and rose to the cream of the crop, just to be here.

The fact that you have blocked all but this lifetime out so you can concentrate on the task at hand does not diminish your journey.

Please don't let anyone tell you that you are not amazing or that you are unworthy. Your sheer presence in this world contradicts that very statement. You are evidence of amazing.

If life feels mundane, accept it as a respite and embrace it. There is so much wonder that reveals itself when the mundane is scrutinized for the opportunity it is. May you transcend the illusion of mundane and turn each moment inside out to reveal the wonder and splendor of an adventure. Play through dear friend. Play through!

Lead with Kindness

(Say each statement three times out loud while continuously tapping on the top of your head at the crown chakra and say it a fourth time while tapping on your chest.)

"I release the belief that showing kindness is displaying weakness; in all moments."

"I release the belief that I am weak; in all moments."

"I release the fear of being bullied for being kind; in all moments."

"I release coming out of my center to be kind; in all moments."

"I stand in my center to reinforce kindness; in all moments."

"I release confusing kindness with vulnerability; in all moments."

"I am both kind and strong; in all moments."

"I exude strength from kindness; in all moments."

"I release forgoing kindness to fit in; in all moments."

"I shift my paradigm from being ashamed of kindness to being proud of kindness; in all moments."

"I release mingling unworthiness into kindness; in all moments."

"I release mistrusting genuine kindness; in all moments."

"I release judging kindness as weak; in all moments."

"I empower kindness everywhere; in all moments."

"I connect to all others in kindness; in all moments."

"I am imbued in kindness; in all moments."

"I am centered and empowered in kindness; in all moments."

"I encourage all others to center and be empowered in kindness; in all moments."

"I resonate and emanate kindness; in all moments."

Holding Space for Better

There is an ebb and flow that happens in life. There are currents that the individual deals with and there are currents that we experience together as a group. Sometimes life outflows well and it feels great. But then there are cycles that feel like nothing is happening. It is a place of stillness. The human consciousness will create a problem out of the stillness. It will call it restlessness, boredom or worse.

When those times of stillness come, forgo identifying them as negative. Be patient with the quiet periods. Allow them to be formless spaces of peace. Instead of filling them back up with negative adjectives, allow them to stay open. This is how more Joy, Love, Abundance and Freedom flow into our lives.

Right now, many are in this place of stillness. Relax into the stillness and allow it to expand into betterment for you and others. I will hold this space with you.

Freeing Ourselves from the Controller

Imagine this is some kind of alternate reality where people are manipulated by this dried up ancient man that is half machine and devoid of all compassion. Perhaps he runs this world to the ground for his own amusement and to compensate for being devoid of humanity. Perhaps these taps will assist in freeing humanity in an abstract way. I could say more but it is a moot point unless people choose to do the work.

(Say each statement three times while tapping on your head and say it a fourth time while tapping on your chest.)

"We declare ourselves surrogates for humanity in doing these taps; in all moments."

"We release being manipulated by the controller; in all moments."

"We release being enslaved by the controller; in all moments."

"We release being impervious to the controller; in all moments."

"We release being weighed down by the controller; in all moments."

"We release being deceived by the controller; in all moments."

"We release being vulnerable to the controller; in all moments."

"We release falling prey to the controller; in all moments."

"We release being controlled by the controller; in all moments."

"We strip all illusion off of the controller; in all moments."

"We withdraw all our energy from the controller; in all moments."

"We take back all our empowerment from the controller; in all moments."

"We remove all vivaxes between ourselves and the controller; in all moments."

"We remove all tentacles between ourselves and the controller; in all moments."

"We remove the claws of the controller from our beingness; in all moments."

"We remove the controller from our lives; in all moments."

"We remove the controller from our world; in all moments."

"We remove the controller from our reality; in all moments."

"We release worshiping the controller; in all moments."

"We release idolizing the controller; in all moments."

"We remove all implants of the controller; in all moments."

"We remove all engrams that the controller put in us; in all moments."

"We remove all engrams of the controller; in all moments."

"We remove all programming and conditioning that the controller has put on us; in all moments."

"We send all energy matrices into the light and sound that connect us to the controller; in all moments."

"We command all complex energy matrices that connect us to the controller to be escorted into the light and sound; in all moments."

"We send all energy matrices into the light and sound that empower the controller; in all moments."

"We command all complex energy matrices that empower the controller to be escorted into the light and sound; in all moments."

"We nullify all contracts with the controller; in all moments."

"We recant all vows and agreements between ourselves and the controller; in all moments."

"We remove all curses between ourselves and the controller; in all moments."

"We remove all blessings between ourselves and the controller; in all moments."

"We remove all dependency on the controller; in all moments."

"We sever all strings, cords and wires between ourselves and the controller; in all moments."

"We dissolve all karmic ties between ourselves and the controller; in all moments."

"We collapse and dissolve all portals from us to the controller; in all moments."

"We collapse and dissolve all portals from the controller to us; in all moments."

"We remove all identities assigned to us by the controller; in all

moments."

"We remove all the pain, burden and limitations that the controller has put on us; in all moments."

"We remove all the fear, futility and unworthiness that the controller has put on us; in all moments."

"We remove all the apathy, regret and illusion of separateness that the controller has put on us; in all moments."

"We remove all that we have put on others due to the controller; in all moments."

"We remove all the oppression that the controller has put on us; in all moments."

"We take back all that the controller has taken from us; in all moments."

"We give back to all others all that we have taken from them due to the controller; in all moments."

"We release resonating with the controller; in all moments."

"We release emanating with the controller; in all moments."

"We extract all of the controller from our sound frequency; in all moments."

"We extract all of the controller from our light emanations; in all moments."

"We extract all of the controller from all 32 layers of our auric field; in all moments."

"We extract all of the controller from our whole beingness; in all moments."

"We extract all of the controller from our whole world; in all moments."

"We extract all of the controller from our reality; in all moments."

"We extract all of the controller from the lower worlds; in all moments."

"We shift our paradigm from the controller to exponential freedom; in all moments."

"We transcend the controller; in all moments."

"We remove all masks, walls and armor that the controller has put on us; in all moments."

"We free ourselves of the coarse energy of the controller's intentions; in all moments."

"We dissipate the residual vibration of the controller's intentions; in all moments."

"We are centered and empowered in exponential freedom; in all moments."

"We resonate, emanate and are interconnected with all life in exponential freedom; in all moments."

"We live, move and express our beingness in exponential freedom; in all moments."

The Exorcism

Humans love drama. The drama is part of the issue. Here is to releasing unfavorable issues from yourself that seem like foreign entities. This is not a Hollywood movie. This is your life. The drama and fear are the antitheses of getting free. No one needs to plunge to their death as a host body to get rid of stubborn energies. Just do these taps in a matter-of-fact way and cut the drama.

(Say each statement three times out loud while continuously

tapping on the top of your head at the crown chakra and say it a fourth time while tapping on your chest.)

"I request all pure spirit guides to assist in this session; in all moments."

"I remove all vivaxes between myself and all complex energy matrices; in all moments."

"I remove all tentacles between myself and all complex energy matrices; in all moments."

"I remove the clutch of all complex energy matrices; in all moments."

"I release being impinged by any complex energy matrices; in all moments."

"I remove all programming and conditioning that any complex energy matrices have put on me; in all moments."

"I remove all engrams that any complex energy matrices have put on me; in all moments."

"I send all energy matrices into the light and sound that support or sustain any complex energy matrices; in all moments."

"I rescind all invitations to all complex energy matrices; in all moments."

"I release deferring to any or all complex energy matrices; in all moments."

"I release using complex energy matrices as a crutch; in all moments."

"I release hiding behind any complex energy matrices; in all moments."

"I release using complex energy matrices as an excuse; in all moments."

"I release feeling helpless against complex energy matrices; in all moments."

"I recant all vows and agreements between myself and all complex energy matrices; in all moments."

"I remove all complex energy matrices from my beingness and send them into the light and sound; in all moments."

"I remove all curses between myself and all complex energy matrices; in all moments."

"I remove all blessings between myself and all complex energy matrices; in all moments."

"I sever all strings and cords and fibers between myself and all complex energy matrices; in all moments."

"I release being shriveled in a corner of myself by any complex energy matrices; in all moments."

"I dissolve all karmic ties between myself and all complex energy matrices; in all moments."

"I remove all the pain, burden, limitations, and weakness that all complex energy matrices have put on me; in all moments."

"I remove the illusion of separateness that all complex energy matrices have put on me; in all moments."

"I remove all the chaos and conflict that complex energy matrices have put on me; in all moments."

"I take back all the good that all complex energy matrices have taken from me; in all moments."

"I separate myself from all complex energy matrices; in all moments."

"I command all complex energy matrices to be escorted into the light and sound; in all moments."

"I release attracting complex energy matrices to my beingness; in all moments."

"I release being vulnerable to complex energy matrices; in all moments."

"I release allowing complex energy matrices to exist in my beingness; in all moments."

"I release allowing complex energy matrices to feed on my energy; in all moments."

"I release allowing complex energy matrices to thrive in my beingness; in all moments."

"I send all residual energy matrices in my beingness into the light and sound; in all moments."

"I repair and fortify my beingness from attracting energy matrices; in all moments."

"I am centered and imbued in Divine Love; in all moments."

"I singe out everything from my beingness that is not Divine Love; in all moments."

Here is a technique to heal everyone in the world of such things.

After you go through these taps once, do these same taps above except add the following tap at the beginning: "I declare myself a surrogate for humanity in doing these taps; in all moments."

Jen Ward

2. A MAN-MADE GOD

A Distant God

I'd like to meet most any God that isn't based on love

And show him what he's doing to earth, as push has come to shove

He must have turned his head away when his message was set in 'cause

There's such an inconsistency between love and the obeying of his laws

Maybe he had a vision that just got misconstrued

To have a noble intention in everything we do

There might be a miscommunication that has to be set straight

Any God worth his weight preaches love, not hate.

Maybe it's the interpretation as so many are seeped in sin

It's not about conquering the world but going quietly within

It's not about seeing the faults of others, bringing them to their knees

It's seeing love in everyone, let them worship as they please

God had this pure intention, all must realize

It was man who buried it in ritual and covered it with lies

Any God that is a God that is instilled in the hearts of man

Doesn't incite the world in violence, "Love" has another plan

Teach responsibility in everything you do

If you judge for your God, that transgression is on you

I can't agree with any man who diminishes others for God

But I realize the learning curve, it's the reverence I applaud

There is also a huge lesson, bookmarked just for me

I can't micromanage everyone, I must just let them be

If I have judgment in what another is ensuing

Then I am doing exactly what I accuse them of doing

If I question what someone values in a cynical maraud

I myself am worshiping a distant, unloving God.

1/20/15

In Regards to Owning God's Favor

When people say, "My god is this or my god is that," they are diminishing God. There is only one Source of all life and we are all protected and loved under the same umbrella. Otherwise, it isn't God but a creation of the ego meant to "lord" superiority over another sect. It is a manipulation meant to stroke the ego of one demographic.

This simple mentality of having a special "in" with God, of being the "chosen," has created the most bloodshed, hatred and bigotry on the planet. If any one being were chosen above the rest, it would only be in their capacity to love beyond all outer conditions and to have compassion for all others in their struggle to find purpose.

Perceiving that one is more special than another exemplifies the ego, which moves one away from the heart of their pious intention. By their mindset and demeanor in regards to others, they demonstrate the hypocrisy in believing they own God's favor.

Unworthy of God

The Bible got it backwards. God didn't make man in his image. Man made God in his image. That is evident in anyone who still believes that God needs to be worshiped, placated, adorned or stroked in any way. That is how limited man was able to conceive of God many, many years ago before the experiences of existing tempered our DNA.

Think about the wisest people that we have as examples of goodness: Gandhi, Mandela, Mother Teresa. They seem somewhat closer to God than others and yet they did not exude the attributes that some still attribute to God. They were kind, benevolent, resilient and focused on living their purpose. These are the attributes of God.

Those who seem most adamant on defending God to others veer away from the attributes of God in that very necessity. Those who judge, belittle or are self-righteous about God are not exhibiting attributes of God but of those who have been the power mongers through human history. God never displayed such arrogance or lack of kindness. It has always been the power mongers. We now have the awareness, ability and courage to recognize the difference.

All books have been written by man. They are not as much a mandate for God but a mandate for man's law in accordance with God. At best, they are a portal to connect to that inner communion with the sanctity of the omnipotent. At worst, they are a decree to diminish the worth of all souls who aren't in agreement with man's depiction of God's intent. This in itself is unworthy of God.

Galvanized in an Agenda

A couple of Jehovah's Witnesses knocked on my door. They both had great energy. But I could also see that it was galvanized with an agenda. They pretended to be open to what I said, but they were impervious to my responses. I answered each question with sincerity and honesty. The questions were met with that firewall of their agenda.

They kept asking me questions, but were disinterested in the answers. As I was answering from the heart, they were computing in their minds what questions would they ask next to keep me engaged. The goal in asking questions was to keep inching forward into receptivity. If they asked enough questions, I would relinquish my stance and relax my guard with them. They would then walk into my energy field and impose their intention into me. Notice I say into and not on? Into means penetrating a boundary. That is more accurate.

These people are so kind and loving on the surface, but they are liars and cheats with their approach and ruthless with their motive. Think about it. The only people who would be receptive to such ploys are the lonely, weak or inexperienced. They kept asking questions to which they didn't care about the answer. That is a lie. They pretended to care about me as a person. They did not. They cared about furthering their agenda. They don't realize that they are liars and cheats. That is what illusion does.

I gave them more sincerity and showed more integrity and truth in our brief interaction than they afforded me. If they were receptive to truth at all, I would have invited them in. But they were not. I could not save them. So I did not waste my energy.

God's Agenda?

If there is one thing that is sad to me, it is misguided people using their intention in a negative way. That is how it is when one uses prayer for an agenda. When one prays for someone and has an outcome in mind, they are trying to override God's will. If one prays with an agenda, it falls into the category of control and is a subtle form of black magic.

In the language of God, all is perfect. All are here to have their experiences, so they can understand their own loving nature. God does not want people to be perfect; that is silly. If God wants people to be like God in any way, it would be in the way of their having the capacity to love and grant acceptance. That is how people are being stretched to the capabilities of God.

When we judge others, when we pray for them to change, when

we thrust a social agenda on a community of people, we are merely showing ignorance and the inability to emulate and honor the message of God's love. When there is any issue we can't relate to, that is where our work needs to be in gaining compassion and understanding. Instead of praying for the other person to change, we should be praying to soften our own rigid stance.

Here is a technique: When you are having trouble relating to someone else, visualize going into a special shoe store. In this store, there are shoes to match every human experience. If there is an issue that you have trouble identifying with, ask the clerk to bring you a special pair of shoes to try on (just for a little bit) of a person who would own these shoes. There will be great resistance to trying on the shoes (you can feel it now). Put on the shoes of someone who is an extreme of who you are. See what it feels like, knowing that it will bring no adverse affects to you.

Here are some taps to help. Say each statement three times while tapping on your head and say it a fourth time while tapping on your chest.

"I release betraying God; in all moments."

"I release hating God; in all moments."

"I release usurping God's creed; in all moments."

"I release overriding Love; in all moments."

"I release being a pawn for power; in all moments."

"I release all arrogance, pride, vanity, ignorance and power plays; in all moments."

The only sacred way to pray is to not have an agenda and to wish goodwill for all. Sending loving energy to a situation without any restrictions on the outcome is the purest form of prayer. Even when one prays to have someone pull through and live, they are putting an agenda on another. What if there is a beautiful gift waiting on the other side for someone, and the only thing keeping them from it is the misguided prayers of a group? If one really wants to do God's work, they will forgo any agenda and just love all unconditionally. That is what God does.

It is okay to put a spin on God for your own comprehension of Its Omniscience. It is not okay to put a special spin on the One True Source of Love, Light and Truth to diminish the worth of others. God Loves all equally. Believing that you are more important to God than another is a desecration of God and merely a long, arduous stroke of the ego.

Feeling Free and Enlightened - In Sympathy with Jesus

I facilitated a private, remote session with a new client. She was feeling like she was in hell. She indeed was. In a past life, she was fed the fear of fire and brimstone and believed that hell was what she deserved. We did a bunch of taps to literally and figuratively remove her from hell.

But we also released all her dynamics with God. She wondered if she wanted to really do that. I explained how anything that we release about her dynamics with God, was not with the true God, but the God that man had made in his image. We were releasing all the concepts and beliefs of revenge, judgment, petty ego that man was prone to needing, not God.

After we did all these taps, she realized her voice changed. It had a richer tone and was more confident. She was thrilled. But we weren't done yet. In past lives, she was devoted to Jesus. When she read the parts of him being tortured and scorned, she resonated with such sympathy with him that she took on some of the pain that he had endured.

In her energy field, she saw Jesus as an enlightened soul who would have been devastated by how man has used him to wield power and destroy innocence. She was appalled at how Jesus was dishonored by all the wars and genocide that were committed in his name. It had made her personal hell more expansive as she was in sympathy with him.

So we did some taps to free Jesus if this is possible. What if Jesus is trapped somehow in the thought forms and all the devastation that man has done in his name? What if our intention to free him could do some good in some subjective way? Here are some of the taps that may be helpful to him.

"I release betraying Jesus; in all moments."

"I release being indifferent to Jesus; in all moments."

"I release letting Jesus down; in all moments."

"I release burdening Jesus; in all moments."

"I remove all the burden that I have put on Jesus; in all moments."

"I remove all the burden that I have taken on in sympathy with Jesus; in all moments."

"I sever all strings and cords between Jesus and all the thought forms that have been put on him; in all moments."

"I free Jesus from the emotional bondage he has been tangled in; in all moments."

"I release envisioning Jesus drowning in sorrow; in all moments."

"I release Jesus being frozen in a state of torture; in all moments."

"I separate the truth of Jesus from the ignorance of Jesus; in all moments."

"I free Jesus from the ignorance that has been encapsulated around him; in all moments."

"I empower, honor and love Jesus in the depth and freedom of his truth; in all moments."

"I release all the arrogance and presumptuousness pervading Jesus; in all moments."

"I release Jesus being used by power; in all moments."

"I heal all those who have suffered in Jesus' name; in all moments."

"I remove all curses on Jesus; in all moments."

"I remove all blessings that have turned to curses on Jesus; in all moments."

"I free Jesus from his private hell; in all moments."

"I recant all vows and agreements between Jesus and ignorance; in all moments."

"I remove all curses between Jesus and ignorance; in all moments."

"I remove all blessings between Jesus and ignorance; in all moments."

"I remove all vivaxes between Jesus and ignorance; in all moments."

"I remove all tentacles between Jesus and ignorance; in all moments."

"I send all energy matrices into the light and sound that immerse Jesus or his name and image in ignorance; in all moments."

"I strip all illusion off of ignorance; in all moments."

"I dissolve all karmic ties between Jesus and ignorance; in all moments."

"I sever all strings and cords between Jesus and ignorance; in all moments."

"I remove all the pain, burden, limitations and engrams that ignorance has put on Jesus; in all moments."

"I take back and give to Jesus all the Joy, Love, Abundance, Freedom, Health and Wholeness that ignorance has taken from him; in all moments."

"I release Jesus resonating with ignorance; in all moments."

"I release Jesus emanating with ignorance; in all moments."

"I release Jesus attracting ignorance; in all moments."

"I remove all ignorance from Jesus' sound frequency; in all moments."

"I remove all ignorance from Jesus' light body; in all moments."

"Jesus transcends ignorance; in all moments."

"Jesus is centered and empowered in truth and divine love; in all moments."

"I resonate and emanate divine love and truth; in all moments."

These taps really seemed to lighten my client. They are not meant to offend anyone's belief system but to help each person cleanse their own relationship with their beliefs and self-responsibility. They may benefit some in feeling free and enlightened. This is their purpose. If they offend, please just walk away and recognize this is the way of someone else to honor Jesus.

We Matter!

Your talents and gifts aren't meant to exist in a vacuum. They are meant to be spilled over into the world to make it beautifully complicated. The world is not meant to be a black and white world of good and bad. It is supposed to be a multidimensional, colorful array of wonderful attempts at being awesome. There is no perfect flower or one song to sing. There is music, color, fragrance and dynamic expression for all types of preferences.

To hold back your skills until everyone will love them will be sealing yourself in a sarcophagus of complacency. The world doesn't realize it loves you yet. You haven't introduced yourself to it. The most aware people are aware of those around them. They take their subtle cues from subtle realms. Quit trying to outsmart the world by rejecting yourself before they get a chance to.

You are not that self-aware yet to realize that even if you were perfect, someone would reject you because they are really rejecting themselves. It has never been about the other person loving or rejecting you. It has always been about what you do to gift yourself. What will you do to empower yourself? What will you do to amuse yourself?

The multitudes are waiting to build their gifts on the back of your accomplishments. This is the tag team of humanity. Why are you stopping up the gears when we are all experiencing the stagnant existence that happens when the multitudes do that? We are still unclogging the gears of past generations who have done this religiously. They are the ones that still choose war over creation and still choose power over love and still chose fear over acceptance. We are not them. Let's wash their stain from the face of humanity and continue with our arts.

We love! We accept. We share. We discern. We plant. We grow. We feed. We heal. We empower. We succeed. We believe. We nurture. We know. It is just time to do all these things together. We are not one little person. We are everyone, and we matter!

Connecting

In the thought patterns of my childhood, I would think that there was nothing beyond the boundaries of the roads I traveled. For instance, I never thought there were homes and towns past my school bus route. I knew there were other communities but it never occurred to me that the roads I traveled could lead to them. There was a convenient disconnect in place within my psyche to "contain" me.

This may be a similar disconnect that people have regarding their concept of God and the Universe. They know there are different ways to worship, but maybe it never occurs to them that the spiritual road they travel intersects with the road others travel.

More importantly, maybe they can't see that their concepts and beliefs can be expanded to include a greater community than just those that directly affect their lives. Maybe they can connect all the roads on the planet, but what then? There is always a way to expand the confines of understanding.

Whenever someone thinks they have an absolute answer, they are like a child who believes that the boundaries end at their understanding. There is an abyss between them and the whole.

Here are some taps to assist: (Say each statement three times while tapping on the head and say it a fourth time while tapping on your chest.)

"I create space in this world for greater truth; in all moments."

"I remove all blockages to greater truth; in all moments."

"I stretch my capacity to accept greater truth; in all moments."

"I release the disconnect between the microcosm (personal self) and the macrocosm; in all moments."

"I align the microcosm with the macrocosm; in all moments."

"I AM centered and imbued with Divine Love; in all moments."

The Golden Rule

If people would understand the natural relationship between cause and effect, they would WANT to give to others because giving to others is the cause that affects one to be given to. It isn't being forced to give or giving out of obligation; it is giving out of a true sense of purpose. People always ask me what their purpose is. I believe it is to give as much of ourselves as we can to others through our talents and gifts while maintaining an absolute balance.

Being disconnected from the natural laws that govern the Universe is the reason there is so much depravity in the world. There are enough aware people in the world to create a tipping point back to the natural law. After all the wars and injustices in the world, society is savvy enough to realize that the Golden Rule, "Do unto others as you would have others do unto you," is the best code of conduct for self-fulfillment. It is the same code of conduct but is followed now as a result of experience and not blind faith.

How to Free Fall into Enlightenment

There is no eventually. There is the moment. Putting anything off with the word eventually or with the phrase "all in good time," is a form of NOT taking responsibility. This is specifically and especially true with our spiritual empowerment. It is being enslaved to time. That is the lie that causes such apathy.

Believing that we have to wait to get to heaven or achieve a state of enlightenment is the last vestige in keeping us subservient in some way. It is a very subtle form of putting one in complacency.

You don't need a permission slip to be enlightened. You don't need anyone's blessing.

Once you recognize the deep fingers of control preventing you from accepting your own innate nature of being completely immersed in divinity, you will forgo the apathy that is part of the waiting. A multi-level tiered system in the advancement of God is a man-made ploy to keep a finger on control.

Question everything you have accepted as truth, even and especially in your own spiritual belief system. Guidelines were meant to keep you attached to a linear agenda. But they imply a range of motion that gives the deception of freedom. Anything of the linear belief system is not freedom. Disconnect yourself from everything that ties you to a linear existence and free fall into enlightenment.

Now is the time. Now is the only reality there truly is.

The Secret of Love

Maybe the reason there are so many people in the world is that love keeps dividing as a means to reflect love back to itself. But when the love takes human form, it becomes defensive and needy. Instead of reflecting love back to itself so love can gather itself back up, it tries to take from everyone else which further divides the love.

Perhaps if people started reflecting love back to each other in kindness, thought and deed, love wouldn't keep feeling the need to divide. Perhaps when we reflect love to others, we will see, feel and express it within ourselves. Perhaps the secret of love is to give it out willingly so that it can recollect in each human heart.

Embodiment of Me

Within mosaic walls of any denomination

When time was counted with sun and stone

We pledged our life force and eternal submission

Gave every worldly possession owned

In taking vows of servitude, poverty, silence

Became whispers of what we potentially could be

Herding the masses was the intention

Enslave each person by their own decree

Now is the time to take back our freedom

To lessen the yoke of the "powers that be"

Recant the effects of our own self-submission

Realize for ourselves what was cruelly omitted…

God and Truth live

In the embodiment of me.

The Love Game

God was bored
So he created a game for himself.
He separated all his atoms and allotted them all a different vantage point.
He created a game board out of matter and energy.
Most of his atoms were in on the game. They would stay in the form of love but be disguised as backdrop.
The playing pieces would be the humans; they would think they were most important but also feel separate and lonely.
There would be two identical kinds of players but they would see each other as inferior.
They would see everything as inferior. This was part of the game.
He gave them the ability to reason so that they could play the game.
They were given feelings so God could experience the game through their vantage point.
They needed a way to move around the board. God created space and time.
Each turn was a lifetime.
Each lifetime they would conquer the other players.
They believed the different playing pieces were giving clues to the game that they didn't have.
This was true. Both playing pieces had different strengths which were clues.
They would pair up sometimes as a means of figuring it out.
They would go on tangents for many turns thinking the game was about the pairing up with a particular player.
The pieces started out as ruthless.
They would destroy everything to figure out the rules.
But as they went along each turn, they started to care about the pieces they paired up with.
They would pause from the game and experience real moments of Joy and Love.

Each time they had these moments, they broke through the illusion.

At first, when the reality of Love shone through, they used this to show superiority over the other players.

They gave the other players false clues and a whole set of rules needed to break through the illusion.

They called this religion.

Religion would send the other players on wild goose chases for many turns.

But some players still got through the maze.

They started to realize they were in a game.

They started to help the other players instead of working against them.

This washed away more illusion.

God became enthralled in the more advanced players.

This helped them figure out the illusion of space and time-- that the board itself was not real.

More and more players are becoming self-realized.

Figuring out the keys to advancing were not making it about advancing, but about:

- opting out of the rules of power by instilling kindness as their first impulse,
- loving others and forgoing self-contempt by turning the love on themselves,
- surrendering all the rules of the hierarchy of the game,
- being loving and kind in every way that they can while seeped in the game,
- recognizing themselves as love itself.

A Message from Jesus Christ

Someone was angry about my posts because I don't praise Jesus. Here was my response:

Jesus Christ does not stop at the edge of our heart. He permeates it. Do you really think he wants us to shut down the love for any reason, especially in his name? Shutting down the love is shutting down the love. Jesus Christ is not the praise whore that you think he is.

I am wondering if people who are so adamant at defending Jesus Christ have ever gone into an altered state and had a conversation with him. He was not mainstream when he was alive. The way he empowered people was irritating to the mainstream. He allowed people to believe in healing and their own purpose and abilities. You would think when someone shows up in the world in a similar way that Jesus Christ did, like so many of us do, it would be the highest form of flattery.

Jesus was not an insider. Jesus did not take offense. He did not categorize people into the worthy or the unworthy. He was fed up with the establishment of the time. He did whatever he could to help people realize how important they were and how they each have a unique connection to God. If Jesus Christ were alive today, I am not certain he would be a follower of the message that was accredited to him as it stands today.

I know for a fact that Jesus is proud of me, that he admires the truth I share, how passionate I am about helping people become more spiritually aware of their own empowerment and that I provide them with techniques so they can more personally connect with him if they want. I feel like I am more like him than all the people who are mad at me for helping others. He actually assists me. He hates how his name has been invoked to judge, belittle and conquer people. He hates that his pure message of love has been desecrated by so many for political gain. They have turned him into a mascot for their greed.

Here is an analogy he gave me yesterday:

If you give a hundred people a hundred dollars to spend anyway that they want, there will be a hundred different ways that money will be spent, saved, thrown away or given away. All people are that different in their relationship with money. It is not our business to micromanage how they interact with it. It would do no good to tell them the best way to use the money because they know for themselves what their recourse is with money. To interfere is to change their relationship with the hundred dollars.

Anything that interferes with people's personal relationship with their highest perception of truth is a form of arrogance. It is like telling them how to spend their money. It just isn't done. In a way, we have a better respect of how people relate with money than how they worship God. Trying to get people to see God as you see God is kind of like manipulating them into investing their hundred dollars in your bank.

The other thing he mentioned for me to share is that if you don't like the way other sects use tyrannical means to get people to follow their religion, then deal with your own tyrannical views around religion. We are a reflection for each other. The extremists' horrendous tactics on demanding people follow their God is a magnified view of what we do when we judge others in regards to their faith. We have a blatant teaching example of how others do un-Godly things in the name of God. May we all take heed of the lesson. Maybe that is the way to salvage some good out of current events.

Eliminating Limiting Constructs

A construct is anything that unnecessarily confines energy.

"We declare ourselves surrogates for all life in doing these taps; in all moments."

"We release being galvanized in limiting constructs; in all

moments."

"We release being compartmentalized by limiting constructs; in all moments."

"We release being diminished by limiting constructs; in all moments."

"We remove all vivaxes between ourselves and limiting constructs; in all moments."

"We remove all tentacles between ourselves and all limiting constructs; in all moments."

"We release using limiting constructs as a crutch; in all moments."

"We release basing our identity on limiting constructs; in all moments."

"We release the fear of not existing beyond limiting constructs; in all moments."

"We remove the claws of all limiting constructs from our beingness; in all moments."

"We release being anchored to limiting constructs; in all moments."

"We remove all programming and conditioning that all limiting constructs have put on us; in all moments."

"We release being enslaved to limiting constructs; in all moments."

"We remove all engrams of limiting constructs; in all moments."

"We withdraw all our energy from all limiting constructs; in all moments."

"We strip all illusion off of all limiting constructs; in all moments."

"We remove all masks, walls, and armor that all limiting constructs have put on us; in all moments."

"We send all energy matrices of limiting constructs into the light; in all moments."

"We send all energy matrices of limiting constructs to dissolve into the light; in all moments."

"We send all energy matrices of limiting constructs to dissolve into the sound; in all moments."

"We command all complex energy matrices of limiting constructs to be escorted into the light to dissolve; in all moments."

"We command all complex energy matrices of limiting constructs to be escorted into the sound to dissolve; in all moments."

"We nullify all contracts with all limiting constructs; in all moments."

"We recant all vows and agreements with all limiting constructs; in all moments."

"We remove all curses between ourselves and all limiting constructs; in all moments."

"We remove all blessings between ourselves and all limiting constructs; in all moments."

"We sever all strings, cords, and wires between ourselves and all limiting constructs; in all moments."

"We dissolve all karmic ties between ourselves and all limiting constructs; in all moments."

"We remove ALL that all limiting constructs have put on us; in all moments."

"We remove ALL that limiting constructs have caused us to put on others; in all moments."

"We take back ALL that limiting constructs have taken from us; in all moments."

"We give back to all others ALL that limiting constructs have caused us to take from them; in all moments."

"We collapse and dissolve all limiting constructs; in all moments."

"We release resonating or emanating with all limiting constructs; in all moments."

"We extract all limiting constructs from our light emanation; in all moments."

"We extract all limiting constructs from our sound frequency; in all moments."

"We shift our paradigm from all limiting constructs to the expansive consciousness of Divine Love; in all moments."

"We transcend all limiting constructs; in all moments."

"We are centered and empowered in the expansive consciousness of Divine Love; in all moments."

"We resonate, emanate, and are interconnected with all life in the expansive consciousness of Divine Love; in all moments."

Being a Good Person

Sometimes being a good person is more than just mouthing words of encouragement that others want to hear. Sometimes it means advocating for someone who others would prefer to shun. Sometimes it is having compassion for an issue when others would prefer to sweep it under the rug. Sometimes it is taking the unfavorable stance, not to prove a point, but because there are real people with real feelings and real problems to factor in. Sometimes it may entail being unpopular. The question is, are you going to be a good person, or do you just want to think of yourself as one?

Some people are lonely and want to fit in. Some people are

suffering with a dilemma trying to maneuver through it. Many are desperately trying to make sense of their life, society, God, and their place in the mix of it. Some just want to turn off the barrage of thoughts and emotional angst that seems to string their existence together.

Did you know it is illegal in many states to say that you can heal? It makes sense because of all the abuse that will come from that statement. But it is legal to administer drugs that have such side effects that are more horrific and devastating than any health condition. It is legal to medicate children and lead them to dependence on medications for life. It is legal to poison our environment as long as the poisons fly under the radar.

To me, holding a positive intention for someone is a form of healing. In that respect, I am a healer because that is my intention for all. So instead of being respected for what I do and how I help people, I am not considered more than a good person.

I have been consciously helping others my whole life. That seems to be my purpose for being here. I have accepted that I don't fit into society or a niche or any group. But I continue to help others even though I know that after I help someone, they are going to be embarrassed to tell others about it. I know when someone wants to see me, it is because they need some kind of help even though they sincerely think they are being genuine in wanting to see or talk to me. I also realize that when I go out of my way to assist someone who is crying out in pain, they will later scoff at my help, ignore me or attribute the help to some other variable.

I will continue to be a good person, even if I know I will be ostracized, used, unappreciated or undervalued. That is my agreement with Love. I will Love even though it is not returned, and I will do what I can to make this world a better place for those I see suffering. This is the bar I have set for my personal integrity. I encourage everyone to be a good person, not because there is a short-term payoff, but because easing the dis-ease of others is the ultimate reward.

Here are some ways to be a good person:

- Do what you agree to do.
- Say only kind things about others.
- Paint only uplifting scenarios for others to walk into.
- Let others outshine you.
- Acknowledge the individual plight of all you encounter.
- Listen with your heart and answer with your heart.
- Allow people to feel good about themselves.
- Do what you can to assist others without coming out of your center.
- Allow people their dreams.
- See others' lives from their vantage point, not yours.
- Allow room for others to grow and change direction.
- Forgo any expectations from others.
- Expect nothing from others.
- Ask yourself, "What would Love do?"
- Do what Love would do until you become Love itself.

The Ultimate Prayer

God doesn't have an ego so doesn't need stroking.

Anything that is written about God is a clumsy, imperfect attempt to articulate the perfect. It is beyond words.

Man has formulated his concept of God by what HE would desire if he were an omniscient being.

There is the conflict.

God has not made man in his own image; man has made God in

his.

Think about what you would want for your children.

Would you need them to constantly stroke you or would you prefer that they were happy and loving, and treated their siblings with this love and respect?

I think that is a more accurate depiction of what God would "want" if God were capable of wanting.

God wanting, I think, is an outmoded concept.

Be loving and kind to each other.

Respect all of God's gifts.

Listen to God speak within your heart, not in your mind.

Realize your own worth.

Appreciate your own gifts.

How would you like it if everything you gave your children was scoffed at or overlooked?

How about if they destroyed everything they were given, and every time they were offered an adventure, it was looked upon as a punishment?

Connection with God doesn't need to happen in an altered state, or with super sensory perceptions.

Everyone is able to connect with God in the natural state of simplicity.

No one is wrong or unworthy to do this.

Take things out of your environment to do this; nothing more needs to be added.

You are perfect in your imperfection.

And gratitude is the ultimate prayer.

3. THE SHIFT TO THE FIFTH DIMENSION

Opportunity

Every fit of anger that's given up to the light

Is one step closer to soul taking flight

Every argument that the world decides to concede

Causes the germination of a dormant peace seed

Every judgment that anyone decides to forgo

Is a small piece of "power" just letting go

Every grudge that we collectively decide to rescind

Allows all spirits to break free and dance in the wind.

12/21/14

A Bridge to the Fifth Dimension

My writings trigger people. They are not just words but a means of releasing and healing old issues and wounds that can't even be articulated because they are so deep, so old, or were inflicted at a time when the human brain was not formulated. Sometimes there are no words to articulate the issue, so there is no means to lead it out of human essence without assistance.

That is one reason I emote sounds. I match the time and space of the incident that caused the issues, calm the energy field and return it to balance. It is like silencing cymbals by holding them still for a moment, or like squeezing everything out of the tube of toothpaste.

The anguish that a baby or animal experiences is not stored in words; it is primal. That is why just releasing sounds may be more efficient than converting them into words first. It is best to just let the emotions seep out unadulterated.

These are the things my writings can release. Those who are drawn to my writings can see that. Others merely believe I am irritating, abrasive, arrogant (a reflection of their own ego) or argumentative. Why would I spend so much of my energy in being so prolific articulating the most unexpressed of humanity just to irritate or upset handpicked targets? It does not make sense.

When people have a reaction to me, it is in their best interest to relax as the irritant (myself) is tolerated. There is freedom in learning how to remove barnacles of energy from our true essence, simply by relaxing into any issues that cause a reaction, instead of doing the opposite by hunkering in defense mode and striking to attack. That is what the "takers" have trained us to do.

There are no power mongers that can hurt us in the fifth dimension. The only ones that can harm us here are ourselves. There is no one to take from us. The days of being raped of our energy are over. This is the moment to get back all we felt we lost. This is what I assist in doing. It is as easy and simple as that because it is already done.

We have arrived at the fifth dimension. In the fifth dimension we are whole, loved and free, but so many people brought their engrams of the third dimension with them as a security for the transition. That is why it feels so much like the third dimension still, but they are dropping away quickly.

That is why my dynamic healing is so effective. Because I know that everyone is whole and already here. I am just the means to help them realize it. My writing, healing, awareness and presence are bridges to embracing the fifth dimension.

A Consciousness Shift

Old establishments will change when individuals change. That is why I do what I do to empower the individuals. It is the individuals who are actually empowered. Once they realize it, the world will change not by people banding together but by being strong individuals who are unwavering in their convictions and refuse to be bought and sold.

Giving power to groups is the old paradigm. Living instinctually in Joy, Love, Abundance, Freedom and Wholeness is the new paradigm. It is wonderfully liberating to experience the shift into a new paradigm. So many capable people being disgruntled is like seeing a fruit laden tree. These are exciting times.

Draw in All Your Empowerment from All Dimensions

(Say each statement three times out loud while tapping on the top of your head at the crown chakra and say it a fourth time while tapping on your chest.)

"I remove all vivaxes between myself and the me in all dimensions; in all moments."

"I remove all tentacles between myself and the me in all dimensions; in all moments."

"I remove the me in all other dimensions from my beingness; in all

moments."

"I release being run by the me in all dimensions; in all moments."

"I remove all programming and conditioning that the me from all dimensions has put on me; in all moments."

"I remove all engrams that the me in other dimensions has put on me; in all moments."

"I recant all vows and agreements between myself and the me in all dimensions; in all moments."

"I remove all curses between myself and the me in all dimensions; in all moments."

"I remove all blessings between myself and the me in all dimensions; in all moments."

"I sever all strings, cords, and wires between myself and the me in all dimensions; in all moments."

"I send incredible love to the me in all dimensions; in all moments."

"I dissolve all karmic ties between myself and the me in all dimensions; in all moments."

"I remove all controlling devices that the me in all dimensions has put in me; in all moments."

"I withdraw all my energy from the me in all dimensions; in all moments."

"I remove all the sickness and dis-ease that the me in other dimensions has put on me; in all moments."

"I remove all the pain, burden, and limitations that the me in all dimensions has put on me; in all moments."

"I remove all the illusion of separateness that the me in all dimensions has put on me; in all moments."

"I remove all the things that I have put on the me in all dimensions; in all moments."

"I take back all the Joy, Love, Abundance, Freedom, Health, Success, Security, Companionship, Creativity, Peace, Life, Wholeness, Beauty, Enthusiasm, Contentment, Spirituality, Enlightenment, Confidence, Family, Intellect, the Ability to Discern, and Empowerment that the me in all dimensions has taken from me; in all moments."

"I give back to the me in all dimensions all that I have taken from them; in all moments."

"I heal me in all dimensions; in all moments."

"I repair and fortify the wei chi of all my bodies of me in all dimensions; in all moments."

"I close the portal to the me in all dimensions; in all moments."

"I remove all residual influence that the me in all dimensions has put on me; in all moments."

"I am centered and empowered in Divine Love; in all moments."

"I meet the alpha and the omega within myself; in all moments."

"I harness the empowerment of the microcosm to catapult me into the macrocosm of within; in all moments."

"I move fluidly through the microcosm and the macrocosm of within; in all moments."

When Is the Last Time You…

Tasted a unique flavor that was foreign to you?

Smelled a new intriguing aroma?

Experienced the brushstroke of vibrant new color?

Felt true passion ignite from within?

Got excited by a sense of wonder?

Challenged the depth of your own insight?

Visited a new awareness?

Stretched your capacity to discern?

Followed the path of a new line of reasoning?

Poked the sleeping lion of adversity?

Meandered through your thoughts to a new outcome?

Threw convention away?

Led someone to a new awakening?

Parted way with convention?

Dove in the deep end of alternative outcomes?

Simply asked why and got an answer?

Asked yourself other tough questions?

Ripped the mask off of conformity?

Attempted something that made you feel naked and afraid?

Spoke your truth?

Even knew your truth?

Wondered why you are here, really here?

Wondered where here is?

Asked yourself why?

Told yourself why not?

Heard the inner symphony?

Danced to its melodic rhythm?

Surrendered all your atoms to the universe?

Blew away the dust?

Realized you exist beyond the realms of time?

Looked around and saw the eyes of love peering back at you?

Gained a new perspective?

Let go of hanging on to your own shirt?

Braced to free fall only to hover?

Felt your particles stretch out into their own galaxy?

Discerned the wisdom of a tree?

Experienced all of love as your brethren?

Engaged in the interactive truth of awakening?

What are you doing right now?

Where do you really exist?

Who are you?

Who am I?

What is love?

What's the difference?

You gaining your courage to share your gifts creates a butterfly effect. It then creates a tipping point until the whole world is reflective and wise instead of introverted and shy. Godspeed in sharing your gifts. The world needs the breeze from the flap of your wings to blow it out of complacency!

Take a Quantum Leap in Consciousness

(Say this statement three times out loud while tapping on the top of your head at the crown chakra and say it a fourth time while tapping on your chest.)

"I declare myself a surrogate for humanity in doing these taps; in all moments."

"We make space in this world for a Universal quantum leap in consciousness; in all moments."

"We remove all blockages to a Universal quantum leap in consciousness; in all moments."

"We exponentially stretch our capacity for a Universal quantum leap in consciousness; in all moments."

"We make space in this world for a quantum leap in Universal Love; in all moments."

"We remove all blockages to a quantum leap in Universal Love; in all moments."

"We exponentially stretch our capacity for a quantum leap in Universal Love; in all moments."

"We make space in this world for a quantum leap in Universal Truth; in all moments."

"We remove all blockages to a quantum leap in Universal Truth; in all moments."

"We exponentially stretch our capacity for a quantum leap in Universal Truth; in all moments."

"We make space in this world for a quantum leap in Universal Peace; in all moments."

"We remove all blockages to a quantum leap in Universal Peace; in all moments."

"We exponentially stretch our capacity for a quantum leap in Universal Peace; in all moments."

"We make space in this world for a quantum leap in Universal Abundance; in all moments."

"We remove all blockages to a quantum leap in Universal Abundance; in all moments."

"We exponentially stretch our capacity for a quantum leap in Universal Abundance; in all moments."

"We make space in this world for a quantum leap in Universal Freedom; in all moments."

"We remove all blockages to a quantum leap in Universal Freedom; in all moments."

"We exponentially stretch our capacity for a quantum leap in Universal Freedom; in all moments."

Cracked Bucket

There is so much pain in the world. It is like a tidal wave of sadness that a lot of people are being hit with. The great news is that it is a limited amount and we are bailing out the boat. Many of us have been diligently scooping the negativity out of the world lifetime after lifetime, bucketful after bucketful.

We are finally making headway. Thank you for all those who keep bailing the boat by using your gifts, sharing a kindness and sending out healing love to all. It doesn't matter if there is a crack in your bucket. It only makes your efforts more endearing.

For those who feel overwhelmed, please know that there is always love for you. It comes from people and forces you may never know or recognize. Please stay open to the love. It is coming to you in the breeze; it is coming to you in droplets of sunshine; it is coming to you from sincere and powerful intentions from incredible hearts all over the planet.

Perched for Enlightenment by Transcending the Lower Worlds

I facilitated a private, remote session for a gifted healer. In her sessions we work at a deep level. At first, I was seeing her connection to other planets and how it may be holding her back as a divine being. The Universe is vast. It consists of different layers of vibrations of which the physical one is the harshest. I was getting a sense to help her release her attachment to all of the lower worlds. All the worlds that anyone could ever imagine, all the galaxies and all the subtle realms are all part of the lower worlds.

The lower worlds are all the realities that exist in the duality of positive and negative. Besides the physical realm, they include the astral worlds which are where we go when we cross over from the physical existence. Beyond that are the causal planes which consist of all our past life memories and records. The causal plane houses all the akashic records and are what I read when I facilitate sessions. Even more refined than the vibratory word of the astral plane and causal plane, is the mental realm. Beyond that is a thin realm called the etheric plane.

The physical, astral, causal, mental and etheric planes are all part of the lower worlds. To transcend them, one moves beyond the realms of the ego, which is very scary. To transcend all of these levels means to let go of all concepts and beliefs. To do this is called transcendence. When one reaches transcendence or enlightenment, they are removing all attachments to the lower worlds. By moving beyond the ego, one fears they will no longer exist. They are afraid of being separated from their consciousness.

In the middle of doing the taps I was giving her, my client hesitated. She realized that she felt hesitant to leave her loved ones behind. A beautiful analogy came through. Some very special healers have entrenched themselves in the lower worlds and assist individuals in plucking them out of their private hell so they can transcend.

But instead of hunkering in the lower worlds, by transcending, we can now open the cage of the lower worlds and allow everyone access to freedom. We can assist them much more easily from a higher vantage point. The more people that transcend the lower worlds, the more we can open gateways of the cage. We can assist so many more souls to enlightenment by transcending the lower worlds ourselves instead of staying entrenched in them. This is the time to free as many souls as possible.

So many people are supported by teachers and guides, but they are not going to do the work for us. That is an outmoded belief of being saved. Teachers and guides are just that. They show us the way and make it easier but we have to still take the steps. Complacency is a trap. Thinking that a spiritual being is going to carry us over the finish line is a trap.

These taps are a safe, effective way for us to do the work. Our guides and teachers have supplied the tools and have led us to them. To make the most of them with courage and confidence is empowerment and a step towards mastership.

(Say each statement three times out loud while tapping on your head and say a fourth time while tapping on your chest.)

"I release being entrenched in the lower worlds; in all moments."

"I release being lost in the lower worlds; in all moments."

"I release being enslaved to the lower worlds; in all moments."

"I release enslaving others to the lower worlds; in all moments."

"I release the fear of being separated from my consciousness; in all moments."

"I release the fear of being separated from my loved ones by transcending the lower worlds; in all moments."

"I uplift all humanity by transcending the lower worlds; in all moments."

"I remove all matrices between myself and the lower worlds; in all moments."

"I remove all tentacles between myself and the lower worlds; in all moments."

"I remove all engrams from myself of being trapped in lower worlds; in all moments."

"I send all energy matrices into the light and sound that keep me trapped in the lower worlds; in all moments."

"I recant all vows and agreements between myself and all the lower worlds; in all moments."

"I recant all vows and agreements between myself and all those in the lower worlds; in all moments."

"I remove all curses between myself and all the lower worlds; in all moments."

"I remove all curses between myself and all those in the lower worlds; in all moments."

"I sever all strings and cords between myself and all of the lower worlds; in all moments."

"I sever all strings and cords between myself and all those in the lower worlds; in all moments."

"I dissolve all karmic ties between myself and all the lower worlds; in all moments."

"I dissolve all karmic ties between myself and all those in the lower worlds in all moments."

"I remove all the pain, burden, limitations and engrams that all the lower worlds have put on me; in all moments."

"I remove all the pain, burden, limitations and engrams that I have put on all the lower worlds; in all moments."

"I remove all the pain, burden, limitations and engrams that all those in the lower worlds have put on me; in all moments."

"I remove all the pain, burden, limitations and engrams that I have put on all those in the lower worlds; in all moments."

"I take back all the Joy, Love, Abundance, Freedom, Life and Wholeness that all the lower worlds have taken from me; in all moments."

"I give back all the Joy, Love, Abundance, Freedom, Life and Wholeness that I have taken from all the lower worlds; in all moments."

"I take back all the Joy, Love, Abundance, Freedom, Life and Wholeness that all those in the lower worlds have taken from me; in all moments."

"I give back all the Joy, Love, Abundance, Freedom, Life and Wholeness that I have taken from all those in the lower worlds; in all moments."

"I withdraw all my energy from the lower worlds; in all moments."

"I withdraw all my energy from all those in the lower worlds; in all moments."

"I release resonating with the lower worlds; in all moments."

"I release resonating with all those in the lower worlds; in all moments."

"I release emanating with the lower worlds; in all moments."

"I release emanating with all those in the lower worlds; in all moments."

"I remove all of the lower worlds from my sound frequency; in all moments."

"I remove all those in the lower worlds from my sound frequency; in all moments."

"I remove all of the lower worlds from my light body; in all moments."

"I remove all those in the lower worlds from my light body; in all moments."

"I shift my paradigm from the lower worlds to Joy, Love, Abundance, Freedom, Life and Wholeness; in all moments."

"I transcend the lower worlds; in all moments."

"I make space in this world for my own transcendence; in all moments."

"I remove all blockages to my own enlightenment; in all moments."

"I stretch my capacity to transcend; in all moments."

"I am centered and empowered in my own enlightenment; in all moments."

"I resonate and emanate in the omniscience of my own enlightenment; in all moments."

Doing these will put one at a great advantage and release many of the issues that prevent one from being empowered in their own life. It is not about bowing out of life but becoming so free of all limitations that one can actively embrace Joy, Love, Abundance, Freedom and Wholeness at the deepest level.

Being a Soul Whisperer

Every post, every exercise I give and every poem have an intention of assisting the individuals in reclaiming their missing pieces. They are able then to collect themselves to pull themselves back to wholeness. They are capable of reclaiming energetically what was taken from them. I also assist in healing all the cracks when the pieces are recollected so they can retain the divine love that is poured in them just like a vase can contain water.

The Love I provide is pure healing energy to soothe a weary soul. It is true that a soul cannot be broken from without and that we can't really lose our true essence which is soul--a nugget of divine love contained in a layer of tools such as emotions, thoughts and physical body which help it gain awareness on all levels. It is true that a soul can't be destroyed from without but they can be so manipulated, abused and dejected that they believe they are destroyed.

That is why my help is so effective. I am able to talk to the main essence of a person, the one that hasn't had voice or reason for so long. I am a soul whisperer. I can remind them of their essence and that they are empowered beyond all the illusion of what they outwardly perceive. I can remind them of the reality of their true self and how to speak in their native tongue, which is love.

If what I said was just words, they would be dismissed

immediately because of their superficiality. But soul recognizes its native tongue, like a child who was taken from his homeland at a young age never to hear the language again. Once he hears it, memories of his sweet mother and homeland come rushing in. That is what happens when people read my posts. They are hearing and responding to the love.

There is such a freedom and delight in speaking one's native tongue. To be so unencumbered and open is how it is to regain one's empowerment. Empowerment is having the true self back at the helm and putting thoughts, beliefs, experiences, feelings and physical existence in alignment with the true self, which is love. So healing is a matter of piercing the illusion of the pain, isolation and unworthiness and allowing the true essence to oversee, saturate and enhance all that we think, feel, say and do. That is what I do.

Your true self is a mighty being. It can be a beacon as bright as a thousand suns in this world for all to burn off the dross and know their true self. Everything we think, say and do is a choice as to whether to empower the true self or shove it in a corner of ourselves and allow it to collect dust. You are empowered now and every moment to choose and speak love. To do so sets your inner compass on love.

You speak fluid love. It is only a matter of remembering and trusting it. You are a soul whisperer too. But love shouldn't be whispered like a dirty little secret. Divine love should be gregariously shared and enjoyed in song, kindness and brotherhood. So let's be soul singers and ride the eternal melodies back into the heart of love.

Life

There are people that you haven't met yet that will forever impact your Life and revitalize you in a way that you could never imagine.

There are doors that will open in walls where you didn't realize there *was* a door.

There are prayers that will be answered that you never even formed into thoughts.

There will be questions answered you may have never felt worthy to ask.

There are wonderfully amazing qualities in you that have never come to Light. They will be wonderfully unearthed through your own trials.

There is Joy, Enthusiasm, Wonder, Laughter, Love and Companionship that you will scoop into your net as you skim along the surface of this incredible life.

Filtering Out Love

Any group that says that it is the way to absolute truth is putting a cap on truth. It may be the purest way to truth and that can be absolutely right. But at one point, the individual has to break away from the rocket and maintain orbit of their own accord. To prevent this natural progression from occurring is defeating the whole purpose of the rocket.

The rocket itself can't maintain the orbit that the individual has been catapulted to. The sheer bulk of its words and guidelines are enough to ground the individual. One can stay in the hull of the rocket out of fear of crashing and burning. Or one can do that task that all its training has led it to and trust in the process of transcending. It is done alone and unencumbered by doctrine.

This is the true test of mastership. It is not about loyalty or allegiance to the process but a willingness to soar to new heights in new realms. It is to encourage others in their individuality to detach from all fear. To surrender all adornments, to be enlightened and sustained in the reality of unconditional perpetual and pristine divine love.

The Group Mentality

The reason we join a group and the reason we stay in a group may be very different and even at cross-purposes with each other. When we join a new group, we may be exhilarated that there are more people who think like we do. It is exciting because we can advance our own views but also maintain the security of doing so in a group. The group mentality is a safety net. We could be wrong, but could so many other people be wrong as well?

When we have been in a group a long time, it is natural to outgrow it. That is the cycle of life. There is always another step to self-unfolding. The reason one is afraid to outgrow the group is the fear of leaving the herd mentality, "the flock." It is the fear of being wrong and the fear of being alone.

Any group with any integrity will accept your need to be an individual. Isn't that the next step of advancement, thinking for yourself and trusting what you have been taught and guided to do? Staying in a group out of fear is still a form of fear. Fear is the opposite of love. When the love for truth is so strong that the fear of being wrong is evaporated in the light, one will know their answer. Fear of damnation will no longer be relevant.

The truth is we are never alone. When we tune into life to such a degree, we realize that we are a fraction of nature. We are atoms of God. Right and wrong have been learned and the spiritual laws have been adopted. We are free to experience the expansion of our own consciousness with the invisible Masters to lead us along.

In the "end," the smallest connection between ourselves and anyone is love. Everything else will be unhooked from our essence and recycled into love until we realize that we are love itself.

How to Dry Up Hell

Last night, I was shown the true nature of Hell. It is not really a place as much as a stagnation of consciousness. Sure, those with a similar state of consciousness may gather together. This is the nature of the spiritual law of vibrations. It means that things that resonate at a similar sound frequency gravitate to others of the same frequency.

That means that when your family is nasty to you and you can't understand why, it is simply the spiritual law of vibrations coming into play. It doesn't mean that you are not worthy of kindness. Perhaps they are not capable of registering your kindness. Perhaps your kindness is like a high-pitched sound to them that only dogs can hear.

The spiritual laws are as exacting as the law of gravity. So they really aren't anything to take personally. In the other realms last night, my friend and I were driving to look at this property that they were giving away to anyone who could settle it. It was difficult to locate and that was part of why it was hard to find.

The land itself was next to this expansive ocean, which is symbolic for the God state that everyone wishes to attain. That is how beautiful and pristine this property was. But as you got off the parkway to ride along the oceanfront, there was a long strip of land where the energies in it were beckoning the drivers to join them.

The energies were vile and performing acts of debauchery. They were dark and hideous, exploiting all aspects of themselves to get passersby to join it. Yes some would be terrified of it but we are savvy travelers and knew enough to just keep driving. But yes, others would get snared here.

But what was unusual about the area is that it was dwindling in area. In fact, the reason that the prime real estate was being doled out was to dry up this area of the beach. It was a huge area and it was an eyesore and a problem. Those who have a very different vibratory rate than the ones in the debauchery zones were being given homes nearby to change the vibration of the hell zone.

People think hell is a fixed place. It is a vibration, a state of consciousness. At one point, we drove past the entrance of the park-like setting we were looking for and had to drive by the hell zone again. The first time it was very intimidating. But the second time, I noticed one or two of the images had the same exact movement. They were not as real as I thought they were. They were similar to film screen images. They were similar to habitual behavior. Isn't that all habitual behavior is? There is no consciousness in it.

When I awoke, I realized that the new homes were being offered to anyone who transcended. They are taking up residency right near the boundaries of pure heaven. From there, they are able to travel all the worlds and have a ship upon the seas of God as well. Their function will be to dry up those places of lower vibration simply by existing as they do and maintaining their own integrity. Isn't that what we all do here?

I realized the one core issue of all those who were in hell. It was not an issue of worthiness. No one is worthy of hell. Or, more accurately, no one is unworthy of heaven. We are all offshoots of love individualizing the experience of love and reporting back to Source as a means to expand the borders of love. If one is experiencing hellish things, it just makes the move sweeter and more greatly appreciated when they return to balance.

No one is bad or evil. No. The one defining issue that collected the abominations that I saw in one place was regret. Regret was the heavy vibration that attracted more of the same. If gratitude is associated with wonderful things, regret is its antonym. See, hell isn't a place but a state of consciousness. It is being stuck in a ditch that seems too steep to get out of. Have you ever met someone stuck in regret? They are entrenched. Regret needs to be addressed with as much gratitude as possible to keep out of the negative trenches.

It is subtle. *Why doesn't anyone like me? Why wasn't I born beautiful, popular or with loving parents? Why do they love them and not me? Why doesn't my family appreciate me? Why did I have that one life-changing incident? Why can't I lose weight? Why can't I just win the lottery?* Understanding this concept IS winning the lottery. You are now capable of moving away from regret and drying up hell by your shift in awareness.

By the way, no hell is private. You subject everyone else to your vibration and add to a disgusting subtle reality when you immerse yourself in regret. When you immerse yourself in regret, you add to hell. Hell, like heaven, doesn't exist in a remote place. It is a vibration that all access through you. You can be a doorway to heaven, hell or both for all others. You choose. You choose, and in their relationship with you, they choose as well.

Have no regrets. Follow your inner promptings. Let love, kindness, awareness, integrity and adventure be your compass. They will keep you out of hell.

A Sacrifice Beyond Death

Those who say they love America say they will lay down their life for America. As if that is so hard to do. Anyone who feels helpless, lost or unimportant, at one time or another, thinks about ending their life. Isn't that what all these radicals are doing as they gun down innocent people? So what is so glorious about doing what every lunatic with a gun and a vendetta fantasizes about doing?

If you truly love America and would do anything to keep America safe, then you would be willing to look at your own subtle bigotries and rigidness to see how it is getting in the way of a United America. Anyone can go out in a blaze of glory. This is a primal fantasy of anyone with an ingrained warrior mentality.

But are you willing to concede to kindness? Are you willing to walk in another man's shoes? Are you willing to look at what your life would be like if you wore another hue of skin, or a different gender or sexual orientation? Would you sweep your special intolerance under the blanket of "them versus us," or would you be able to love any child of any race or species as if it were produced by your own loins?

Please don't tell me you will die for this country. Please tell me you will live and fight intolerance. You will sit with what makes you uncomfortable until you can adopt a wider viewpoint of it. Please tell me that you are a brave American, brave enough to face the unknown together with the uncertainty of a fresh start.

Doing that will make me respect you beyond anything else. The world is waiting for you to shift your stance and be present with the rest of humanity. You are important. You matter as much as anyone else, not because you will sacrifice your life to death, but because you will sacrifice your life to love.

Taps for Truth Seekers Everywhere

(Say each statement three times while tapping on your head and say it a fourth time while tapping on your chest.)

"We declare ourselves surrogates for truth seekers everywhere in doing these taps; in all moments."

"We declare ourselves surrogates for clergy of all faiths in doing these taps; in all moments."

"We release being led astray of truth; in all moments."

"We nullify all contracts that lead us astray of truth; in all moments."

"We remove all vivaxes between ourselves and being led astray of truth; in all moments."

"We remove all tentacles between ourselves and being led astray of truth; in all moments."

"We strip all illusion off of all that has led us astray of truth; in all moments."

"We remove all masks, walls, and armor from all those who have led us astray of truth; in all moments."

"We remove all programming and conditioning of all that has led us astray of truth; in all moments."

"We remove all engrams of all that separates us from truth; in all moments."

"We withdraw all our energy from all that separates us from truth; in all moments."

"We crumble the facade of all that separates us from truth; in all moments."

"We crumble the facade of all that has led us away from truth; in all moments."

"We send all energy matrices into the light and sound that separate us from truth; in all moments."

"We send all energy matrices into the light and sound that lead us astray of truth; in all moments."

"We command all complex energy matrices that separate us from truth to be escorted into the light and sound; in all moments."

"We command all complex energy matrices that lead us astray of truth to be escorted into the light and sound; in all moments."

"We release being used to demonize truth; in all moments."

"We send all energy matrices into the light and sound that demonize truth; in all moments."

"We command all complex energy matrices that demonize truth to be escorted into the light and sound; in all moments."

"We send all energy matrices into the light and sound that thwart truth; in all moments."

"We command all complex energy matrices that thwart truth to be escorted into the light and sound; in all moments."

"We recant all vows and agreements between ourselves and all that leads us astray of truth; in all moments."

"We remove all curses between ourselves and all that leads us astray of truth; in all moments."

"We remove all blessings between ourselves and all that leads us astray of truth; in all moments."

"We sever all strings, cords, wires, and communication between ourselves and all that leads us astray of truth; in all moments."

"We dissolve all karmic ties between ourselves and all that leads us astray of truth; in all moments."

"We remove from ourselves and all others all that those who lead us astray of truth have put on us; in all moments."

"We take back for ourselves and all others all that those who lead us astray of truth have taken from us; in all moments."

"We collapse and dissolve all portals to all those who lead others astray of truth; in all moments."

"We release resonating or emanating with those who lead others astray of truth; in all moments."

"We extract all that leads others astray of truth from our sound frequency; in all moments."

"We extract all that leads others astray of truth from our light emanation; in all moments."

"We extract all that leads others astray of truth from the universal sound frequency; in all moments."

"We extract all that leads others astray of truth from the universal light emanation; in all moments."

"We extract all that leads others astray of truth from our whole beingness; in all moments."

"We extract all that leads others astray of truth from all worlds, realities, and dimensions; in all moments."

"We shift our paradigm from all those who lead others astray of truth to the enlightenment of truth; in all moments."

"We transcend all those who lead others astray of truth; in all moments."

"We collapse and dissolve all untruth; in all moments."

"We collapse and dissolve all vehicles of untruth; in all moments."

"We are centered and empowered in the enlightenment of universal truth; in all moments."

"We resonate, emanate, and are interconnected with all life in the enlightenment of universal truth; in all moments."

God is within. Heaven is within. Always within. Sending prayers up and out was taught as a form of control to prevent the energy of prayers from being effective. If everyone prayed within, the effectiveness rate of prayers would skyrocket.

Dissolving Archaic Structures

I facilitated a private remote session with a woman who admitted having a lot of resentment for people who don't contribute and live off the system. I explained to her that people are not the problem. The structure in place is archaic and inflexible. The reason why there are so many dropouts, homeless, unemployed, imprisoned, and "disabled" is because the structure in place only provides for a narrow band of the society to thrive. The rest have the option to conform or opt out.

People in general want to help, want to thrive, want to hone and share their gifts. It is a sad commentary on society that so much of the genius that is our innate abilities is left untapped. Whenever there is a natural disaster, the resourceful and giving nature of people is unleashed and everyone in the area comes together and pitches in. That is the true nature of people and should be the natural state of society. People are a rich, natural resource that mostly goes untapped unless the archaic structure of our society is interrupted.

My client's irritation with people who weren't contributing revealed her attachment to the archaic structures. She was more invested in the structures than people. In many past lives, she was in positions of power that depended on the power structures of the time to support her success. Attachment to them was holding her back in the present life. She is not the only one.

Here are the taps I led her through:

"I release being enslaved to archaic structures; in all moments."

"I release worshiping archaic structures; in all moments."

"I release relinquishing my compassion to archaic structures; in all moments."

"I recant all vows and agreements between myself and all archaic structures; in all moments."

"I remove all curses between myself and all archaic structures; in all moments."

"I sever all strings and cords between myself and all archaic structures; in all moments."

"I dissolve all karmic ties between myself and all archaic structures; in all moments."

"I remove all the pain, burden, limitations and engrams that all archaic structures have put on me; in all moments."

"I remove all the pain, burden, limitations and engrams that I have put on all others due to archaic structures; in all moments."

"I take back all the joy, love, abundance, freedom, life and wholeness that all archaic structures have taken from me; in all moments."

"I give back all the joy, love, abundance, freedom, life and wholeness that I have taken from all others due to archaic structures; in all moments."

"I release resonating with archaic structures; in all moments."

"I release emanating with archaic structures; in all moments."

"I remove all archaic structures from my sound frequency; in all moments."

"I remove all archaic structures from my light body; in all

moments."

"I shift my paradigm from all archaic structures to Joy, Love, Abundance, Freedom, Life and Wholeness; in all moments."

"I transcend all archaic structures; in all moments."

"I am centered and empowered in divine love; in all moments."

The more we all forgo our attachment to all archaic structures, the more a new support system that empowers all individuals can be implemented. It can happen in all moments.

Perpetuate Love

We have been conditioned to use our energy to keep people and experiences out when it is the nature of life to flow. This is a waste of our potential. It keeps us locked in an unnatural paralyzed state of holding up intangible walls. Let the turret crumble. Let the torrent energy flow. Let it rise, recede, wax, wane, flood, evaporate and reach its natural level. Add all your love and capabilities into the wonderful mix.

Make mistakes, bleed, lose at love, stumble, gracefully hold an unpopular stance, make peace with your demons and send them on their way with a flask and a slap on the back.

Hold the concept of love as gently and with the same conviction as a trembling new bird. Watch it travel on the wind as a wandering seed hell-bent on its whimsical convictions. See love settle amongst grains of truth to set out its roots. Watch love grow like a weed and flourish in a garden of its own making. Be the proprietor of love in this world. See kindness as its steward.

Ride the love and unroll your own masts. Revel in a perpetual state of your own unfurling. See the love, be the love, blend with the love, continue the loving journey. Encourage as many along the way as you will. Love and kindness will prevail. It is the natural bounty of all.

Flashpoint

How do you know that--

The next altruistic act,

Serendipitous encounter,

Grandiose epiphany,

Rant,

Cry,

Struggle,

Simple act of kindness,

Quiet resolve,

Sincere smile,

Honest self-reflection,

Is not the flashpoint,

That uplifts all of humanity,

With its purity of intent,

And alignment to the moment?

Move Past Linear Limitations

One of the limitations on society is linear thinking. It is the belief that one has to be right at the expense of someone else. It is the belief that there is only one answer to each question. It is being stuck in one vantage point. It is seeing everyone else as wrong who is not at that same vantage point. This is the cause of all wars and disagreements. Instead of win-lose, thinking exponentially is a win-win scenario.

Thinking exponentially is the ability to toggle vantage points so one can see the truth of any point of view. It is a way to understand what is unfathomable to some. It is creating a fluidity in the consciousness so everyone can thrive. As beneficial as thinking exponentially is, living exponentially is exponentially more freeing.

(Say each statement three times out loud while tapping on the top of your head at the crown chakra and say it a fourth time while tapping on your chest.)

"I declare myself a surrogate for humanity in doing these taps; in all moments."

"We release being paralyzed in linear existence, in all moments."

"We remove all vivaxes between ourselves and linear existence; in all moments."

"We remove all tentacles between ourselves and linear existence; in all moments."

"We send all energy matrices into the light that keep us trapped in linear existence; in all moments."

"We remove all programming and conditioning from linear existence; in all moments."

"We remove all engrams that linear existence has put on us; in all moments."

"We recant all vows and agreements between ourselves and linear existence; in all moments."

"We remove all curses between ourselves and linear existence; in

all moments."

"We remove all blessings between ourselves and linear existence; in all moments."

"We sever all strings and cords between ourselves and linear existence; in all moments."

"We dissolve all karmic ties between ourselves and linear existence; in all moments."

"We strip all illusion off linear existence; in all moments."

"We remove all masks, walls, and armor from linear existence; in all moments."

"We withdraw all our energy from linear existence; in all moments."

"We distance ourselves from linear existence; in all moments."

"We remove all the pain, burden, limitations, and illusion of separateness that linear existence has put on us; in all moments."

"We take back all that linear existence has taken from us; in all moments."

"We separate all the ways consciousness overlays linear existence; in all moments."

"We release resonating with linear existence; in all moments."

"We release emanating with linear existence; in all moments."

"We extract all of linear existence from our sound frequency; in all moments."

"We release being titillated by the doings of linear existence; in all moments."

"We shift our paradigm from linear existence to exponential freedom; in all moments."

"We transcend linear existence; in all moments."

"We separate ourselves from all attributes of linear existence; in all moments."

"We distance ourselves from all attributes of linear existence; in all moments."

"We are centered and empowered in exponential freedom; in all moments."

"We resonate and emanate exponential freedom; in all moments."

Being a Visionary

We limit each other all the time. This statement is limiting in itself. Language started out in the caveman days to convey vital information, but anytime one puts a cap on the actions of another or holds the other person's experiences as truth, we are all held to the lowest common denominator. Only the lowest bar is achieved.

How many times have we all heard, "You are going to get sick if you...," "If you don't do, this you will...," or "You will fall and break your neck if you..."? We aren't even putting our own experiences on others; we are burdening the human spirit with fears we have grandfathered in from wherever.

The four-minute mile, breaking the sound barrier, every stride in civil rights were all thought impossible to achieve. It took someone to see beyond the immediate horizon to raise the bar for all and for others to agree that it is a worthy reality. All it takes is someone--anyone--to hold true to a higher vision and for others to open up their consciousness to allow it to manifest. It may start as only a door cracked open but there will be a tipping point to a Universal belief system. And when resistance is met, and the opposing view screams louder, it is evidence that the consciousness is being stretched into realization.

Here are some of the visions I hold. Please feel free to hold them with me.

- Spontaneous healing
- Disease wiped out of the annals of human experience
- Joy, Love, Abundance and Freedom for every individual
- Communicating through nonverbal cues
- All beings supporting each other
- Accessing energy sources that don't deplete the planet
- People thinking and creating for themselves
- Everyone contributing their gifts
- All life, including plant, animal and mineral, being valued
- Interplanetary travel and community
- Mass forms of control and manipulation being wiped out
- Nature being valued and protected
- Universal kindness resurfacing on a mass scale
- Music, dance and self-expression being the norm

Please don't mistake a visionary with someone in denial and feel the need to point out all the ills in the world. I am not naive. I have consciously witnessed atrocities that would keep many adults up nights. But I have also seen and loved past them. So can everyone if they choose. Light can only be snuffed out for a while but it is eternal. Light and love always prevail.

Tears

Encourage the tears. They are well deserved for all of us; they flush out the pain from the inner chambers. They flush out the rejection, abandonment and feelings of unworthiness. They move all old issues out of the little corners of ourselves so the love can seep back in. Saturate yourself with love by releasing the old wounds, habits and conditioning. Immerse yourself in love and wash out the wounds. You are love. You are loved and you are loving. Be loving as a way to immerse yourself more easily into the love.

Release Losing Heart

(Say each statement three times out loud while tapping on the top of your head at the crown chakra and say it a fourth time while tapping on your heart chakra.)

"I release being led astray by false prophets; in all moments."

"I release betraying Jesus; in all moments."

"I release losing faith; in all moments."

"I release losing heart; in all moments."

"I release living outside of truth; in all moments."

"I release being a hypocrite; in all moments."

"I release disappointing Jesus; in all moments."

"I release believing lies about Jesus; in all moments."

"I release being weak; in all moments."

"I release desecrating my spirit; in all moments."

"I release desecrating my body; in all moments."

"I live in the true Love and Light of Jesus; in all moments."

"I dedicate myself as a vessel for Love and Light; in all moments."

"I grace this world as a vessel for the Love and Light of Jesus; in all moments."

"I am centered and empowered in being a vessel of the Love and Light of Jesus; in all moments."

"I resonate and emanate the Love and Light of Jesus; in all moments."

Release Being Affected by Politicians

(Say each statement three times out loud while tapping on the top of your head at the crown chakra and say it a fourth time while tapping on your chest at the heart chakra.)

"I declare myself a surrogate for humanity in doing these taps; in all moments."

"I strip all illusion off of all politicians and the political process; in all moments."

"I clearly see the hypocrisy in all politicians and the political process; in all moments."

"I strip all illusion off of the money trail of all politicians and the political process; in all moments."

"I remove all blinders when viewing all politicians and the political process; in all moments."

"I release being coerced by any or all politicians and the political process; in all moments."

"I release being deduced to fear by any or all politicians and the political process; in all moments."

"I release being immersed in 'them versus us' mode by politicians and the political process; in all moments."

"I release being duped by politicians and the political process; in all moments."

"I release being manipulated by politicians and the political process; in all moments."

"I release being used as a pawn by politicians and the political process; in all moments."

"I release all that I hold sacred being reduced to a talking point by politicians and the political process; in all moments."

"I release all that I hold sacred being devalued by politicians and the political process; in all moments."

"I strip all illusion off of the selfish intent of all politicians and the political process; in all moments."

"I release being pitted against others by politicians and the political process; in all moments."

"I release demonizing others on behalf of politicians and the political process; in all moments."

"I release being compliant with hate through politicians and the political process; in all moments."

"I transcend the bullshit of all politicians and the political process; in all moments."

"I shift my paradigm from all politicians and the political process to the absolute sanctity of Divine Love; in all moments."

"I am centered and empowered in the absolute sanctity of Divine Love; in all moments."

"I resonate and emanate the absolute sanctity of Divine Love; in all moments."

Returning the World to Balance in Honoring Goddess Energy

Goddess energy is not a peripheral subjugation of God. It is an equal counterpart. The way that we conceptualize it as less than God itself is the way we subjugate female energy in general. The reason that female energy is so minimized is because she has been picked clean by male energy. All of her empowerment has been extracted except for physical beauty and sexuality. It is because these are the two things that male energy can utilize more if she maintains them.

It is obvious that there has been a huge disservice done to female energy. It does not only affect those with female anatomy. It is a form of gutting humanity of half of our existence and expecting to be whole. The lack of respect and reverence for female energy is the reason that the world is in the condition that it is.

God is not male. God is transgender. Goddess energy should be given the same reverence as male energy in the world. That is the balance and shift that has to occur on an energetic level so we all can be whole.

Here is a set of powerful taps for female energy to regain her empowerment so that all humanity can return to balance. Please do these taps and feel the shift in your own magnetic makeup in doing them.

(Say each statement three times while tapping on your head and say it a fourth time while tapping on your chest.)

"We declare ourselves surrogates for female energy in doing these taps; in all moments."

"We release being controlled by male energy; in all moments."

"We release being manipulated by male energy; in all moments."

"We release being used by male energy; in all moments."

"We release being silenced by male energy; in all moments."

"We release being beaten up by male energy; in all moments."

"We release being conquered by male energy; in all moments."

"We release being subservient to male energy; in all moments."

"We release being admonished by male energy; in all moments."

"We release being enslaved by male energy; in all moments."

"We release being enslaved to male energy; in all moments."

"We remove all vivaxes between ourselves and male energy; in all moments."

"We remove all tentacles between ourselves and male energy; in all moments."

"We remove the claws of male energy from our beingness; in all moments."

"We remove the satellites of male energy from our beingness; in all moments."

"We remove all controlling devices that male energy has put in us; in all moments."

"We release giving our heart to male energy; in all moments."

"We take back our heart from male energy; in all moments."

"We take back our spirit, mind and body from male energy; in all moments."

"We release being a mouthpiece for male energy; in all moments."

"We release being a pawn for male energy; in all moments."

"We remove all programming and conditioning that male energy has put on us; in all moments."

"We remove all engrams of male energy from our beingness; in all moments."

"We release deferring to male energy; in all moments."

"We release being fractured and broken by male energy; in all

moments."

"We release being rendered helpless and invisible by male energy; in all moments."

"We remove all energy matrices of controlling male energy from our beingness and send them into the light and sound; in all moments."

"We send all energy matrices of male energy into the light and sound; in all moments."

"We command all complex energy matrices of male energy to be escorted into the light and sound; in all moments."

"We shatter all illusion that male energy has put on female energy; in all moments."

"We shatter all glass ceilings that male energy has put on female energy; in all moments."

"We strip all illusion off of male energy; in all moments."

"We remove all masks, walls and armor from ourselves and male energy; in all moments."

"We withdraw all our energy from male energy; in all moments."

"We release giving our hearts to male energy; in all moments."

"We release the primal urge to be conquered by male energy; in all moments."

"We nullify all contracts between ourselves and male energy; in all moments."

"We recant all vows and agreements between ourselves and male energy; in all moments."

"We remove all curses between ourselves and male energy; in all moments."

"We release being paralyzed by male energy; in all moments."

"We release being demonized by male energy; in all moments."

"We release being mutilated by male energy; in all moments."

"We remove all blessings between ourselves and male energy; in all moments."

"We release identifying male energy as our savior; in all moments."

"We release the fear of being forsaken by male energy; in all moments."

"We sever all strings, cords and wires between ourselves and male energy; in all moments."

"We dissolve all karmic ties between ourselves and male energy; in all moments."

"We release perpetuating a male agenda; in all moments."

"We remove all the pain, burden and limitations that male energy has put on us; in all moments."

"We remove all the fear, futility and unworthiness that male energy has put on us; in all moments."

"We remove all the subjugation, inequality and illusion of separateness that male energy has put on us; in all moments."

"We take back ALL that male energy has taken from us; in all moments."

"We release resonating with male energy; in all moments."

"We release emanating with male energy; in all moments."

"We extract all male energy from our sound frequency; in all moments."

"We extract all male energy from our light emanation; in all

moments."

"We heal all 32 layers of our embodiment; in all moments."

"We repair and fortify the wei chi of all our bodies; in all moments."

"We align all our bodies; in all moments."

"We shift our paradigm from male agenda to our own empowerment; in all moments."

"We transcend male agendas; in all moments."

"We are centered and empowered in our own empowerment; in all moments."

"We resonate, emanate and are interconnected with all life in the divinity of our empowerment; in all moments."

Honoring the Universe

The Universe is a perpetual state of gratitude. It is we who open the door to the blessings and kindness that are always offered freely in the organic state of natural giving. When we are being loving and open, we create a two-way passageway between ourselves and the Universe. There is more fluidity when traffic flows in both directions.

When we are patient with others, when we politely allow others to pass and give intangible gifts of smiles and kindness freely, we are personifying the Universe. We are manifesting the omniscience of life and honoring it through our actions and presence.

Unconditional Love's Creed

To...

>Give without need to receive,

>Accept all gifts graciously,

>Listen without judgment,

>Speak only kindness, truth and necessities,

>See the best in all,

>Ignore negative behavior and situations,

>Use your talents to uplift others,

>Be an individual,

>Lead others to greatness.

By the Grace of God

Someone messaged me that they loved what I shared but wondered why I don't talk about God more and give God the glory. Here is my response in case others have been wondering about it too. It is true; it is a choice.

I could not do anything that I am capable of without God. But the interpretation of God leads to misunderstandings. God does not want me to leave anyone out. So if I talk about the semantics of God, it will offend someone or create debate and opinions and set me up to defend myself. It would render me ineffective. I am doing God's work in a quiet but powerful way.

I live like a monk and speak to God every instance. If you notice, I speak about Love a LOT. God is Love right? Just insert God into every time I use the word Love. What is the difference? God does not have an ego. God is not tyrannical in any way. Love is the most gracious name for God. It is man who has interpreted God's message and who has caused the dysfunction in the world. Love needs no interpretation. It is the purest message one can communicate to convey that sacred connection with the source.

There is a reason that I am in a female body and also have such a dynamic passion for truth and the ability to heal. Everything I am, can do, and have endured has been handcrafted by the grace of God. I assure you. I could not endure otherwise.

Stop Seeking Perfection

We have been lied to. Perfection has nothing to do with spiritual attainment. Perfection is an illusion that originates in the mind. Needing to be perfect doesn't lead to spiritual attainment but leads one into an energetic eddy that is an endless loop.

Even the most beautiful specimen outgrows the experience of perfection. It is a fleeting experience that is more impressive in observance than in experiencing. Trying to recapture a fleeting moment leaves one immersed in regret. Regret is the seedbed to each personal hell. It is the opposite of gratitude.

We completed these taps in a group session. My friend was driving in her car at the time. She felt the energy of the group shift performing these even though she was not privy to them at the time we did them.

Here is to peeling off another layer.

(Say each statement three times while continuously tapping on your head and say it a fourth time while tapping on your chest.)

"I declare myself a surrogate for humanity in doing these taps; in all moments."

"I release the need to be perfect; in all moments."

"I release confusing perfection with spiritual attainment; in all moments."

"I release equivocating spiritual attainment with perfection; in all moments."

"I release being stabbed in the back; in all moments."

"I strip all illusion off of perfection; in all moments."

"I relinquish the quest to be perfect; in all moments."

"I remove all masks, walls and armor of being perfect; in all moments."

"I convert all the energy I waste trying to be perfect into being kind; in all moments."

"I un-trench myself from the mind by disengaging the need to be perfect; in all moments."

"I nullify all contracts with perfection; in all moments."

"I remove all the pain, burden, and limitations that trying to be perfect has put on me; in all moments."

"I shift my paradigm from seeking perfection to being kind; in all moments."

"I am kind to myself; in all moments."

"I release confusing being safe with Love; in all moments."

"I release being paralyzed in the need to be safe; in all moments."

"I shatter all glass ceilings on being safe; in all moments."

"I am centered and empowered in kindness; in all moments."

"I transcend the need to be perfect; in all moments."

"I resonate, emanate, and am interconnected with all life in being kind; in all moments."

The Religion of Love

God is Love. Anything that is not loving is not mandated by God. In fact, God is freedom as well. And the thing that mandates less freedom is not God either. Religion is to God what a camera is to all of nature. Defining nature by one photo is as ridiculous as defining God through one religion.

If a religious practice is telling someone to condemn or ostracize others, then it is not from God but from the dictates of man. It is easy sometimes to make the distinction. For example, it is easy for many of us to see that God would not order others to kill on his behalf, but others do just that. Others judge, diminish, abandon and humiliate others in the name of God. To them, that distinction is a little more in accordance with God. Nope. God is Love. Anything other than kindness has man's hand in it.

Here is a rule of thumb. Hate is not God. Separation is not God. Superiority is not God. Government is not God. Fear is the opposite of Love. God is Love. When one is fearful of another, it is their gauge that they are coming out of their center. Love is their center. For some, they have been trained to be out of their center from babyhood so they may have to do some literal soul searching to get back into a center.

Here are some more rules of thumb. Anyone who thinks they are absolutely right is bound to be proven wrong. When one has something to prove to someone else, they have more to prove to themselves. There are no absolutes in the realm of God. If someone is living in absolutes, they are already thinking like a man.

These are just my humble opinions. Don't worry. My opinions aren't written in stone to be defended to the hilt. Love is fluid and so a more accurate statement is that these are my humble opinions in this present moment. Love, like an open mind, is predicated to change each moment because that is where God is--in the moment.

Calibrate the Day

We choose the course of the day, week and even life with what we decide to "put out there" each moment. Did you already complain that it was Monday? Did you already have a negative thought about the weather? These things set precedent for the next moment.

Our mood is not set in stone. If we wake up a little bit irritated or with a little scratchy throat, it may take a moment to forgo the disdain and calibrate the day to joy. But this is a choice. Wake up your awareness by sitting still for a moment, breathing deep and paying attention to what your body is telling you. Address the need so it doesn't vie for attention using negative thoughts and feelings.

Breakfast is a way to tune into your body and give it what it needs. Your daily routine of opening the curtains and letting the dog out are all ways to pour love into your moment. Every little task that is done consciously is pouring love into the day.

It is a beautiful fresh start to the new week. The days are getting longer. It will be warmer soon. How are you going to use your talents to uplift others? What thoughts are you going to add to the universal mind? What kindnesses are you going to express as a part of a universal heart? Love is here, encouraging you for your positive efforts.

(Say each statement three times while tapping on your head and say it a fourth time while tapping on your chest.)

"I am a powerhouse of Divine Light, Love, Song, Healing, Health, Joy, Beauty, Abundance and Wholeness; in all moments."

"Every cell of my body assimilates, resonates and emanates Divine

Light, Love, Song, Healing, Health, Joy, Beauty, Abundance and Wholeness; in all moments."

"I am a conscious conduit for Divine Light, Love, Song, Healing, Health, Joy, Beauty, Abundance and Wholeness in the world; in all moments."

"All who broach me are invited to assimilate, resonate, and emanate with Divine Light, Love, Song, Healing, Health, Joy, Beauty, Abundance and Wholeness; in all moments."

"I perpetuate Divine Light, Love, Song, Healing, Health, Joy, Beauty, Abundance and Wholeness in all lifetimes; in all moments."

There is only one source of Love, Light and Truth. When someone calls this source "their God," it is evidence that they have made God in their own image and have deduced its omnipotence to the level and scope limited by their own ego.

Crumble Down the Resistance to World Peace

People frequently complain about the length of the tap exercises I post. Or they tell me how hard it is to sit there and do them. I am not sure if it has occurred to anyone that it is difficult for me to write them, that I have resistance in forging them from nothing with no payoff to myself in doing so. I know people will criticize and complain, yet I work through the resistance to bring them to you on the off chance they will assist someone in feeling more empowered in their life.

Hearing people tell me how difficult it is to do the taps or diminish them and me by comparing them to any old taps used to take wind out of my sails, but knowing that it is helping others who do forge through the resistance is the motivation. Think about it. If you do nothing, you get more of the same. So why not try something abstract as an exercise in doing something.

I have a lot of resistance to writing this series of taps, yet I know it's necessary for the advancement of peace in the world. Let's all work through our resistance together and send out a proactive intention to crumble down the resistance to world peace.

You will be surprised at how much energy doing all these taps will free in you.

(Say each statement three times while tapping on your head and say it a fourth time while tapping on your chest.)

"I declare myself a surrogate for all Christians and Jews in doing these taps; in all moments."

"I release hating Muslims; in all moments."

"I release demonizing Muslims; in all moments."

"I release being the enemy of Muslims; in all moments."

"I release the belief that I am superior to Muslims; in all moments."

"I nullify all contracts with Muslims; in all moments."

"I withdraw all my energy from hating Muslims; in all moments."

"I extract all the hate that I have projected onto Muslims; in all moments."

"I dry up all psychic streams that mandate the diminishing of Muslims; in all moments."

"I send all energy matrices into the light and sound that compel me to hate Muslims; in all moments."

"I command all complex energy matrices that compel me to hate

Muslims to be escorted into the light and sound; in all moments."

"I remove all engrams of hating Muslims; in all moments."

"I remove all programming and conditioning to hate Muslims; in all moments."

"I strip all illusion off of hating Muslims; in all moments."

"I remove all masks, walls and armor that hating Muslims has put on me; in all moments."

"I eliminate the first cause in regards to hating Muslims; in all moments."

"I release being immersed in hating Muslims; in all moments."

"I untangle all my energy from hating Muslims; in all moments."

"I release the genetic propensity to hate Muslims; in all moments."

"I dissolve all of the hating of Muslims with the purity of Divine Love; in all moments."

"I view all Muslims from the vantage point of Love; in all moments."

"I remove all vivaxes between myself and hating Muslims; in all moments."

"I dry up all instincts to hate Muslims; in all moments."

"I recant all vows and agreements to hate Muslims; in all moments."

"I remove all curses that I put on Muslims; in all moments."

"I remove all blessings I put on hating Muslims; in all moments."

"I sever all strings and cords between myself and hating Muslims; in all moments."

"I dissolve all karmic ties between myself and hating Muslims; in

all moments."

"I remove all the pain, burden and limitations that I have put on all Muslims; in all moments."

"I remove all the fear, futility and unworthiness I have put on all Muslims; in all moments."

"I release ostracizing Muslims; in all moments."

"I give back all that I have taken from Muslims; in all moments."

"I extract all hate of Muslims from my sound frequency and the Universal sound frequency; in all moments."

"I extract all hate of Muslims from my light emanation and the Universal light emanation; in all moments."

"I release individually or universally resonating or emanating with hating Muslims; in all moments."

"I transcend hating Muslims; in all moments."

"I shift my paradigm from hating Muslims to seeing all souls as pure love; in all moments."

"I am centered and empowered in seeing all souls as pure love; in all moments."

"I resonate, emanate and am interconnected with all life in seeing all souls as pure love; in all moments."

■■

"I declare myself a surrogate for all Christians and Muslims in doing these taps; in all moments."

"I release hating Jews; in all moments."

"I release demonizing Jews; in all moments."

"I release being the enemy of Jews; in all moments."

"I release the belief that I am superior to Jews; in all moments."

"I nullify all contracts with Jews; in all moments."

"I withdraw all my energy from hating Jews; in all moments."

"I extract all the hate that I have projected onto Jews; in all moments."

"I dry up all psychic streams that mandate the diminishing of Jews; in all moments."

"I send all energy matrices into the light and sound that compel me to hate Jews; in all moments."

"I command all complex energy matrices that compel me to hate Jews to be escorted into the light and sound; in all moments."

"I remove all engrams of hating Jews; in all moments."

"I remove all programming and conditioning to hate Jews; in all moments."

"I strip all illusion off of hating Jews; in all moments."

"I remove all masks, walls and armor that hating Jews has put on me; in all moments."

"I eliminate the first cause in regards to hating Jews; in all moments."

"I release being immersed in hating Jews; in all moments."

"I untangle all my energy from hating Jews; in all moments."

"I release the genetic propensity to hate Jews; in all moments."

"I dissolve all of the hating of Jews with the purity of Divine Love; in all moments."

"I view all Jews from the vantage point of Love; in all moments."

"I remove all vivaxes between myself and hating Jews; in all moments."

"I dry up all instincts to hate Jews; in all moments."

"I recant all vows and agreements to hate Jews; in all moments."

"I remove all curses that I put on Jews; in all moments."

"I remove all blessings I put on hating Jews; in all moments."

"I sever all strings and cords between myself and hating Jews; in all moments."

"I dissolve all karmic ties between myself and hating Jews; in all moments."

"I remove all the pain, burden and limitations that I have put on all Jews; in all moments."

"I remove all the fear, futility and unworthiness I have put on all Jews; in all moments."

"I release ostracizing Jews; in all moments."

"I give back all that I have taken from Jews; in all moments."

"I extract all hate of Jews from my sound frequency and the Universal sound frequency; in all moments."

"I extract all hate of Jews from my light emanation and the Universal light emanation; in all moments."

"I release individually or universally resonating or emanating with hating Jews; in all moments."

"I transcend hating Jews; in all moments.

"I shift my paradigm from hating Jews to seeing all souls as pure love; in all moments."

"I am centered and empowered in seeing all souls as pure love; in

all moments."

"I resonate, emanate and am interconnected with all life in seeing all souls as pure love; in all moments."

■■■

"I declare myself a surrogate for all Jews and Muslims in doing these taps; in all moments."

"I release hating Christians; in all moments."

"I release demonizing Christians; in all moments."

"I release being the enemy of Christians; in all moments."

"I release the belief that I am superior to Christians; in all moments."

"I nullify all contracts with Christians; in all moments."

"I withdraw all my energy from hating Christians; in all moments."

"I extract all the hate that I have projected onto Christians; in all moments."

"I dry up all psychic streams that mandate the diminishing of Christians; in all moments."

"I send all energy matrices into the light and sound that compel me to hate Christians; in all moments."

"I command all complex energy matrices that compel me to hate Christians to be escorted into the light and sound; in all moments."

"I remove all engrams of hating Christians; in all moments."

"I remove all programming and conditioning to hate Christians; in all moments."

"I strip all illusion off of hating Christians; in all moments."

"I remove all masks, walls and armor that hating Christians has put on me; in all moments."

"I eliminate the first cause in regards to hating Christians; in all moments."

"I release being immersed in hating Christians; in all moments."

"I untangle all my energy from hating Christians; in all moments."

"I release the genetic propensity to hate Christians; in all moments."

"I dissolve all of the hating of Christians with the purity of Divine Love; in all moments."

"I view all Christians from the vantage point of Love; in all moments."

"I remove all vivaxes between myself and hating Christians; in all moments."

"I dry up all instincts to hate Christians; in all moments."

"I recant all vows and agreements to hate Christians; in all moments."

"I remove all curses that I put on Christians; in all moments."

"I remove all blessings I put on hating Christians; in all moments."

"I sever all strings and cords between myself and hating Christians; in all moments."

"I dissolve all karmic ties between myself and hating Christians; in all moments."

"I remove all the pain, burden and limitations that I have put on all Christians; in all moments."

"I remove all the fear, futility unworthiness I have put on all Christians; in all moments."

"I release ostracizing Christians; in all moments."

"I give back all that I have taken from Christians; in all moments."

"I extract all hate of Christians from my sound frequency and the Universal sound frequency; in all moments."

"I extract all hate of Christians from my light emanation and the Universal light emanation; in all moments."

"I release individually or universally resonating or emanating with hating Christians; in all moments."

"I transcend hating Christians; in all moments."

"I shift my paradigm from hating Christians to seeing all souls as pure love; in all moments."

"I am centered and empowered in seeing all souls as pure love; in all moments."

"I resonate, emanate and am interconnected with all life in seeing all souls as pure love; in all moments."

■■

"I declare myself a surrogate for all religious denominations in doing these taps; in all moments."

"I release hating Pagans; in all moments."

"I release demonizing Pagans; in all moments."

"I release being the enemy of Pagans; in all moments."

"I release the belief that I am superior to Pagans; in all moments."

"I nullify all contracts with Pagans; in all moments."

"I withdraw all my energy from hating Pagans; in all moments."

"I extract all the hate that I have projected onto Pagans; in all moments."

"I dry up all psychic streams that mandate the diminishing of Pagans; in all moments."

"I send all energy matrices into the light and sound that compel me to hate Pagans; in all moments."

"I command all complex energy matrices that compel me to hate Pagans to be escorted into the light and sound; in all moments."

"I remove all engrams of hating Pagans; in all moments."

"I remove all programming and conditioning to hate Pagans; in all moments."

"I strip all illusion off of hating Pagans; in all moments."

"I remove all masks, walls and armor that hating Pagans has put on me; in all moments."

"I eliminate the first cause in regards to hating Pagans; in all moments."

"I release being immersed in hating Pagans; in all moments."

"I untangle all my energy from hating Pagans; in all moments."

"I release the genetic propensity to hate Pagans; in all moments."

"I dissolve all of the hating of Pagans with the purity of Divine Love; in all moments."

"I view all Pagans from the vantage point of Love; in all moments."

"I remove all vivaxes between myself and hating Pagans; in all

moments."

"I dry up all instincts to hate Pagans; in all moments."

"I recant all vows and agreements to hate Pagans; in all moments."

"I remove all curses that I put on Pagans; in all moments."

"I remove all blessings I put on hating Pagans; in all moments."

"I sever all strings and cords between myself and hating Pagans; in all moments."

"I dissolve all karmic ties between myself and hating Pagans; in all moments."

"I remove all the pain, burden and limitations that I have put on all Pagans; in all moments."

"I remove all the fear, futility and unworthiness I have put on all Pagans; in all moments."

"I release ostracizing Pagans; in all moments."

"I give back all that I have taken from Pagans; in all moments."

"I extract all hate of Pagans from my sound frequency and the Universal Sound frequency; in all moments."

"I extract all hate of Pagans from my light emanation and the Universal light emanation; in all moments."

"I release individually or universally resonating or emanating with hating Pagans; in all moments."

"I transcend hating Pagans; in all moments.

"I shift my paradigm from hating Pagans to seeing all souls as pure love; in all moments."

"I am centered and empowered in seeing all souls as pure love; in all moments."

"I resonate, emanate and am interconnected with all life in seeing all souls as pure love; in all moments."

∎∎∎

"I declare myself a surrogate for all religious denominations in doing these taps; in all moments."

"I release hating Atheists; in all moments."

"I release demonizing Atheists; in all moments."

"I release being the enemy of Atheists; in all moments."

"I release the belief that I am superior to Atheists; in all moments."

"I nullify all contracts with Atheists; in all moments."

"I withdraw all my energy from hating Atheists; in all moments."

"I extract all the hate that I have projected onto Atheists; in all moments."

"I dry up all psychic streams that mandate the diminishing of Atheists; in all moments."

"I send all energy matrices into the light and sound that compel me to hate Atheists; in all moments."

"I command all complex energy matrices that compel me to hate Atheists to be escorted into the light and sound; in all moments."

"I remove all engrams of hating Atheists; in all moments."

"I remove all programming and conditioning to hate Atheists; in all moments."

"I strip all illusion off of hating Atheists; in all moments."

"I remove all masks, walls and armor that hating Atheists has put on me; in all moments."

"I eliminate the first cause in regards to hating Atheists; in all moments."

"I release being immersed in hating Atheists; in all moments."

"I untangle all my energy from hating Atheists; in all moments."

"I release the genetic propensity to hate Atheists; in all moments."

"I dissolve all of the hating of Atheists with the purity of Divine Love; in all moments."

"I view all Atheists from the vantage point of Love; in all moments."

"I remove all vivaxes between myself and hating Atheists; in all moments."

"I dry up all instincts to hate Atheists; in all moments."

"I recant all vows and agreements to hate Atheists; in all moments."

"I remove all curses that I put on Atheists; in all moments."

"I remove all blessings I put on hating Atheists; in all moments."

"I sever all strings and cords between myself and hating Atheists; in all moments."

"I dissolve all karmic ties between myself and hating Atheists; in all moments."

"I remove all the pain, burden, and limitations that I have put on all Atheists; in all moments."

"I remove all the fear, futility, unworthiness I have put on all Atheists; in all moments."

"I release ostracizing Atheists; in all moments."

"I give back all that I have taken from Atheists; in all moments."

"I extract all hate of Atheists from my sound frequency and the Universal sound frequency; in all moments."

"I extract all hate of Atheists from my light emanation and the Universal light emanation; in all moments."

"I release individually or universally resonating or emanating with hating Atheists; in all moments."

"I transcend hating Atheists; in all moments.

"I shift my paradigm from hating Atheists to seeing all souls as pure love; in all moments."

"I am centered and empowered in seeing all souls as pure love; in all moments."

"I resonate, emanate and am interconnected with all life in seeing all souls as pure love; in all moments."

Feel free to continue doing these taps for other denominations. Notice how spacious it feels in the atmosphere from doing these taps. This exercise is you being a dynamic advocate for world peace.

4. AWAKENING

Love's Hue

Stretch your arms into the sky, pluck out the farthest star

Display it on your bedpost to remember who you are

Dig with your mind into the earth, find the deepest root

Remind yourself often of where you come and mark it with your boot

Delve into the pain that you hide from the world and that you shelter with your tears

Disarm the things that keep you from knowing, that this world is a house of mirrors

Question all matters, everything that you've ever learned since your birth

Discard all the lies that you readily accepted that prevent you from knowing your worth

Reawaken the aspect of your sweet self that knows you as being the best

Forget all the memories that kept you enslaved, they were merely a spiritual test

You are divine Love rooted in earth, the rest is the house of illusion

Shatter the mirrors, stop believing the lies, let go of the pain and confusion

Reclaim your spirit, realize your worth, you were merely asleep, so Awaken

Emanate Joy. Realize Love. Remember that dream you've forsaken!

You are abundance, so cash yourself in, you are the gain that you seek

A course of miracles in your own book of life, just open you up, take a peek

You are a windfall, you are your own church, you are a prayer, so just say you

A brush stroke of truth, swept across the night sky, Love's colorful well blended hue.

2/5/15

Breaching the Realms to Awakening

People are starting to realize that you can't give your energy through devotion or dedication to another group or person and also have it to empower yourself. At some point, you are going to have to decide if you want to take a backseat in your own spiritual endeavors or fully realize your own potential. Everything we are is a spiritual endeavor. Just because we deny it is so or lost our way does not make it any less real.

Your whole reason for existing is to realize yourself as the God being that you are. You have a unique vantage point to life. You have been brutalized and walked beside and behind the downtrodden. This has built up great empathy in you and understanding into the subtle mechanisms of compassion.

Who is more qualified to don the humble greatness of omnipotence than one who has been violated and abused at every turn and still has the capacity to love? This world has been your training ground. But you are breaching the realms of awakening. How do I know that? You are reading this.

Untangling the Wires

I finished facilitating a session with a longtime client. She has really opened up in the last year and is enjoyable to work with. In her first sessions, she was asking about her love life and career. But now she is asking questions about the Universe, getting glimpses of her past lives and she told me today that she sees energy now.

But the biggest change she described was where before she would feel love for her dog or family, now it is magnified to consume her. It is so beautiful to know that my work with her is directly related to more love being experienced in the world.

In her session, I was given the understanding that the reason people don't have a particular desire in their life is because they are processing certain concepts differently due to their experiences. For instance, if a small child was hit by its mother, it might process love as pain. Or if someone was in love for the first time and that person they adored dumped them, they might process relationships as abandonment. The wires get crossed.

Some of the issues seemed to work in reverse. For example, one of them is confusing health for youth. But how that processes to the self is the belief that one cannot be healthy unless they are young.

Here are the taps that I led her through at the end of the session. I love that my clients allow me to share what we encounter in their sessions. It depicts their generous nature and desire to assist others with their experiences. It is how we uplift humanity. Once a truth is thrown into the hat, it is there for all to partake of. We are all assisting the upliftment of humanity by delving into truth and sharing our findings.

(Say each statement three times out loud while tapping on you head and say it a fourth time while tapping on your chest.)

"I release processing Joy as loss; in all moments."

"I release processing Love as pain; in all moments."

"I release processing Abundance as a stockpile of things; in all moments."

"I release processing Freedom as loneliness; in all moments."

"I release processing Health as youth; in all moments."

"I release processing Success as conquering others; in all moments."

"I release processing Security as withholding my truth; in all moments."

"I release processing Companionship as giving away my power; in all moments."

"I release processing Creativity as being unstable; in all moments."

"I release processing Peace as a stagnant state; in all moments."

"I release processing Life as being difficult; in all moments."

"I release processing Beauty as a weapon; in all moments."

"I release processing Enthusiasm as a waste of energy; in all moments."

"I release processing Contentment as boredom; in all moments."

"I release processing Spirituality as being impoverished; in all moments."

"I release processing being human as superior; in all moments."

"I release processing Humility as unworthiness; in all moments."

"I release processing being human as being separate from nature; in all moments."

"I release processing feelings as reality; in all moments."

"I release processing the mind as the ultimate truth; in all moments."

"I release processing Intelligence as power; in all moments."

"I release processing being human as being encased in matter; in all moments."

"I release processing Dreams as a whim; in all moments."

"I release processing God as separate from myself; in all moments."

"I release processing the Universe as outside of myself; in all moments."

"I release processing Enlightenment as unattainable; in all moments."

"I release processing God realization as unfathomable; in all

moments."

You may have different ones and you may have some not listed. It is a great exercise in self-reflection.

Energy, Chakras and God

Energy spirals. Its flow is not as linear as conceptualized. Maybe when you visualize it coming into the body just through the top of the head and going right down, you are doing yourself a disservice. Maybe you are thwarting the natural flow of energy in some way.

Chakras are not linear. They do not just have an opening at the top where they accept energy in. They accept energy in from all directions. Think of a disco ball, but instead of just throwing out rays of light, it accepts energy from all directions.

The way to more accurately visualize the chakras is like a wand on a cotton candy machine that gathers all the sugar fluff collecting around the edge of the barrel. Except that the wand works in a multidimensional sort of way instead of a flat plane surface. The chakras are reaching out and collecting energy in all directions. It is a very active process.

The way you enter and leave the body is through a spiral. That is why when you are laying down to sleep, all the images come from the day, and then more abstract images. The energy of you is spiraling out of the body in a gentle way. The same is true when you are waking up and it takes you a few tries to wake up. The energy of you is spiraling in.

When you wake up quickly, you are being slammed into the body and it can lead to a headache or grouchiness when awakening. Imagine a big jet airplane slamming into a wall. That is what you are doing when you wake up too quickly. When you think you are awake, lay there for awhile and literally collect yourself. Since the astral plane is so close to the physical plane, it may seem like you are back in the body but you may be hovering.

When you visualize energy coming into you, see it like sideways rain flooding into you from every direction. See the chakras as active receiving systems with intelligence and purpose rather than stationary globes. They attract energy into the body within a certain range of vibration which is depicted by the color of energy collected.

The colors of the chakras are not just a color-coded system. It is the actual color vibration of the energy that you are collecting and drawing in. The color of your vegetables depicts what vibration of energy they are collecting. So if you know that you are weak in one particular chakra, take in the energy the body is lacking through that weak chakra by eating vegetables of that color or wearing clothes of that color.

God is energy. Understanding energy helps in understanding God. God is not in a weigh station out in the sky somewhere. God is meeting us every day in every way and in every form. Every single person, place or thing is God meeting us in different ways to teach us how dynamic we really are. If you don't like what life is showing you, change your agreement with the people and situations around you.

The more that you treat God as an abstract concept to send your energy to and to receive at Its will, the more room there is to fail in being empowered. The more you have an interactive relationship with God and see every living being as a reflection of God and an ambassador of God's Love, the more you can hone your understanding of God and the more opportunities there are to partake of God's love.

God is bombarding you with experiences, lessons, private time, one-on-one learning and a constant barrage of love simply to empower you. Everyone receives the lessons they need to realize themselves as dynamic and empowered. Receiving a goody bag of materialism is such a low bar of receiving. Look at the actions of the filthy rich. They will have to live with the despicable consequences of their spiritual lessons for lifetimes to come.

We who serve, we who love all, we who are empathic to the plights of others, we who use our gifts to uplift others in some way are interacting with God every day. The more your thoughts, deeds and purpose take in the lessons and use them to create a greater outflow of energy to assist others, the more you are embracing your true nature as an atom of God.

When you are no longer passive in your concept of God, but active, you have gained much insight into your true nature.

Manifesting the World of Light

I facilitated a private remote session for a new client. Usually I can feel a person's issues as soon as we connect. But this person was so in tune with a wonderful realm of light and love that it was not going to be an ordinary session. In tapping into her, I could see a fairy world with large flowers and sprites everywhere. It was a pleasure to just be privy to this world through her.

Her issues were rooted in her deep desire to be in that world of beautiful light and love instead of the one that we see on the news. She did not so clearly see this until I articulated this for her. But then it was clear to her. All of her frustration had to do with being in this world when the world of light was her true home.

She was one who protested and did what she could to turn this world into one of Light. It disheartened her because it felt like a losing battle. It was in a sense. By protesting and being so frustrated, she was actually feeding energy into the coarse world instead of curing the ills of man. Her frustration with the current course of the world was actually helping the world that she disdained thrive.

She was actually holding a place for the world of light in this world by her connection with it. During her session, we removed her connection with the coarse world and made space for the world of light to manifest for all. We withdrew all the energy that she was feeding into the coarse world and freed it up to manifest the world of light. If more people do this, the coarse world will evaporate and the world of light will prevail. My new client realized that the work we did in that one hour was more effective in changing the vibration of the world than all her protesting had done.

(Say each statement three times out loud while tapping on the top of your head at the crown chakra and say it a fourth time while tapping on your chest at the heart chakra.)

"I release being enslaved to the coarse world; in all moments."

"I remove all engrams of being enslaved; in all moments."

"I release feeding the coarse world; in all moments."

"I recant all vows and agreements between myself and the coarse world; in all moments."

"I remove all curses between myself and the coarse world; in all moments."

"I remove all blessings between myself and the coarse world; in all moments."

"I sever all strings and cords between myself and the coarse world; in all moments."

"I dissolve all karmic ties between myself and the coarse world; in all moments."

"I remove all the pain, burden, limitations, engrams and vivaxes that the coarse world has put on me; in all moments."

"I remove all the pain, burden, limitations, engrams and vivaxes that I have put on all others due to the coarse world; in all moments."

"I take back all the Joy, Love, Abundance, Freedom, Health and Wholeness that the coarse world has taken from me; in all moments."

"I give back all the Joy, Love, Abundance, Freedom, Health and Wholeness that I have taken from all others due to the coarse world; in all moments."

"I withdraw all my energy from the coarse world; in all moments."

"I release resonating with the coarse world; in all moments."

"I release emanating with the coarse world; in all moments."

"I extract all of the coarse world from my sound frequency; in all moments."

"I extract all of the coarse world from my light emanation; in all moments."

"I shift my paradigm from the coarse world to the World of Light; in all moments."

"I transcend the coarse world; in all moments."

"I hold space in this world to manifest the World of Light for all; in all moments."

"I remove blockages to manifesting the World of Light for all; in all moments."

"I stretch my capacity to manifest the World of Light for all; in all moments."

"I collapse and dissolve the coarse world; in all moments."

"I am centered and empowered in the World of Light; in all

moments."

Transcending the Lower Worlds

(Say each statement three times while tapping on your head and say it a fourth time while tapping on your chest.)

"I remove the glass ceiling of the physical realms; in all moments."

"I transcend the physical realms; in all moments."

"I transcend the astral realms; in all moments."

"I transcend the causal realms; in all moments."

"I transcend the mental realms; in all moments."

"I transcend the etheric realms; in all moments."

"I transcend the spiritual realms; in all moments."

"I remove all resistance to higher consciousness; in all moments."

"I transcend the 9 to 5 existence; in all moments."

"I transcend all archaic structures; in all moments."

"I withdraw all my energy and support from all archaic structures; in all moments."

"I transcend all of linear existence; in all moments."

"I withdraw all my energy and support from all linear existence; in all moments."

Eliminating the First Cause

The first cause is the initial intention that was sent out to start the action or event that is undesirable. For example, during the Iraq war, the president at the time was pressured into pulling out

American troops from the Middle East. The solution was to hire and train local thugs and assassins to fight for us. Those thugs turned on America and became a savvy fighting force of their own (compliments of America).

This group has developed into the terrorist group called ISIL. If not for America training them and equipping them in the first place, we would not be in the position we are in dealing with them in the world perhaps. The United States funding their training would be considered a first cause in the formation of ISIL. These taps are meant to energetically erase the first cause, so what ensued is eliminated. It is kind of like preventing that first domino from being knocked down and starting a chain reaction of events.

(Say each statement three times out loud while continuously tapping on the top of your head at the crown chakra and say it a fourth time while tapping on your chest.)

"I declare myself a surrogate for humanity in doing these taps; in all moments."

"I eliminate the first cause in creating ISIL; in all moments."

"I eliminate the first cause in all depression and sadness; in all moments."

"I eliminate the first cause in all hate; in all moments."

"I eliminate the first cause in all poverty and lack; in all moments."

"I eliminate the first cause in all slavery and imprisonment; in all moments."

"I eliminate the first cause in all sickness and disease; in all moments."

"I eliminate the first cause in all failure; in all moments."

"I eliminate the first cause in all insecurity; in all moments."

"I eliminate the first cause in all abandonment, rejection and isolation; in all moments."

"I eliminate the first cause in all conformity; in all moments."

"I eliminate the first cause in all war; in all moments."

"I eliminate the first cause in all death and decay; in all moments."

"I eliminate the first cause in all fractures and fragmentation; in all moments."

"I eliminate the first cause in all ugliness and judgment; in all moments."

"I eliminate the first cause in all apathy; in all moments."

"I eliminate the first cause in all corruption and power; in all moments."

"I eliminate the first cause in all programming and conditioning; in all moments."

"I eliminate the first cause in creating the Dark Ages; in all moments."

"I eliminate the first cause in all self-consciousness; in all moments."

"I eliminate the first cause in creating rogues and loners; in all moments."

"I eliminate the first cause in all ignorance; in all moments."

"I eliminate the first cause in all karmic conditioning; in all moments."

Who You Are

As a dynamic being, you are not flawed. You are a whole,

complete, loving, sovereign energy watching the dynamics of you play out and trying to pour as much of that wisdom into the little human self as possible. That is the game--to see how much empowerment you can infuse into yourself. See? That is the shift. Shift into that dynamic, omniscient expression of you and operate this physical life from that vantage point.

Empowerment

Many clients have a feeling of being disconnected. They feel different, removed from society and their true home or source.

It is not possible to be disconnected. The fact that we exist is validation in itself. The disconnect is with our own subtle senses that gauge and process our interactions in the Universe. These senses are more sensitive than the five and need to be recognized, developed and exercised.

Gut feelings, imagination, self-confidence and thinking outside of the box are all ways to enhance our subtle skills. Survival is no longer about a 9 to 5 existence. It is more about who is able to forgo the habitual enslavement of small ideas and empower themselves with their own dynamic freethinking self.

Encouragement

You don't need prayers as much as understanding. You need to lift a lantern into that dark abyss and look into every crevice. What you thought was your ambrosia was laced with cyanide. The Universe just knocked the goblet out of your hands as you were raising it to your lips. You are not stricken down. You are blessed by the invisible hands of protection. You are loved.

Certainly it is inviting at the mouth of a cul-de-sac. But once you have entrenched yourself in a dead end, it sometimes takes pain to knock you back into the awareness to find yourself. I'm sending you love.

I am excited for your growth. You can gauge it by the depth of the pain that you are feeling. It is incredible. It leaves the old you in the dust.

Judaism

The teachings of Judaism are of a higher vibratory rate than many other teachings. It is an ethical, spiritual teaching. The fighting has been a means to anchor such a teaching of higher vibratory rate into the negativity of this world. The fighting has been a means of balance for it to exist in its purity. As the whole world changes in vibratory rate, the fighting won't be a necessary anchor anymore. It will cease of its own accord.

Overcoming Primal Mode

A lot of our thoughts and behavior were formulated by being in survival mode for so many lifetimes. Now, many of our thoughts and behaviors have become ingrained and it is just us behaving out of habit. WE MUST BREAK THE HABIT so that we can manifest joy, love, abundance, freedom and wholeness for all. Kindness, gratitude and regard for all others are our "soul patch" to break the habit of unconscious living.

Perpetual Contemplation

Everything we do can be done as a meditative or contemplative state to bring more love and awareness into our lives. They key is simply doing it with more conscious intention.

For example:

When one is bathing they can visualize washing away negative thought forms from themselves.

When one speaks, they can think of each word as a burst of positive or negative energy that they are adding into the environment. They can speak with the intention of only adding positive energy to the whole.

When one is driving home, they can feel the communion of all the other drivers and treat them with the reverence of leaving church.

When one eats, they can visualize the love being extracted out of the food and sending it to all the cells of their body. They can send gratitude back to the sponsors of their meal, the earth and the plants.

When anything unusual happens during the day, one can treat it like a dream message and interpret its meaning.

When one is doing something that they don't enjoy, visualize how much worse conditions may have been in past eras and be grateful for the contrast.

When one is relaxing, imagine resting in the arms of love.

When someone offers anything uplifting, see it as a gift from the Universe and accept graciously.

When one is walking the dog, realize how they feel when they are enjoying their favorite past time and allow the pet the space to enjoy themselves unhindered by control.

When loving one's children, imagine oneself as a child as well and realize it is nurturing one's self by nurturing them.

This is a way to make the whole day richer and to enliven the lives of those around us more than we already do.

It seems unfathomable how much we will change once the mass consciousness realizes we are all interconnected. All that drive to hoard wealth and succeed at all costs will shift into helping empower others. It is all exciting as we can watch everyone not so much racing to the future anymore but racing to the moment.

Entering the Sublime

We know our loving nature. We give and give and give until something happens and we start to feel unappreciated. Then we may feel bad inside and start to ruminate and become self-reflective and that is when the beautiful giving flow may disintegrate.

Giving is a beautiful flow of love coming from our core. It seems effortless because it comes from a place of omniscience, but when we start to want appreciation and accolades for the flow, then we are mixing the human consciousness into the mix. The human consciousness is finite and we may start to feel depleted.

When you start to feel bad about giving, it is a sign you are outgrowing your old pot and stretching your capacity to give even more. If you start to feel bad and resent others, you stay in the same pot, but if you keep loving through it, then you move to a bigger pot and attain a greater capacity to give, love and serve. Then it becomes a joy to watch the human consciousness try to revolt and to NOT concede from being loving. In this way, you are taking initiative and mastering the lessons that all spiritual greats once had to master.

You are entering the sublime!

Move On

Feelings from past lives that we are sinners or damned do some damage to our present day psyche. In private sessions with people, I help people release the feelings of being unlovable, sinners or damned. I think these feelings are etched so deeply into us sometimes that they have a major effect on self-worth. How can we join in as problem solvers in life if we feel that God has rejected us? It leads to depressing, apathetic lives.

The good news is that it is all a misunderstanding. We are never rejected by life, just by some people. It is never too overwhelming to undo or too late for a fresh perspective. I love helping people change their vantage point. In past lives, our family, church and village were our mainstays, our survival. These days we have the freedom to change direction and choose where we plant ourselves.

There is no need to stay stuck with people who don't value or appreciate us. Choose to be around those who love. If one group disapproves, there is no need to internalize their opinions. Just find a group that inspires and supports you, and appreciates your special gifts!

Also, try these taps:

(Say each statement three times while tapping on your head and say it a fourth time while tapping on your chest.)

"I release the belief that I am damned; in all moments."

"I release feeling that I am unworthy; in all moments."

"I release the belief that I am unworthy; in all moments."

Enhance Your Own Value

We send prayers up like messages to a signal tower hoping they will be prioritized and delivered. When will we realize that WE are the signal tower? Whether prayers are effective or random has to do with two things: The signal strength of the sender and the receptiveness of the recipient.

Send your positive intentions directly to the recipient. On the other end, always be receptive to the well wishes of others. When we pray for ourselves, we are sending out a signal and it is being sent back to us.

This can be a very empowering realization because so many believe that the process is random. It feels as if some invisible force is deciding whether we are worthy or not, and that concept, through a psyche that has been broken down by the exploits of man can leave one feeling helpless.

It is not hit or miss. You are empowered by your own intention. And if you have seen your prayers work miracles for others, please turn them on yourself because you are worth it! Enhance your own value!

The Legacy of Love

You are not separate from your spirit guides. There are many more than you realize. They appreciate your love as much as you benefit from theirs. You are connected and embraced in all the protection, love and wisdom that they can possibly offer.

They do not separate from you. It is you in your belief that has kept them at bay. The more you acknowledge and appreciate them, the more that the connection is realized. Fear of not knowing them, fear of doing or saying the wrong thing, fear of believing in something that is not widely talked about are all fear. Fear is the opposite of love, so dry up the fear and separateness by simply loving more.

The only risk in loving too much is that the ego will feel out of sorts if the love is misplaced, but the ego is not in charge, or shouldn't be. The best remedy for an over-healthy ego is to simply love more. Love under all conditions. Love even if you feel raw and vulnerable. Love even, and especially, if you feel wronged. The people who wrong you are in the most need of love. For how could they defy someone as beautiful as you if they were in agreement with love?

Love is never a waste. Love is never displaced. The more that it feels foolish and awkward to give, the more evidence that that is exactly what is needed. So what if your love splashes in the "wrong" places or pours over into the "wrong" spots. Your love will never be a waste until this whole world is drenched in love. It can happen.

My first writing of the day is usually what the spirit guides want me to share. No, they are not just my guides. They are here to serve all. They are yours as well. To call them mine is to create a level of separation that is not necessary or helpful. Please accept the love firsthand. It is vital to the transcendence of the world that all realize and accept the sweetest and most sincere gift--one of love and acceptance.

Anyone who tries to make you feel unaccepted or invalidated is not of love. Please remember that as they engage and walk away. You are such a beautiful expression of love and unique beauty. Please don't you dare allow anyone--not your mother, friends, community, country or world--make you feel otherwise. To stay in the love must be your strength of conviction. For when you accept the love and ingest it as your truth and essence, you hold the door open for a billion other souls to do the same.

Make your walk on this earth count for something. Walk in confidence and reverence. This is your legacy if you choose. It has always been your choice. Mastership is simply recognizing this. If you want to be more connected with your spirituality, simply love more and all will be revealed to you.

Awakening

Within crusted walls of embedded emotion,
Bombarded by waves of perpetual commotion,
Is a permanent "me" determined to stand,
Slough off adversity like layers of sand.

Draw in the Light from a faraway source,
To stand firm in the Love seems "par for the course,"
Reverberating in music, a most precious choir,
Break through the dross, confusion and mire.

Emanate, vibrate, reverberate, resound,
Be inundated with such beauty I unfurl and rebound,
Show others imprisoned what awakening can be,
Humbly resonating, beautiful and free.

10/21/13

Technique to Expand into Your God Self

Whenever someone doesn't do something that they know is beneficial, even though they are getting wise council from their own innate wisdom, they hesitate to follow it out of fear. Fear is so subtle sometimes. There is fear of being wrong, what others will think, fear of failing or looking foolish. There are so many ways to sabotage ourselves from heeding our own wise council.

The truth of the matter is that one is never going to gain confidence in trusting their own innate wisdom unless they practice it. If you don't listen to your own advice, that gnawing voice of truth, why would your voice keep bothering? When you don't listen, it is like turning down the volume of your own truth and walking away.

Then we listen to others who seem like they know more. The only reason they may know more is that they are either listening to wisdom more within themselves, or they are using their ego to mock up such confidence. If you turn up the volume on your own wisdom, you will know the difference.

The technique to overcome this limitation is very simple. Imagine that you are a God being operating a human body. Everything the God being wants to convey in wisdom and kindness has to work through the limitations of the physical body. This body may still have the fears and awkwardness of being human, but there is the God being component of it that sees the struggle of the limiting parts and has an overview of how to deal with them.

Your God wisdom would know that you are afraid but would also see how afraid all other people are and put the fear in perspective. Your God part would have less resistance to doing the right thing without fear of failing. God does not fail. God heals, loves and can even redirect the little human body, but it never fails.

This vantage point affords many benefits. The more one thinks, feels, acts and exists at this God vantage point, the more they are tapped into the absolute wisdom of the Universe. Doing this technique is a grand example of, "fake it until you make it."

Also, if you think it does not work, but you like what I write, how do you think I tap into such insights to help as many people and beings as I can? Why are people having dream experiences of me healing them? How can I talk to animals, trees and life itself? I use this technique and stay in this vantage point as much as possible while being aware of the physical component.

I was pushed to this vantage point by being phased out, in a way, from the world that you enjoy, but all you have to do is adopt the techniques that I share. It is a way for you to have the best of both worlds. Heeding the techniques that I share is an incredible opportunity to stretch beyond your present capacities to an incomprehensible freedom.

Take all the limitations off yourself. From the God vantage point you will be able to recognize what they are. They will feel like little uncomfortable glitches in your energy field, like knots in the stomach feel. Whenever you sense one of them, address it right away and expand further. There are no limitations, especially when your intentions are the purest.

Primed for Enlightenment

There have always been spiritual factions assisting the inhabitants of the world to reach the point of enlightenment. Enlightenment is a physiological process of the ego being stripped away from the true self. It is what Saint Paul described as getting knocked down by the Light of God on the road to Damascus. When it happens, the person is left with a purity of truth and serves others from a sacred place. There are many misconceptions about enlightenment. After the process, the ego is reintegrated into the psyche but it is with a heightened awareness of the difference between ego and one's true self that the individual continues.

Reaching enlightenment is becoming more possible with our interconnectedness. When it happened for me, I was locked up by others and I can't help but feel that this was orchestrated. As I assist others in reaching enlightenment, I can't help but think that this is in divine accordance with my purpose. When I came back from imprisonment, I was never angry. Maybe this is why. Maybe I realized on some level that I would make good use of the experience.

No true spiritual path is gratuitous. Every single grain of truth that was folded over into a religion was a seed to lead individuals to the heart of God. Complacency is offensive to the spiritual greats who have dedicated their existence to bringing others to truth. They have not done so, so one individual can feel warm and fuzzy. They have not done so, so one group or individual feels superior to another. They have not done so, so someone has a leg up on another. They have done so to uplift all.

Maybe it is a huge experiment to see if humans can pull themselves up by the bootstraps and embrace the spiritual nature that is in their grasp. Maybe then, the desire to serve others is as compulsive as a salmon swimming upstream. Maybe all the war, strife and injustice that this world has seen are the perfect breeding grounds for enlightened souls. Once enough people transform through the process of enlightenment, we will reach a tipping point and all of humanity will follow suit. This is my intention for sharing all the techniques.

Recently, some of my clients have been getting a sense of being ready for enlightenment. It is almost like they found me to help them prepare. One client, who did experience the process, believes that she would not have been ready without our work. Another client realized that she still has an ingrained fear of being an individual. It is an astute awareness. Here are the taps to assist with that subtle issue.

(Say each statement three times out loud while tapping on your head and say it a fourth time while tapping on your chest.)

"I release the fear of being separated from the ego; in all

moments."

"I release the fear of losing my mind; in all moments."

"I release the fear of the responsibility of enlightenment; in all moments."

"I release the fear of something better; in all moments."

"I release the fear of the unknown; in all moments."

"I release being programmed for the mundane; in all moments."

"I release the fear of being separated from the herd; in all moments."

"I release the fear of my own greatness; in all moments."

"I release the fear of my own insignificance; in all moments."

"I make space in this world for my own enlightenment; in all moments."

"I remove all obstacles to my own enlightenment; in all moments."

"I stretch my capacity for my own enlightenment; in all moments."

"I release the fear of losing it all; in all moments."

"I connect to my own vortex; in all moments."

"I remove all limitations; in all moments."

"I open up the heavens and walk into my own stillness; in all moments."

"I release the fear of losing myself; in all moments."

"I release the fear of the realization of not knowing who I am; in all moments."

"I release micromanaging the Universe; in all moments."

"I cut all strings and cords between myself and the ego; in all moments."

"I release the belief that my greatness is contingent on another; in all moments."

"I recant my vow to not transcend until every sentient being has transcended; in all moments."

"I release waiting for someone to save me; in all moments."

"I release waiting to be discovered; in all moments."

"I release the fear of facing myself; in all moments."

"I make space in this world to transcend the mind; in all moments."

"I remove all blockages to transcending the mind; in all moments."

"I stretch my capacity to transcend the mind; in all moments."

"I release reacting to outer stimuli; in all moments."

"I release an aversion to my own stillness; in all moments."

"I release feeling and believing that I am unworthy to serve; in all moments."

"I am centered and empowered in my own enlightenment; in all moments. "

These taps may create a powerful shift in the individual. May the experiences they bring be life changing. Also, please realize that feeling alone and being alone are two different things. There are always spiritual guides to assist even if one does not recognize or acknowledge their presence.

No One Can Diminish You!

(Say these statements three times out loud while continuously tapping on the top of your head at the crown chakra and say them a fourth time while tapping on your chest.)

"I release the fear of the responsibility of being awesome; in all moments."

"I release diminishing my awesomeness before someone else does; in all moments."

"I release living in constant fear of being diminished; in all moments."

"I release living in constant fear of being called out; in all moments."

"I release making myself invisible to cover my awesomeness; in all moments."

"I release hiding my awesomeness from the world; in all moments."

"I release being in denial of my own awesomeness; in all moments."

"I release limiting my own awesomeness to remain safe; in all moments."

"I release choosing security over my own awesomeness; in all moments."

"I release choosing mediocrity over awesomeness; in all moments."

"I release allowing others to define me; in all moments."

"I release subjecting myself to false humility; in all moments."

"I break through all the limitations of false humility; in all

moments."

"I see awesomeness in all; in all moments."

"I shift my paradigm from mediocrity to Universal awesomeness; in all moments."

"I accept living in an awesome world; in all moments."

"I am centered and empowered in awesomeness; in all moments."

"I infuse Universal awesomeness into my sound frequency and light emanation; in all moments."

"I resonate and emanate Universal awesomeness; in all moments."

Technique: Walk Through God

We are conditioned to think of God as an abstract concept or as a caricature of an old man on a throne. There is a lot of wiggle room between those two depictions. How about thinking of ourselves already immersed in God?

If we can imagine that we are atoms of God--which many are taught that we are--that means everyone else is an atom of God. So what we are doing every day and every moment is walking through a sea of God.

If one can remember this, then they can meet God every day in the face of all those they encounter. When someone is kind to you, it is God being kind to you. When you are kind to others, it is you recognizing your own true nature. When others are unkind or hateful, they just need reminding who they are. They need to be shown kindnesses to remember their true essence.

This vantage point can create a great shift in someone. Think about it. When you are stuck in traffic, you are actually present with God. When there is an event that many are tuned into, it is a sea of God coming together. When you are walking down a crowded street, instead of focusing on a destination, relax in the experience of passing through God.

Perhaps those who feel the need to pour what is bothering them out onto social media are reaching out to God. Perhaps when people ask for prayers, they are more effective in talking to God than if they tried praying.

Perhaps the reason so many people are becoming so aware by interacting on social media is because they are interfacing with God. It is a nice thought. This vantage point will afford some to be kinder to each other. That is why nature is so peaceful. Maybe other forms of life naturally present themselves in their purest state of God. Maybe humans can get there as well.

Being Centered

Being centered is being in the eye of the storm. It is your own calm. It is where your love and truth are. There are definite signs that you are in your center. When one is centered, they are at peace with themselves. They are kind, and content and happy. There is no jealousy and no pettiness. One does not enjoy gossip because they do not take fascination in the struggles of others.

People use many different techniques to stay centered. Some pray, some meditate, work out, use visualizations, listen to inspirational music or read inspirational works. Some may even play Candy Crush to stay centered. What looks like wasting time to one person may be a survival tool for another.

Here are some taps to assist in staying centered.

(Say each statement three times while tapping on your head and a fourth time while tapping on your chest.)

"I am centered in Joy, Love, Abundance and Freedom; in all

moments."

"I release coming out of Love in search of Love; in all moments."

"I release coming out of Contentment to find Joy; in all moments."

"I release surrendering my Freedom to search for Freedom; in all moments."

"I am connected to all in Divine Love; in all moments."

"I am whole and perfect in my present state; in all moments."

"I am my own success; in all moments."

I don't usually recommend doing the taps more than one session. However, these are the taps to keep handy in case you need a boost.

Let's Create a Spiritual Renaissance

In private sessions, I assist people who are committed to being the most ethical, spiritual beings they can possibly be. They are dedicated to connecting with Source in its purest state. When I work with them, some unique concepts come through for them to release. At the end of a session, they sometimes just want to sleep because they want to slip out of their body and the lower consciousness.

In a recent session, my client had that reaction to doing these taps. We focused on unworthy intentions. An example of an unworthy intention is the Crusades--plundering and killing in the name of a just cause. I suggest the taps to anyone who has reached a plateau in their own spiritual endeavors. I invite you to try them and see if they help you lighten your consciousness.

(Say each statement three times while tapping on your head, and say it a fourth time while tapping on your chest.)

"I recant all vows and agreements between myself and all unworthy intentions; in all moments."

"I remove all curses between myself and all unworthy intentions; in all moments."

"I release giving up my freedom to unworthy intentions; in all moments."

"I release being enslaved by unworthy intentions; in all moments."

"I dissolve all karmic ties between myself and all unworthy intentions; in all moments."

"I remove all the pain, burden and limitations that all unworthy intentions have put on me; in all moments."

"I take back all the Joy, Love, Abundance, Freedom and Wholeness that all unworthy intentions have taken from me; in all moments."

"I remove all unworthy intentions from my Sound frequency; in all moments."

"I remove all unworthy intentions from my Light body; in all moments."

"I shift my paradigm from all unworthy intentions to Joy, Love, Abundance, Freedom and Wholeness; in all moments."

"I surrender to the fluidity of Joy, Love, Abundance and Freedom; in all moments."

Healing a World

Hate saw Love and was enraged

Love saw Hate and felt compassion

Hate shook its fist at Love.

Love kept its distance out of deference

Hate attacked Love but lost its balance and fell

Love kept its composure

Hate cried

Love answered its call

Love helped hate up

Hate looked at Love and was confused

Hate thought that it was Love

Hate now knew what Love looked like

Love saw love in Hate's eyes

Hate melted into love

Love collected itself and went on its way.

Release Primal Abandonment

(Say each statement three times out loud while tapping on the top of your head at the crown chakra and say it a fourth time while tapping on your chest.)

"I release the trauma of being born; in all moments."

"I release the trauma of being abandoned in my crib; in all moments."

"I release the trauma of crying it out; in all moments."

"I release the trauma of my cries being unanswered; in all moments."

"I release confusing my cries being unanswered with God not hearing my prayers; in all moments."

"I release the primal belief of being abandoned; in all moments."

"I release the belief that I am abandoned by God; in all moments."

"I release the belief that I am left to my own wits; in all moments."

"I release feeling alone and isolated in the Universe; in all moments."

"I release translating being alone in my crib with being alone in the Universe; in all moments."

"I release suffering without a voice; in all moments."

"I release confusing being invisible as a baby with being invisible in the world; in all moments."

"I remove all the negative programming and conditioning that my babyhood put on me; in all moments."

"I release the belief I need to cry it out to be loved; in all moments."

"I release the trauma of being ignored; in all moments."

"I release the trauma of being treated like a non-person; in all moments."

"I release using manipulation to get love; in all moments."

"I release the belief that I need to manipulate to be loved; in all moments."

"I release confusing manipulation with self-worth; in all moments."

"I shift my paradigm to nurturing and comforting myself; in all moments"

"I pour infinite Love, Nurturing, Encouragement and Positive Reinforcement into my baby self; in all moments."

"I am centered and empowered in comforting and nurturing myself; in all moments."

Loving Balance

In our natural state, our energy is a perpetual flow of love. There is a desire that borders on compulsion to give and share. We hold a memory of this completeness within our energy field and it is what we aspire to return to.

Due to trauma and fear, our loving flow diminishes to a trickle. This diminishes our access to the energy that fuels and inspires us. We greatly shut down and become less effective in helping ourselves and uplifting others.

Those who are trying hard to become effective again may get skewed in sharing. They are trying their best but their sharing is mental rants or emotional dumping. Since their energy flow is still introverted their sharing is based on fear or problems.

When someone is in this mode of processing, try to listen to them obliquely (if you feel you must listen). Sympathy has a low frequency, so giving too much sympathy can actually hinder more than help someone. A greater way to help them is to validate their greatness rather than their issues. Remind them of their resilient spirit and that anything they are experiencing is temporary. They will try to bring you into their pain but that is only out of fear or loneliness. They don't understand what they do.

To get out of that state ourselves, the best thing we can do is just give. Give of our talents, our time, our gifts in any way that allows us to prime the pump of generosity and love that is our natural state. But in doing so, realize that we have to include loving ourselves. Because when we can love others AND love ourselves, then we are in balance.

A New Truth

We collectively are God. Anyone who understands their nature is a landing point for God on the surface of humanity. We are all landing points for God to the extent that we can believe that we are. That is why I get frustrated when people separate themselves from their greatness by telling me I am gifted.

Believing I am gifted is great if we can see that everyone is gifted. Otherwise, people are separating themselves from their greatness by believing that I or anyone is something they are not. That is the antithesis of truth and opposite of all that I share. So believing that I am more gifted for what I share is a lack of understanding of the message that I share.

Male energy has skewed our belief system by saying one person is great at the expense of others. It has trained humanity to comply with being subjugated by beliefs and ritualistic conditioning and by turning to one man. What I share is more than words but a potent energy that burns through apathy and indifference to uncover clear understanding. Words, music, kindness, sincerity, inspiration and creativity are other means of breaking through as well.

Consciousness is like ice and truth is like ice fishing in cold weather. It needs to be drilled through repeatedly. The more people awaken to the fact that we are all landing points for God, the more that God will be relevant in the world again. We have been taught that we don't matter. We have been taught by male energy that to feel our greatness is a pathology called God complex. They give the subject medication and lock them away.

Embracing one's greatness is not something that society easily accepts. It is up to all of us to start feeling our greatness so we can storm the door of all limitations together. This is a war cry to humanity. Let our spiritual freedom ring. Let us make God relevant through our hearts and intentions. We are our humanity's saving grace.

Hear these words.

Release the Limitations of Being Human

(Say each statement three times out loud while tapping on the top of your head at the crown chakra and say it a fourth time while tapping on your chest at the heart chakra.)

"I release being human out of habit; in all moments."

"I release being human; in all moments."

"I release feeling beholden to being human; in all moments."

"I release being enslaved to being human; in all moments."

"I recant all vows and agreements between myself and being human; in all moments."

"I remove all curses between myself and being human; in all moments."

"I remove all blessings between myself and being human; in all moments."

"I sever all strings and cords between myself and being human; in all moments."

"I dissolve all karmic ties between myself and being human; in all moments."

"I remove all vivaxes between myself and being human; in all moments."

"I remove all the pain, burden, limitations and engrams that being human has put on me; in all moments."

"I remove all the pain, burden, limitations and engrams that being human has put on all others; in all moments."

"I take back all the Joy, Love, Abundance, Freedom, Health, Success, Security, Companionship, Creativity, Peace, Life, Wholeness, Beauty, Enthusiasm, Contentment, Spirituality, Enlightenment, Confidence, Intellect and the Ability to Discern that being human has taken from me; in all moments."

"I give back all that I have taken from all others by being human; in all moments."

"I shift my paradigm from being human to manifesting my higher self; in all moments."

"I strip all illusion off of being human; in all moments."

"I transcend being human; in all moments."

"I repair and fortify the wei chi on all my bodies; in all moments."

"I repair and fortify the wei chi on my higher self; in all moments."

"I align all my bodies with my higher self; in all moments."

"I make space in this world to manifest my higher self; in all moments."

"I remove all blockages to manifesting my higher self; in all moments."

"I stretch my capacity to manifesting my higher self; in all moments."

"I am centered and empowered in manifesting my higher self; in all moments."

"I resonate and emanate my higher self; in all moments."

Release Using Pain to Pay Homage to God

In past lifetimes, God was associated with painful practices and suffering. Today, as more people become spiritually enlightened, their bodies are still carrying the belief that enlightenment comes through pain. So the more aware they are, the more pain they put themselves in. These taps address that core issue.

Please realize that God NEVER wanted or wants us to suffer. Pain is something that man has inflicted on the world, not God. Man in his arrogance thought he could be the mouthpiece of God, but if you think about it, God is not even God. God is a word that has been used to symbolize the formless, nameless love. Even uttering Its name limits Its sacred stretch to the mental realms. God exists beyond the mind, and so do you.

(Say each statement three times out loud while tapping on the top of your head at the crown chakra and say it a fourth time while tapping on your chest.)

"I release the belief that I need to suffer to gain spiritual awareness; in all moments."

"I remove all vivaxes between God and pain; in all moments."

"I remove all vivaxes between myself and pain; in all moments."

"I release associating God with pain; in all moments."

"I release associating pain with God; in all moments."

"I remove all tentacles between God and pain; in all moments."

"I remove all engrams of me suffering to find God; in all moments."

"I send all energy matrices into the light that confuse God and suffering; in all moments."

"I remove all programming and conditioning that tell me I need to suffer to find God; in all moments."

"I release the belief that God could ever reject me; in all moments."

"I release the belief that God could ever abandon me; in all moments."

"I release the belief that God could ever hate me; in all moments."

"I release the belief that God could ever want me to suffer; in all moments."

"I release the belief that God could ever withdraw love from me; in all moments."

"I remove all engrams of God rejecting, abandoning, or hating me; in all moments." (It wasn't God. It was man.)

"I remove all engrams of God withdrawing love from me; in all moments."

"I remove all engrams of suffering for God; in all moments."

"I release the belief that I am separate from God; in all moments."

"I release feeling unworthy of God; in all moments."

"I release the belief that others are closer to God than myself; in all moments."

"I shift my paradigm from believing God is vengeful to knowing God as pure love and kindness; in all moments."

"I shift my paradigm from pain to Love; in all moments."

"I release using pain to pay homage to God; in all moments."

"I extract all the pain from my beingness that I was using to pay homage to God; in all moments."

"I make space in this world to experience the ultimate resolve of God's Love; in all moments."

"I remove all blockages to perpetually experiencing the Source of Love; in all moments."

"I stretch my capacity to experience and perpetuate the Source of Love; in all moments."

"I declare myself a sacred conduit and channel for the Source of Love; in all moments."

Love's Appeal

Tell me I don't matter

Tell me you don't care

Tell me it's all bullshit

That you're not really there

Tell me there's no freedom

That everything's a lie

Carelessly chuckle and walk away

As you watch me die

Or...

Tell me there is purpose

In all we say and do

Give me reason to believe

In Love, in life, in you

Plant a garden with your words

Make each day a song

Give all a reason to exist

Tell all that they belong

Give all purpose, don all truths

Make all scenarios win/win

From the ashes of defeat

Sprouts of providence begin

See Peace, when others envision war

Talk advantage when others spout loss

Risk vulnerability and feeling raw

Show kindness at every cost

Encourage, enlighten, visualize, unfold

Empathize, appreciate, heal

Cater to one's higher truth

To deliver Love's appeal

It doesn't really matter

What you say or do

As long as you act from the depth of Love

And know that place is you.

Jen Ward 6/27/14

Capturing John Lennon's Vision

I actually stumbled upon John Lennon's vision of world peace one day in contemplation. It was everyone living their purpose and passions. It was all uplifting everyone with their gifts merely because to do so brought so much joy. Perhaps world peace has been stifled by a male or yang-dominated slant on life. But that imbalance is being corrected and perhaps love and peace can prevail.

It is a great spiritual undertaking for us all to come together in peace and freedom, but I believe we are up for the task. There really is nothing that a pure intention fueled by a loving heart cannot accomplish. The magnitude of such a capacity has never been registered. It is a fertile time for everyone to test the limitlessness of possibilities.

Release Negatively Programming Yourself

(Say each statement three times out loud while tapping on the top of your head at the crown chakra and say it a fourth time while tapping on your chest.)

"I release programming problems into myself; in all moments."

"I release telling myself that I am flawed; in all moments."

"I release telling the world that I am flawed; in all moments."

"I release programming sadness or depression into myself; in all moments."

"I release telling myself that I am depressed; in all moments."

"I release telling the world that I am depressed; in all moments."

"I release programming isolation into myself: in all moments."

"I release telling myself that I am unlovable; in all moments."

"I release telling the world that I am unlovable; in all moments."

"I release programming poverty into myself; in all moments."

"I release telling myself that I am poor or broke; in all moments."

"I release telling the world that I am poor; in all moments."

"I release programming slavery into myself; in all moments."

"I release telling myself that I am trapped; in all moments."

"I release telling the world that I am trapped; in all moments."

"I release programming disease into myself: in all moments."

"I release telling myself that I am sick; in all moments."

"I release telling the world that I am sick; in all moments."

"I release programming obesity into myself; in all moments."

"I release telling myself that I am fat; in all moments."

"I release telling the world that I am flawed; in all moments."

"I release programming failure into myself; in all moments."

"I release telling myself that I am a failure; in all moments."

"I release telling the world that I am flawed; in all moments."

"I release programming myself to be broken; in all moments."

"I release telling myself that I am broken; in all moments."

"I release telling the world that I am broken; in all moments."

Free Yourself From Other Realities and Dimensions

(Say each statement three times out loud while tapping on the top of your head at the crown chakra and say it a fourth time while tapping on your chest.)

"I remove all vivaxes between myself and all other realities and dimensions; in all moments."

"I remove all tentacles between myself and all other realities and dimensions; in all moments."

"I remove all programming and conditioning that all other realities and dimensions have put on me; in all moments."

"I remove all engrams that all other realities and dimensions have put on me; in all moments."

"I remove all the fear and isolation that all other realities and dimensions have put on me; in all moments."

"I release being manipulated by all realities and dimensions; in all moments."

"I release being a pawn for any realities or dimensions; in all moments."

"I release being at the mercy of any realities or dimensions; in all moments."

"I remove all the trauma that has been inflicted on me by any realities or dimensions; in all moments."

"I release being galvanized to complacency by any other realities or dimensions; in all moments."

"I release being drained of my life force by any other realities or dimensions; in all moments."

"I take back my life force from all realities and all dimensions; in all moments."

"I recant all vows and agreements between myself and all realities and all dimensions; in all moments."

"I am DONE diminishing myself; in all moments."

"I release being the amusement of other realities or dimensions; in all moments."

"I remove all curses between myself and all realities and all dimensions; in all moments."

"I remove all blessings between myself and all realities and all dimensions; in all moments."

"I sever all strings and cords and wires between myself and all realities and dimensions; in all moments."

"I dissolve all karmic ties between myself and all realities and dimensions; in all moments."

"I remove all the fear and isolation that I have put on all others in all realities and all dimensions; in all moments."

"I remove all the pain, burden, and limitations that have been put on me by all realities and all dimensions; in all moments."

"I remove all the pain, burden, and limitations that I have put on all others in all realities and all dimensions; in all moments."

"I give back all the good that I have taken from all others in all realities and all dimensions; in all moments."

"I take back all the good that has been taken from me in all realities and all dimensions; in all moments."

"I heal all those I have wounded in all realities and all dimensions; in all moments."

"I right all wrongs that I have committed in all realities and all dimensions; in all moments."

"I heal my body in all realities and in all dimensions; in all moments."

"I right all wrongs that have been done to me in all realities and in all dimensions; in all moments."

"I wipe my slate clean in all realities and in all dimensions; in all moments."

"I transcend all realities and dimensions; in all moments."

"I close up all portals between all realities and dimensions that don't mutually support both parties in being empowered in Divine Love; in all moments."

"I withdraw all my energy from all realities and all dimensions; in all moments."

"I strip all illusion off of all realities and all dimensions; in all moments."

"I withdraw my allegiance from any particular reality or dimension; in all moments."

"I release resonating with any realities or dimensions; in all moments."

"I release emanating with any realities or dimensions; in all moments."

"I extract all realities and dimensions from my beingness; in all moments."

"I extract all realities and dimensions from my sound frequency; in all moments."

"I extract all realities and dimensions from my light emanation; in all moments."

"I declare myself a pure particle of pure love; in all moments."

"I declare myself a pure channel for Divine Love in all realities and in all dimensions; in all moments."

"I align all my beingnesses in all realities, in all dimensions, and in all moments."

"I am centered and empowered and imbued in Divine Love in all realities, in all dimensions, and in all moments."

"Divine Love dissolves all reactionary states within my beingness in all realities, in all dimensions, and in all moments."

Melting the River

We are a small stream in the infinite vast river of Divine Love. To ourselves we are a huge river and it is only in comparison to the whole that we are perceived as small. What happens in our small stream is reflective of what is happening in the whole river. We are all connected. We are all of the same river. We move, flow, express, exude, run free and share ourselves with the myriad of life.

But when we forget we are part of the whole, when we believe we are isolated from the source, when we are fearful and forget our beautiful, loving nature, we become frozen and cling to the rocks for a bit.

It is not necessary to memorialize every transgression or to wield our might for justification just to see ourselves temporarily frozen and use all our intention to melt the waters back into exuberance.

In contemplation, see the sweet little stream frozen against the rocks and visualize melting it. Watch it well up and run back into the source river carefree and unhindered.

In this way, you will be loving yourself free without thoughts of unworthiness or resistance getting in your own way. You are free, you are free, you are free. See yourself melting into the source river, running parallel with it and having all the components that it does. Be the river, be the stream, be happy, be free!

Love is as permeating as the warming effects of the sun. Everyone and everything indiscriminately absorbs it and emanates it out to all hopefully just as indiscriminately. So when others inconvenience you by subconsciously being drawn to you, allow them the same detached respect you'd give a turtle warming himself on a rock.

Portal Activation

We are all human portals to all that we wish and desire. The trick is to forgo all the conditioning and remember our true potential. Here is a shortcut in doing that. Can you imagine if everyone in the world would just do these taps and let go of all the outer drama that is trying to be shoved into them right now?

(Say each statement three times while tapping on your head and say it a fourth time while tapping on your chest.)

"The portal to my ideal weight is activated and accessed; in all moments."

"The portal to my optimal health is activated and accessed; in all moments."

"My portal to exponential joy is activated and accessed; in all moments."

"My portal to exponential love is activated and accessed; in all moments."

"My portal to exponential abundance is activated and accessed; in all moments."

"The portal to absolute freedom is activated and accessed; in all moments."

"The portal to living my purpose is activated and accessed; in all moments."

"The portal to my absolute success is activated and accessed; in all moments."

"My portal to exponential interconnection is activated and accessed; in all moments."

"My portal to exponential creativity is activated and accessed; in all moments."

"My portal to exponential beauty is activated and accessed; in all moments."

"My portal to exponential contentment is activated and accessed; in all moments."

"My portal to exponential peace is activated and accessed; in all moments."

"The portal to activate all of these things for all other living beings is exponentially activated; in all moments."

A Portal of God

To dance upon the horizon all through the night

To live in the exhilaration of an eagle's first flight

To pursue a purity all others abscond

To breathe in each moment forever and beyond

To dive into the heavens as your own private pool

To see life from the vantage point of a perpetual school

To be the Lover, the Teacher, the Healer of man

Living in the moment where all ends and began

To rise to the surface of humanity's cream

To support each being's purpose, their intimate dream

To cheerlead all others and actually applaud

Is the moment you become a portal for God.

Sitting in the Middle of the Seat

My dog Simha is in her element during her car rides. She gets lost in the experience. When she gets in the back seat, she chooses the window that she wants to hang out of. By sitting right next to it, she expects the window to automatically roll down, and it does. It rolls down because I love her, know her wishes and roll it down automatically for her. But it was *her* intention that rolled it down not mine. If I were in the car alone, there would be no interest in rolling down the back window so it would remain closed. I am empowered, but it is *her intention* that rolls down the window.

That is how it is in our life. God, the Universe or Source knows how to run the whole world. We are merely sitting in the back seat. Or are we? Are we just passive passengers or does our intention enliven reality? I believe that we are so loved and doted on that our intentions are like Simha sitting by the window. Our intentions are acted upon by a greater power than ourselves. If we want wonder and empowerment, we have to set that intention. It is in the confidence and knowing that the window will roll down that Simha *makes* it roll down because I love her.

So it is with our own spirituality. The love of the Universe realizes all your intentions. You simply have to intend them. If Simha sits in the middle of the seat, that means she is indifferent to a window being open. I get a little disappointed that she isn't hanging out the window in her glory. But what is more disappointing is that most humans sit in the middle of the seat and never bother to explore the Universe. They never even put the intention out there. Explore the Universe people! Open up the possibilities with your intention!

Acccpt Pcace

We think that if we all had the opportunity for peace that we would embrace it wholeheartedly. Even the most spiritually savvy souls have to remind themselves not to process peace as boredom. They have to discipline themselves not to kick up the dust of old issues to feel like they are being proactive.

We are in a different energy cycle. We have to learn to relax into a more expansive state of consciousness. It is not done by doing more. It is done by relaxing into the moment and allowing your atoms to expand more than you ever have. It is about trusting the process of trusting the moment.

Here is a rule of thumb: If nothing needs to be done, don't go looking for something to do. If you have no clear direction from your inner compass, do nothing until you do. This allows the old energies to untangle themselves and allows old behavior of kneejerk reactions to dissipate.

This creates an upgrade in your energy system and recalibrates all your current thoughts, feelings and behavior. When someone tries to create a reaction in you, it means they are afraid of the upgrade in the programming of humanity. Just notice what is happening and allow the attempt to pass by unsuccessfully. Doing anything reactionary does yourself and the world a disservice.

(Say each statement three times while tapping on your head and say it a fourth time while tapping on your chest.)

"I declare myself a surrogate for humanity in doing these taps; in all moments."

"I release dredging up disappointment to avoid peace; in all moments."

"I release the aversion to accepting peace; in all moments."

"I release avoiding peace; in all moments."

"I release processing peace as boredom; in all moments."

"I make space in my beingness to accept peace; in all moments."

"I remove all blockages to accepting peace; in all moments."

"I stretch my capacity to accept peace; in all moments."

"I send all energy matrices into the light and sound that have an aversion to peace; in all moments."

"I command all complex energy matrices that have an aversion to peace to be escorted into the light and sound; in all moments."

Stretching Beyond the Pain

Of course people are feeling the intensity of being expanded. It is formula to stretching beyond the pain. It is about getting pulled to the point of a rubber band, breaking, and relaxing against the sheer intensity of the stretch. It is then that the rubber band or the human consciousness stretches even more, and one realizes themselves expanded beyond what they recently thought was unfathomable.

The good news is that we are all going through this together. No one is alone in this. It is the natural process of transcendence. We have all been working many lifetimes for this to happen. It isn't going to feel warm and fuzzy at first. There is a deep contentment and a richness of existence that is waiting right beyond the illusion, but the illusion wants you to stay immersed in it. That is why there is so much anguish. But it does go away with the illusion.

These are such exciting times. I am so glad others are feeling it as well and that we have this venue to connect to one another. How blessed we really are. In hindsight the pain will disappear, like the pain of childbirth is replaced with the joy of the fruit of the labor. When it does, we will all be IN LOVE together. The growing pains are worth it.

Surrogate for Peace

Some of us, and many more, are starting to get an understanding that we are all connected. We are not separate units but exist in a love soup. It is a learning exercise for soul to believe it is separate so it can stretch its awareness of itself as love.

Many of us get a sense of lifetimes of war. We want nothing to do with it because we have had such a thorough saturation of it in the past. We have known war so well. Maybe through osmosis, we can afford those still learning the lessons of it an EZ pass to our resolve.

The more we intensify our inclination towards peace, the more it is possible to draw everyone to peace. If this resonates with you at all, please do the following taps as a surrogate for humanity. The ability of a loving intention to make a dramatic change in human history has only been tested a handful of times. Maybe we are kissing the world with a loving intention here. Maybe this is the tipping point to create internal and external peace for all.

(Say each statement three times while continuously tapping on your head and say it a fourth time while tapping on your chest.)

"I declare myself a surrogate for Peace; in all moments."

"I infuse my loving intention for Peace into the heart of humanity; in all moments."

"I recant all vows and agreements between myself and war; in all moments."

"I remove all curses between myself and war; in all moments."

"I dissolve all karmic ties between myself and war; in all moments."

"I remove all the pain, burden, and limitations that war has put on me; in all moments."

"I take back all the Joy, Love, Abundance, Freedom, Health, Success, Security, Companions, Peace, Life and Wholeness that war has taken from me; in all moments."

"I withdraw all my energy from war; in all moments."

"I release resonating with war; in all moments."

"I release emanating with war; in all moments."

"I remove all of war from my sound frequency; in all moments."

"I remove all of war from my light body; in all moments."

"I shift my paradigm from war to Peace; in all moments."

"I shift my paradigm from war to Joy, Love, Abundance, Freedom, Health, Success, Security, Companionship, Peace, Life and Wholeness; in all moments."

"I awaken my enthusiasm for and acceptance of Peace; in all moments."

"I make space in this world for Universal Peace; in all moments."

"I remove all blockages to Universal Peace; in all moments."

"I stretch my capacity to accept Universal Peace; in all moments."

"I add my loving intention to the cause of Universal Peace; in all moments."

"I am centered and empowered in divine love; in all moments."

"I am a conduit for divine love; in all moments."

"I uplift all of humanity with my love; in all moments."

The Natural Process of Transcending

The world thus far has always been negative. The fact that so many people are now aware of it is a good thing because they are now paying attention. You can't fix something if you don't realize there is an issue. Now that so many people are paying attention, a universal shift can, and is, being made.

When you hear someone talk about the world in negative terms, just smile and realize that they are waking up. It is a good thing. They are just grumpy and groggy because their long slumber is being disturbed. That's okay. It is better that they are awakening. Soon they will shift from just complaining to contributing to making this world a better place for all to be in. It is the natural process of transcending.

Transcendence

Beyond Godly borders on which nationality depends

Is the Universal war cry for humanity to transcend.

All the etchings in marble, the writings in stone

Are left to remind us--we don't do it alone.

Walls are not made to keep us living in fear

They're to uphold a vision for all to hold dear.

Beyond the facade of what we all know

Is good versus evil going toe to toe.

The same struggle that takes place between us and our brethren

Is reflective of what's fought between our hell and our heaven.

The same battle that's fought in our family and home

Is the same that played out in Ancient Greece, Athens and Rome.

The same selfish desires and pettiness of plans

Are seen a billion times over in the struggle of man.

When we conquer our dreams, put the ego in check

Take a moment from the drama, take time to reflect.

It is clearly visible that on which we depend

Is an illusion that evaporates once we transcend.

Jen Ward

5. FREE YOURSELF AND HUMANITY

One Little Human

One little human
Falling away from the pack
Can restore hope to the world
Bring humanity back.

One little human
Stepping away from the crowd
Can feel the anguish of the multitudes
And voice it out loud.

One little human
Scarred and nearly broken
Can take faith, hope and love
Where it's never been spoken.

One little human
Abiding by love's creed
Can heal the whole planet
Let's wish it Godspeed.

One little human
It may very well be you

Can teach all other humans
What they are able to do.

See your interactions as surrogates for the interactions of the multitudes. What you do as an individual is a role model for humanity even though people may never know of you. When you have even a small victory, it is a victory for all. You and what you do are that important.

Be a Portal for the Ancient Ones to Uplift Humanity

All the Ancient Ones support you in doing these taps. You are doing them in the coarse energy of the physical realm and so it is more efficient and effective than shifting consciousness from a loftier vibration as the Ancient Ones do.

By doing these taps, you are actually being used as a portal for higher consciousness to seep into this world. The more people who do these taps, the more that higher consciousness can gush into the world and facilitate great shifts in consciousness. It is a way of using your God abilities before you realize your own potential. *That* is how powerful they are.

Perhaps by doing these taps, you can recognize your own significance.

(Say each statement three times out loud while continuously tapping on the top of your head at the crown chakra and say it a fourth time while tapping on your chest.)

"We declare ourselves surrogates for humanity in doing these taps; in all moments."

"The marriage between arrogance and ignorance is annulled; in all moments."

"All vivaxes between arrogance and ignorance are removed; in all moments."

"All vivaxes between ourselves and both arrogance and ignorance are removed; in all moments.

"Being bred in arrogance or ignorance is halted; in all moments."

"All illusion on both arrogance and ignorance is stripped away; in all moments."

"All tentacles between ourselves and both arrogance and ignorance are severed; in all moments."

"All energy matrices that support or perpetuate arrogance or ignorance are dissolved into the light and sound; in all moments."

"Being manipulated by both arrogance and ignorance is prevented; in all moments."

"All portals created by arrogance or ignorance are sealed; in all moments."

"All engrams of both arrogance and ignorance are removed from our beingness; in all moments."

"All programming and conditioning of both arrogance and ignorance are removed from our beingness; in all moments."

"All vows and agreements between ourselves and both arrogance and ignorance are recanted; in all moments."

"All of confusing arrogance for empowerment is removed; in all moments."

"All belief that ignorance is bliss is removed; in all moments."

"All curses between ourselves and both arrogance and ignorance are removed; in all moments."

"All blessings between ourselves and both arrogance and

ignorance are removed; in all moments."

"All strings and cords between ourselves and both arrogance and ignorance are severed; in all moments."

"All strings and cords between arrogance and ignorance are severed; in all moments."

"All karmic ties between ourselves and both arrogance and ignorance are dissolved; in all moments."

"All masks, walls, and armor from both arrogance and ignorance are removed; in all moments."

"All the pain, burden, and limitations that both arrogance and ignorance have put on us are removed; in all moments."

"All unworthiness that both arrogance and ignorance have put on us is removed; in all moments."

"All illusion of separateness that both arrogance and ignorance have put on us is removed; in all moments."

"All that both arrogance and ignorance have taken from us is regained; in all moments."

"Resonating or emanating with both arrogance or ignorance is released; in all moments."

"All arrogance and ignorance are extracted from both our sound frequency and light emanation; in all moments."

"Our paradigm is shifted from both arrogance and ignorance into empowerment and freedom; in all moments."

"Arrogance and ignorance are transcended; in all moments."

"Both arrogance and ignorance are collapsed and dissolved; in all moments."

"Divine Love and freedom are our center and empowerment; in

all moments."

"Empowerment and freedom resonate and emanate through our beingness; in all moments."

"Interpreting the blissful state of nothingness with negative attributes is released; in all moments."

Shatter All Illusion

In contemplation, visualize yourself in a huge glass maze. You are walking through this maze looking for truth and love. The maze itself is immersed in truth and love but you cannot see it because you are at the vantage point of being in the maze.

On the walls of the maze are all these images that identify as you. They have your home life, work and all that is comfortable. Unfortunately, they also have all the things that cause fear and unhappiness as well. On one side of each corridor is the concept that you are striving for--to have more love. On the opposite corridor, is the thing that represents something of love and truth to you but falls short of the absolute love and truth outside the maze.

From a vantage point of standing outside the maze, throw heavy rocks at the maze and shatter all the walls of it so the illusion is destroyed. Continue doing this until the you that was in the maze is standing free and clear of any walls of illusion. Imagine walking around crushing the shattered glass into a fine powder by stepping on it.

Feel yourself expansive in the clear surroundings of truth and love. All illusion is gone.

(Say each statement three times while tapping on your head and say it a fourth time while tapping on your chest.)

"I declare myself a surrogate for all life in doing these taps; in all moments."

"I shatter the illusion of religion; in all moments."

"I shatter the illusion of God; in all moments."

"I shatter male domination; in all moments."

"I shatter the illusion of female inferiority; in all moments."

"I shatter all power plays; in all moments."

"I shatter all universal lies; in all moments."

"I shatter all universal manipulation; in all moments."

"I shatter all illusion of the benefits of war; in all moments."

"I shatter all war; in all moments."

"I shatter all universal ego; in all moments."

"I shatter all egos; in all moments."

"I shatter all illusion of dis-ease; in all moments."

"I shatter all illusion of beauty; in all moments."

"I shatter all illusion of perfection; in all moments."

"I shatter all ugliness; in all moments."

"I shatter all flaws; in all moments."

"I shatter all illusion of aging; in all moments."

"I shatter all illusion of youth; in all moments."

"I shatter all aging; in all moments."

"I shatter all illusion of death; in all moments."

"I shatter all illusion of separation; in all moments."

"I shatter all want; in all moments."

"I shatter all need; in all moments."

"I shatter all judgment; in all moments."

"I shatter all illusion of lack; in all moments."

"I shatter all slavery; in all moments."

"I shatter all illusion of freedom; in all moments."

"I shatter all indifference; in all moments."

"I shatter all apathy; in all moments."

"I shatter all darkness; in all moments."

"I shatter all illusion of wealth; in all moments."

"I shatter all poverty; in all moments."

"I shatter all ignorance; in all moments."

"I shatter all power; in all moments."

"I shatter all fear; in all moments."

"I shatter all unworthiness; in all moments."

"I shatter all illusion of humility; in all moments."

"I shatter all illusion of love; in all moments."

"I shatter all debauchery; in all moments."

"I shatter all evil; in all moments."

"I am centered and empowered in absolute loving truth; in all moments."

"I resonate, emanate, and am interconnected with all life in absolute love and truth; in all moments."

Release Being Obligated

(Say each statement three times while tapping on your head and say it fourth time while tapping on your chest.)

"I release being obligated; in all moments."

"I cut all tentacles to being obligated; in all moments."

"I release feeling obligated; in all moments."

"I release the belief that I am obligated; in all moments."

"I remove all vivaxes between myself and obligation; in all moments."

"I release confusing my purpose with obligation; in all moments."

"I remove all programming and conditioning that obligation has put on me; in all moments."

"I remove all engrams of obligation; in all moments."

"I nullify all contracts with obligation; in all moments."

"I collapse all portals of obligation; in all moments."

"I eliminate the first cause in regards to obligation; in all moments."

"I send all energy matrices into the light and sound that obligate me; in all moments."

"I command all complex energy matrices that obligate me to be escorted into the light and sound; in all moments."

"I recant all vows and agreements between myself and obligation; in all moments."

"I remove all curses between myself and obligation; in all moments."

"I remove all debt of obligation; in all moments."

"I remove all blessings between myself and obligation; in all moments."

"I sever all strings and cords between myself and obligation; in all moments."

"I dissolve all karmic ties between myself and obligation; in all moments."

"I remove all the pain, burden, and limitations that obligation has put on me; in all moments."

"I remove all the fear, futility and unworthiness that obligation has put on me; in all moments."

"I remove all the illusion of separateness that obligation has put on me; in all moments."

"I remove all the rejection, abandonment, and isolation that obligation has put on me; in all moments."

"I remove all that I have put on all others due to obligation; in all moments."

"I take back all that obligation has taken from me; in all moments."

"I give back to all others all that I have taken from them; in all moments."

"I release resonating with obligation; in all moments."

"I release emanating with obligation; in all moments."

"I dissolve all obligation from my sound frequency; in all moments."

"I dissolve all obligation from my light emanation; in all moments."

"I shift my paradigm from obligation to spiritual empowerment; in

all moments."

"I dissolve all obligation from my whole beingness; in all moments."

"I transcend obligation; in all moments."

"I am centered and empowered in spiritual liberation; in all moments."

"I resonate, emanate, and am interconnected with all life in spiritual liberation; in all moments."

Humanity Needs You to Do These More Than Ever

(Say each statement three times out loud while tapping on the top of your head at the crown chakra and say it a fourth time while tapping on your chest.)

"I declare myself a surrogate for humanity in doing these taps; in all moments."

"I extract all the sadness from all the layers of my auric field; in all moments."

"I extract all the depression from all the layers of my auric field; in all moments."

"I extract all the fear from all the layers of my auric field; in all moments."

"I extract all the hate from all the layers of my auric field; in all moments."

"I extract all the lack from all the layers of my auric field; in all moments."

"I extract all the inhibition from all the layers of my auric field; in all moments."

"I extract all dis-ease from all the layers of my auric field; in all moments."

"I extract all failure from all the layers of my auric field; in all moments."

"I extract all insecurity from all the layers of my auric field; in all moments."

"I extract all the isolation from all the layers of my auric field; in all moments."

"I extract all the conformity from all the layers of my auric field; in all moments."

"I extract all the chaos from all the layers of my auric field; in all moments."

"I extract all entanglements from all the layers of my auric field; in all moments."

"I extract all the strife from all the layers of my auric field; in all moments."

"I extract all of hell from all the layers of my auric field; in all moments."

"I extract all the obsession with death from all the layers of my auric field; in all moments."

"I extract all fragmentation from all the layers of my auric field; in all moments."

"I extract all the ugliness from all the layers of my auric field; in all moments."

"I extract all the apathy from all the layers of my auric field; in all moments."

"I extract all the floundering from all the layers of my auric field; in all moments."

"I extract all the discontent from all the layers of my auric field; in all moments."

"I extract all the ignorance from all the layers of my auric field; in all moments."

"I extract all the disconnectedness from all the layers of my auric field; in all moments."

"I extract all intruders from all the layers of my auric field; in all moments."

"I send all energy matrices into the light that intrude upon any layers of my auric field; in all moments."

"I infuse absolute Joy into all the layers of my auric field; in all moments."

"I infuse perpetual, Divine Love into all the layers of my auric field; in all moments."

"I infuse complete Abundance into all the layers of my auric field; in all moments."

"I infuse absolute Freedom into all the layers of my auric field; in all moments."

"I infuse complete Health into all the layers of my auric field; in all moments."

"I infuse incredible Success into all the layers of my auric field; in all moments."

"I infuse complete Security into all the layers of my auric field; in all moments."

"I infuse Interconnectedness into all the layers of my auric field; in all moments."

"I infuse my individualized Creativity into all the layers of my auric field; in all moments."

"I infuse reverent Peace into all the layers of my auric field; in all moments."

"I infuse a zest for life into all the layers of my auric field; in all moments."

"I infuse absolute Wholeness into all the layers of my auric field; in all moments."

"I infuse breathtaking youthful Beauty into all the layers of my auric field; in all moments."

"I infuse exuberant Enthusiasm into all the layers of my auric field; in all moments."

"I infuse absolute Contentment into all the layers of my auric field; in all moments."

"I infuse a perpetual striving for Truth into all the layers of my auric field; in all moments."

"I infuse the transcendence of Enlightenment into all the layers of my auric field; in all moments."

"I infuse complete Confidence into all the layers of my auric field; in all moments."

"I infuse an incredible ability to discern into all the layers of my auric field; in all moments."

Powerful Taps for the Universal Betterment of the World

There is a spiritual principle that if you want something for yourself, desire it for others. These taps are the ultimate in wishing good things for others. They are a powerful way to bring much goodness to the world and your own realms.

(Say each statement three times out loud while continuously tapping on the top of your head at the crown chakra and say it a fourth time while tapping on your chest.)

"I declare myself a surrogate for humanity in doing these taps; in all moments."

"I make space in this world for universal appreciation of nature; in all moments."

"I remove all blockages to universal appreciation of nature; in all moments."

"I stretch my capacity to embrace universal appreciation of nature; in all moments."

"I make space in this world for universal respect of trees; in all moments."

"I remove all blockages to universal respect of all trees; in all moments."

"I stretch my capacity to embrace universal respect for all trees; in all moments."

"I make space in this world for universal acceptance of natural healing; in all moments."

"I remove all blockages to universal acceptance of natural healing; in all moments."

"I stretch my capacity to embrace universal acceptance of natural healing; in all moments."

"I make space in this world for universal joy; in all moments."

"I remove all blockages to universal joy; in all moments."

"I stretch my capacity to embrace universal joy; in all moments."

"I make space in this world for universal kindness; in all moments."

"I remove all blockages to universal kindness; in all moments."

"I stretch my capacity to embrace universal kindness; in all moments."

"I make space in this world for universal abundance; in all moments."

"I remove all blockages to universal abundance; in all moments."

"I stretch my capacity to embrace universal abundance; in all moments."

"I make space in this world for universal freedom; in all moments."

"I remove all blockages to universal freedom; in all moments."

"I stretch my capacity to embrace universal freedom; in all moments."

"I make space in this world for universal optimal health; in all moments."

"I remove all blockages to universal optimal health; in all moments."

"I stretch my capacity to embrace universal optimal health; in all moments."

"I make space in this world for universal success and living one's purpose; in all moments."

"I remove all blockages to universal success and living one's purpose; in all moments."

"I stretch my capacity to embrace universal success and living one's purpose; in all moments."

"I make space in this world for universal security and home; in all moments."

"I remove all blockages to universal security and home; in all

moments."

"I stretch my capacity to embrace universal security and home; in all moments."

"I make space in this world for universal connectedness; in all moments."

"I remove all blockages to universal connectedness; in all moments."

"I stretch my capacity to embrace universal connectedness; in all moments."

"I make space in this world for universal individualized creativity; in all moments."

"I remove all blockages to universal individualized creativity; in all moments."

"I stretch my capacity to embrace universal individualized creativity; in all moments."

"I remove all blockages to universal knowing and speaking of truth; in all moments."

"I stretch my capacity to embrace universal knowing and speaking of truth; in all moments."

"I make space in this world for universal peace; in all moments."

"I remove all blockages to universal peace; in all moments."

"I stretch my capacity to embrace universal peace; in all moments."

"I make space in this world for universal value and respect for all life; in all moments."

"I remove all blockages to universal value and respect for all life; in all moments."

"I stretch my capacity to embrace universal value and respect for all life; in all moments."

"I make space in this world for universal quality of life; in all moments."

"I remove all blockages to universal quality of life; in all moments."

"I stretch my capacity to embrace universal quality of life; in all moments."

"I make space in this world for universal wholeness; in all moments."

"I remove all blockages to universal wholeness; in all moments."

"I stretch my capacity to embrace universal wholeness; in all moments."

"I make space in this world for universal spirituality; in all moments."

"I remove all blockages to universal spirituality; in all moments."

The Universal We

I know it is hard to wrap our head around this because we are us, but we are the cure for the imbalance in society. How do we mend the ills of man? We are doing it. We love when others won't. We show our hand of beauty, truth and conviction. We serve as examples of what walking and breathing love entails. We stand in our truth and don't back down in the little ways. We live with conviction every day and tend to the little issues. In doing that, the big issues take care of themselves.

What Would Dr. Seuss Say?

You think I am there

And you are here

But you are there

There is here

We are here

Here is now

We are in

The Here and Now

You think I'm great

And you are small

That makes no sense

No sense at all

How can it be when I am you

We are the same

Just one

Not two

As a fact, we are all one

It's always been

Since life's begun

We are not separate

You and me

We are the same

We are the we

The world is made of

One big we

We span the globe

This we that's me

When you are hurt

We feel the same

We cry and stomp

And give out blame

We defend ourselves

Exhaust our wits

Stomp about

In angry fits

But when we perch

To strike a blow

Then's the time

We need to know

When we hurt them

We hurt the we

I hurt you

You hurt me

Let's turn the tables

On this game

Disarm the drones

And refrain

When you want

To hate yourself

See me crying

On a shelf

When you want

To say you're bad

Realize

You've just been had

The hate you give...

To your me

Is the plight

Of the universal we

If you want to

Heal the all

Crumble that

Inner wall

The wall that says

You can not be

Wonderfully abundant, happy, free.

I Will Pray

Whenever anyone asks me to pray for them, I give my pat answer which is, "I don't pray for people." It is like sending the intention to a satellite of unknown origins and expecting it to bounce to the recipient after that. I will send you love from the depth of my well of pure and infinite goodness though. Doing that is like hand delivering it.

Pope Francis is very wise in asking others to pray for him. In doing this, he is showing them his vulnerability. He is making it very clear that he is not shielded by the shiny facade of power. He is empowering the individuals to a vantage point that is not subservient to his. He is elevating them with confidence in their abilities, and a sincere acknowledgement of their worth. There is a lot of insight, wisdom and healing in that humble request.

People used to tell me all the time that they would pray for me. I dismissed them with the confidence that I did not need their prayers, so they stopped offering. But I have a different understanding of accepting others' prayers now. They are fuel to be used to ignite billions of sparks of light, open billions of hearts and awaken billions of dreams.

I am back in the business of graciously accepting prayers. I will accept love in all forms without getting caught up on semantics. I will use whatever I am given to perpetuate Universal Joy, Love,

Abundance, Freedom, Health and Wholeness. I will graciously use my abilities to transform any prayers I receive into exponential healing for the world and all its worthy inhabitants.

I will pray for Pope Francis and use my abilities to ease any of his bodily distractions of discomfort. It is merely a silent offering as a contribution for all the hope and enthusiasm he evokes around the world. We are truly living in exciting times. Let's all indulge in tossing out loving prayers and intentions in all directions. Let them land and flourish where they will.

Invite God to Walk Among Us

Someone was commenting on current events in a news interview. They were saying that everyone needs to say a prayer. That would be ineffective because what people say does not truly align with what they do. Someone who prays for deferential treatment but then diminishes others is negating the whole purpose of prayer.

The purpose of prayer is to align one with the vibration of truth and love so that there is an innate protection in the process of mouthing the divine. When someone defames kindness in any way, they change their vibratory rate to being less centered in love and truth. They may resonate with others that behave similarly so they believe they are in good company. There are whole hypocritical sects of people that may do this but being a part of a group that resonates with hypocrisy doesn't make your prayer any closer to vibrating with truth.

Instead of everyone needing to say a prayer, everyone needs to be a prayer. Being a prayer is simply the act of your kindness, sincerity and virtue of heart aligning with your actions. When more and more people do this, it will truly be like God is walking among us.

Shift Your Paradigm

(Say each statement three times while tapping on your head and say it a fourth time while tapping on your chest.)

"I release attacking truth; in all moments."

"I shift my paradigm from poverty consciousness to embracing the spiritual law of abundance; in all moments."

"I shift my paradigm from fear to love; in all moments."

"I shift my paradigm from problems to joy; in all moments."

"I extract and dissolve the energy that's choking truth; in all moments."

"I shift my paradigm from slavery to freedom; in all moments."

"I shift my paradigm from lack to abundance; in all moments."

"I shift my paradigm from disease to optimal health; in all moments."

"I shift my paradigm from failure to success; in all moments."

"I shift my paradigm from uncertainty to security; in all moments."

"I shift my paradigm from loneliness to companionship; in all moments."

"I shift my paradigm from conformity to creativity; in all moments."

"I shift my paradigm from war to peace; in all moments."

"I shift my paradigm from warmongering to peace; in all moments."

"I shift my paradigm from linear to exponential; in all moments."

"I shift my paradigm from degeneration to regeneration; in all

moments."

"I shift my paradigm from death to life; in all moments."

"I shift my paradigm from fragmentation to wholeness; in all moments."

"I shift my paradigm from ugliness to beauty; in all moments."

"I shift my paradigm from apathy to enthusiasm; in all moments."

"I shift my paradigm from disgruntled to contentment; in all moments."

"I shift my paradigm from hypocrisy to spirituality; in all moments."

"I shift my paradigm from ignorance to enlightenment; in all moments."

"I shift my paradigm from insecurity to confidence; in all moments."

"I shift my paradigm from isolation to interconnectedness; in all moments."

"I shift my paradigm from manipulation to empowerment; in all moments."

"I shift my paradigm from desecration to sacredness; in all moments."

Stop Being Affected by an Ominous Force

You know how something sometimes seems to interfere with our health, wealth, happiness or love life? We waste so much energy trying to figure it out. Perhaps the cause exists beyond the tangible realms. So trying to figure it out is a useless distraction. Here are powerful taps to address the core issue of our discontent without the need to filter it through the mind.

I highly recommend taking the time to doing these.

(Say each statement three times out loud while tapping on the top of your head at the crown chakra and say it a fourth time while tapping on your chest.)

"I declare myself a surrogate for humanity in doing these taps; in all moments."

"I release the ominous source interfering with my joy; in all moments."

"I release being a mouthpiece for the ominous source; in all moments."

"I release being a recruiter for the ominous source; in all moments."

"I release being the figurehead for the ominous source; in all moments."

"I release worshiping the ominous source; in all moments."

"I release being a channel for the ominous source; in all moments."

"I release the ominous source interfering with my love; in all moments."

"I release the ominous source being an interference between myself and joy; in all moments."

"I release the ominous source being an interference between myself and love; in all moments."

"I release the ominous source being an interference between myself and abundance; in all moments."

"I release the ominous source interfering between myself and abundance; in all moments."

"I release the ominous source being an interference between myself and freedom; in all moments."

"I release being shackled to the ominous source; in all moments."

"I release the ominous source interfering with my freedom; in all moments."

"I release the ominous source being an interference between myself and health; in all moments."

"I release being crippled by the ominous source; in all moments."

"I release being diseased by the ominous source; in all moments."

"I release the ominous source interfering with my health; in all moments."

"I release being paralyzed by the ominous source; in all moments."

"I release the ominous source being an interference between myself and success; in all moments."

"I release the ominous source interfering with my success; in all moments."

"I release the ominous source being an interference between myself and security; in all moments."

"I release the ominous source interfering with my security; in all moments."

"I release the ominous source being an interference between myself and my companionship; in all moments."

"I release the ominous source interfering with my companionship; in all moments."

"I release the ominous source being an interference between myself and my creativity; in all moments."

"I release the ominous source interfering with my creativity; in all moments."

"I release the ominous source being an interference between myself and peace; in all moments."

"I release the ominous source interfering with my peace; in all moments."

"I release the ominous source being an interference between myself and life; in all moments."

"I release the ominous source interfering with my life; in all moments."

"I release the ominous source being an interference between myself and wholeness; in all moments."

"I release the ominous source interfering with my wholeness; in all moments."

"I release the ominous source being an interference between myself and beauty; in all moments."

"I release the ominous source interfering with my beauty; in all moments."

"I release the ominous source being an interference between myself and enthusiasm; in all moments."

"I release the ominous source interfering with my enthusiasm; in all moments."

"I release the ominous source being an interference between myself and contentment; in all moments."

"I release the ominous source interfering with my contentment; in all moments."

"I release the ominous source being an interference between myself and spirituality; in all moments."

"I release the ominous source interfering with my spirituality; in all moments."

"I release the ominous source being an interference between myself and enlightenment; in all moments."

"I release the ominous source interfering with my enlightenment; in all moments."

"I release the ominous source being an interference between myself and confidence; in all moments."

"I release the ominous source interfering with my confidence; in all moments."

"I release the ominous source being an interference between myself and family; in all moments."

"I release the ominous source interfering with my family; in all moments."

"I release the ominous source being an interference between myself and intellect; in all moments."

"I release the ominous source interfering with my intellect; in all moments."

"I release the ominous source being an interference between myself and the ability to discern; in all moments."

"I release the ominous source interfering with my ability to discern; in all moments."

"I remove all vivaxes between myself and the ominous source; in all moments."

"I remove all tentacles between myself, and the ominous source; in all moments."

"I remove the clutches of the ominous source from my beingness; in all moments."

"I remove all programming and conditioning that the ominous source has put on me; in all moments."

"I remove all engrams that the ominous source has put on me; in all moments."

"I send all energy matrices into the light and sound that enslave me to the ominous source; in all moments."

"I send all energy matrices into the light and sound that threaten me in support of an ominous source; in all moments."

"I recant all vows and agreements between myself and the ominous source; in all moments."

"I remove all curses between myself and the ominous source; in all moments."

"I remove all blessings between myself and the ominous source; in all moments."

"I sever all strings and cords between myself and the ominous source; in all moments."

"I dissolve all karmic ties between myself and the ominous source; in all moments."

"I strip all illusion off the ominous source; in all moments."

"I withdraw all my energy from the ominous source; in all moments."

"I remove all masks, walls, and armor from the ominous source; in all moments."

"I remove all the pain, burden, limitations, and illusion of separateness that the ominous source has put on me; in all moments."

"I remove all the pain, burden, limitations, and illusion of separateness that I have put on all others due to the ominous source; in all moments."

"I take back ALL that the ominous source has taken from me; in all moments."

"I give back to all others all that I have taken from them on behalf of the ominous source; in all moments."

"I release resonating or emanating with the ominous source; in all moments."

"I extract all of the ominous source from both my sound frequency and light emanation; in all moments."

"I extract all of the ominous source from the universal sound frequency and light emanation; in all moments."

"I shift my paradigm from the ominous source to transcendence; in all moments."

"I transcend the ominous source; in all moments."

"I am centered and empowered in the divinity of transcendence; in all moments."

"I am centered and empowered in the divinity of universal transcendence; in all moments."

"I resonate and emanate the divinity of universal transcendence; in all moments."

Be an Energetic Anarchist

If you complain about society, you are feeding it energy. If you are unhappy or disgruntled, you are gluing yourself further to what you disdain. If you are unhappy with the state of the world, simply do these taps and know that you have done your part in bringing about change. There is no protest, debate, campaign or demonstrative action that is more effective in bringing about a shift in the empowerment of humanity than doing this exercise.

(Say each statement three times while tapping on your head and say it a fourth time while tapping on your chest.)

"We declare ourselves surrogates for humanity in doing these taps; in all moments."

"We release giving our lifeblood to society; in all moments."

"We released being brainwashed by society; in all moments."

"We released being pigeonholed by society; in all moments."

"We release being enslaved to society; in all moments."

"We release giving our spiritual freedom to society; in all moments."

"We withdraw all our energy from society; in all moments."

"We release having our consciousness stolen by society; in all moments."

"We remove all vivaxes between ourselves and society; in all moments."

"We remove all tentacles between ourselves and society; in all moments."

"We untangle ourselves from society; in all moments."

"We remove the claws of society from our beingness; in all moments."

"We remove the influence of society from our essence; in all moments."

"We remove all programming and conditioning that society has put on us; in all moments."

"We remove all engrams of society from our beingness; in all moments."

"We send all energy matrices into the light and sound that enslave us to society; in all moments."

"We command all complex energy matrices that enslave us to society to be escorted into the light and sound; in all moments."

"We send all energy matrices of society into the light and sound; in all moments."

"We command all complex energy matrices of society to be escorted into the light and sound; in all moments."

"We send all energy matrices into the light and sound that use individuals to do negative work; in all moments."

"We command all complex energy matrices that use individuals to do negative work to be escorted into the light and sound; in all moments."

"We release being targeted for control; in all moments."

"We convert all black mold to divine love; in all moments."

"We eradicate black mold from all beings; in all moments."

"We extract all black mold from our genetic makeup; in all moments."

"We strip all illusion off society; in all moments."

"We remove all masks, walls, and armor from society; in all moments."

"We eliminate the first cause in creating society; in all moments."

"We nullify all contracts with society; in all moments."

"We remove the dead weight of society from our beingness; in all moments."

"We recant all vows and agreements between ourselves and society; in all moments."

"We remove all curses between ourselves and society; in all moments."

"We remove all blessings between ourselves and society; in all moments."

"We shatter all glass ceilings that society has put on us; in all moments."

"We sever all strings, cords, and wires between ourselves and society; in all moments."

"We dissolve all karmic ties between ourselves and society; in all moments."

"We remove all the pain, burden, and limitations that society has put on us and all others; in all moments."

"We remove all the fear, futility and unworthiness that society has put on us and all others; in all moments."

"We remove all the apathy, ignorance and indifference that society has put on us and all others; in all moments."

"We remove all the illusion of separateness that society has put on us and all others; in all moments."

"We take back for ourselves and all others all that society has taken from us; in all moments."

"We collapse and dissolve all society; in all moments."

"We remove from ourselves and all others all the linear stipulations that society has put on us; in all moments."

"We recharge all land grids with exponentiality; in all moments."

"We release resonating with society; in all moments."

"We release emanating with society; in all moments."

"We extract all of society from our sound frequency; in all moments."

"We extract all of society from our light emanation; in all moments."

"We extract all of society from all 32 layers of our auric field; in all moments."

"We deactivate the muscle memory of society; in all moments."

"We extract all of society from our whole beingness; in all moments."

"We shift our paradigm from society to exponential Joy, Love, Abundance, Freedom, and Peace; in all moments."

"We transcend society; in all moments."

"We are centered and empowered in exponential Joy, Love, Abundance, Freedom, and Peace; in all moments."

"We resonate, emanate, and are interconnected with all life in exponential Joy, Love, Abundance, Freedom, and Peace; in all moments."

You at High Tide

Ethics will never be mandated by law. Law only brings accountability to the lowest common denominator. Ethics will be raised as the human spirit is uplifted to realize the value of its own worth through love, kindness and accomplishment.

When individuals realize the satisfaction of sharing their gifts, they will organically begin to resonate with a frequency of love. Our purpose, as members of humanity, is to keep the pathway clear for all souls to share their gifts. We do this by loving example, simple kindness and taking a non-scrutinizing stance.

All want to be loving. So many who are floundering believe themselves to be loving at the core. They have an innate sense of their own goodness but the conditioning of false humility prevents them from stepping out of the shadow of self-doubt.

Surrendering to the love is a means of diving into the ebb and flow of life and trusting the tide to take you to the shores of love. It is inevitable so just trust and fall back with a sense of abandon. By releasing everything you believe you should be, you become the you that you are: unique, distinct and a wonderment to behold.

This is high tide. This is time for us all to be collected back into the heart of love and to flow again in balance with all that is good. Let go of the struggle and just be present with the dynamic experience of being you. Joy, Love, Abundance and Freedom are inevitable when we stop fighting the current.

I Am in Love with You!

The reason I don't pray for people is because the process is so tedious. It takes converting a huge intention into the clumsy, limited form of thoughts merely to send it back to an intangible form to do some good. I am not naive to think that an omniscient God needs me to tell It what to do, so I know that my intentions work on a more personal level than that. They are effective but not in micromanaging God.

I always tell people I am sending them love when they ask for prayers. That is not technically what I do. Since we are love, it doesn't make sense. What I do is hold my place of incredible love in the Universe. I pour God love in me with all the intention my heart can muster up. It is then I visualize the other person with me. I am not manipulating them or willing my agenda on them. I am simply being in love with them.

Once something is practiced repeatedly, it becomes habitual. How empowered would this world be if everyone would merely hold a position of love for themselves and make it big enough to engulf the whole world? In that way, I am in love with you.

The Underbelly of Asking for Prayers

People don't understand how spiritual law works yet. It is as exacting as physical laws like gravity. When people talk about themselves at their lowest point, that is what people are going to lock onto as that person's identity. They are freezing themselves in that lowest point.

When they talk about their sick or dying relative, they are holding that person in a position of being sick and dying forever. Forever. It is difficult to recover from someone who is supposed to love them yet is locking them into a freezing pattern of being sick and dying forever. It becomes a part of the person's identity. If loved ones realized they were freezing their ailing relative in a limited state of consciousness, they wouldn't do it.

People would really help their loved ones by understanding this. Another person's image of us is a thought form that holds us in a fixed position if you are not strong or aware enough to counter it. People who are sick or struggling are not well enough to counter an onslaught of strangers seeing them as sick. It exacerbates their plight.

It is an extreme violation of someone's psychic space to talk about their struggles without their permission. It is a violation of their psychic space to take pictures of them when they are in the hospital and share them. It is a violation of your pets' psychic space to tell everyone about their medical issues and how they are suffering. It is also a violation of your pets' psychic space when you keep telling their sad backstory over and over. Please, let them enjoy their life and stop pulling them back into their worst moment. You are doing them a lot of damage.

I learned this when I encountered a particular woman and her cute little dog. The mom had incredible health issues. It was no coincidence that she also loved to talk about them. The little dog was happy until the mom started to tell its story. It went from being excited and playful in the moment to wilting and cowering inside. She never even noticed. I stopped her right in the middle of her diatribe and gave her a pretty hearty lecture. The sweet dog loved the lecture. (It was for his benefit.) It was meant to interrupt what she was doing to him. He became happy again.

So when you are asking for those prayers or telling your friends about your issue, ask yourself if this is how you want to be recognized from now on. Ask yourself if the process of talking about something is worth being locked in that experience. If you ask for prayers, ask yourself if the request is going to assist your plight or if it is going to lock you or your loved one in an unfavorable position.

People have a long memory for negative issues and a short memory for the good ones. It takes so much more priming a life with positive goodwill to fix a life in a positive light, but it is worth it. If you are desperate for prayers, a generic request is much more beneficial than giving the details. Your loved ones deserve the respect to be seen in their best light. Please don't desecrate them out of lack of understanding. Their self-empowerment is too important.

Apologies if this truth upsets anyone. If it does, I suggest energetically taking back what you have put out there. It is no small thing to do this. The other thing is that people who ask for prayers don't recognize when they are given. I pour healing energy on all my friends who read my work, so if they are still asking for prayers, they are not recognizing what they have already been given.

I Love You

Love is an energy. It flows when there is an intention. It is like water in some ways. If you send love to someone, they will receive it. But people send love out into the sky and it renders it ineffective the same way that spraying a hose is of little effectiveness if sprayed into the sky.

Why are we so ashamed of love? We are too embarrassed to say, "I love you" to anyone casually. What is the monstrosity of society that caused love to be such a shameful thing? I can see ruthless regimes in the past killing off our loved ones as part of an indoctrination. That is one reason to shun the love sentiment so drastically, but isn't avoiding love and kindness paying homage to the opposite in some small way?

I see hearts or "love ya" or "love to you," but why are the words, "I love you" considered a faux pas to say? Why is it considered corny to say? It is time to untangle the shame from the love. So here it goes. I love each and every one of you who reads this, is my friend or is a part of humanity. I love you. Thank you for your kindness and goodness. Thank you for showing up every day. You are awesome. I love you.

Stop Berating Yourself

(Say each statement three times out loud while continuously tapping on the top of your head at the crown chakra and say it a fourth time while tapping on your chest.)

"I release railroading my own greatness with the need to compete; in all moments."

"I release converting my greatness into concern over superficial beauty; in all moments."

"I release judging myself; in all moments."

"I release basing my worth on my outer appearance; in all moments."

"I release associating outer beauty with self-worth; in all moments."

"I release basing my self-worth on exterior indicators; in all moments."

"I release the need to be pretty to be loved; in all moments."

"I release needing to be successful to be worthy; in all moments."

"I release overlooking my own greatness; in all moments."

"I release overlooking my own beauty; in all moments."

"I release denying myself support; in all moments."

"I release berating myself; in all moments."

"I release sizing myself up in relationship to others; in all moments."

"I release diminishing myself compared to others; in all moments."

"I remove all others from their pedestal; in all moments."

"I elevate myself in equal, measurable worth to all others; in all moments."

"I recommit myself to valuing myself; in all moments."

"I pour love, approval and nurturing love into myself; in all moments."

"I shift my paradigm from berating myself to loving myself; in all moments."

"I transcend berating myself; in all moments."

"I am centered and empowered in nurturing and loving myself; in all moments."

Powerful Taps for the Universal Betterment of the World

There is a spiritual principle that if you want something for yourself, desire it for others. These taps are the ultimate for wishing good things for others. They are a powerful way to bring much goodness to the world and your own realms.

(Say each statement three times out loud while tapping on the top of your head at the crown chakra and say it a fourth time while tapping on your chest.)

"I declare myself a surrogate for humanity in doing these taps; in all moments."

"I make space in this world for universal appreciation of nature; in all moments."

"I remove all blockages to universal appreciation of nature; in all moments."

"I stretch my capacity to embrace universal appreciation of nature; in all moments."

"I make space in this world for universal respect of trees; in all moments."

"I remove all blockages to universal respect of all trees; in all moments."

"I stretch my capacity to embrace universal respect for all trees; in all moments."

"I make space in this world for universal acceptance of natural healing; in all moments."

"I remove all blockages to universal acceptance of natural healing; in all moments."

"I stretch my capacity to embrace universal acceptance of natural healing; in all moments."

"I make space in this world for universal joy; in all moments."

"I remove all blockages to universal joy; in all moments."

"I stretch my capacity to embrace universal joy; in all moments."

"I make space in this world for universal kindness; in all moments."

"I remove all blockages to universal kindness; in all moments."

"I stretch my capacity to embrace universal kindness; in all moments."

"I make space in this world for universal abundance; in all moments."

"I remove all blockages to universal abundance; in all moments."

"I stretch my capacity to embrace universal abundance; in all moments."

"I make space in this world for universal freedom; in all moments."

"I remove all blockages to universal freedom; in all moments."

"I stretch my capacity to embrace universal freedom; in all moments."

"I make space in this world for universal optimal health; in all moments."

"I remove all blockages to universal optimal health; in all moments."

"I stretch my capacity to embrace universal optimal health; in all moments."

"I make space in this world for universal success and living one's purpose; in all moments."

"I remove all blockages to universal success and living one's purpose; in all moments."

"I stretch my capacity to embrace universal success and living one's purpose; in all moments."

"I make space in this world for universal security and home; in all moments."

"I remove all blockages to universal security and home; in all moments."

"I stretch my capacity to embrace universal security and home; in all moments."

"I make space in this world for universal connectedness; in all moments."

"I remove all blockages to universal connectedness; in all moments."

"I stretch my capacity to embrace universal connectedness; in all moments."

"I make space in this world for universal, individualized creativity; in all moments."

"I remove all blockages to universal, individualized creativity; in all moments."

"I stretch my capacity to embrace universal, individualized creativity; in all moments."

"I remove all blockages to universal knowing and speaking of truth; in all moments."

"I stretch my capacity to embrace universal knowing and speaking of truth; in all moments."

"I make space in this world for universal peace; in all moments."

"I remove all blockages to universal peace; in all moments."

"I stretch my capacity to embrace universal peace; in all moments."

"I make space in this world for universal value and respect for all life; in all moments."

"I remove all blockages to universal value and respect for all life; in all moments."

"I stretch my capacity to embrace universal value and respect for all life; in all moments."

"I make space in this world for universal quality of life; in all moments."

"I remove all blockages to universal quality of life; in all moments."

"I stretch my capacity to embrace universal quality of life; in all moments."

"I make space in this world for universal wholeness; in all moments."

"I remove all blockages to universal wholeness; in all moments."

"I stretch my capacity to embrace universal wholeness; in all moments."

"I make space in this world for universal spirituality; in all moments."

"I remove all blockages to universal spirituality; in all moments."

"I stretch my capacity to embrace universal spirituality; in all

moments."

"I make space in this world for universal transcendence; in all moments."

"I remove all blockages to universal transcendence; in all moments."

"I stretch my capacity to embrace universal transcendence; in all moments."

"I make space in this world for universal empowerment; in all moments."

"I remove all blockages to universal empowerment; in all moments."

"I stretch my capacity to embrace universal empowerment; in all moments."

The Synergy of Mass Healing

We are merely different atoms of energy exchanging and interplaying with each other. Just like a charged particle, we attract different experiences to ourselves and give experiences to others. Our interplay is how we learn, expand and transcend.

We are constantly exchanging with others around us. Our thoughts, emotions and actions are the way we make a swap. When we give love, support, attention and well wishes to others, we are strengthening their charge and supporting them as atoms of God. When we judge, ignore, dismiss or invalidate others, we are weakening their charge. When we complain to or sympathize with others, we are weakening their charge to benefit the strengthening of our own. When we commiserate or gossip with others, we are weakening both charges.

If someone offers you a gift and you refuse, you are stopping a beautiful flow of energy midstream. When someone is not listened to, the energy is stunted as well. Spontaneous, giving, exuberant energy keeps the mechanism of the Universe operating. Apathy, fear, expecting the worst deaden a charge and render particles exposed inoperable. These things, as Universal concepts, are cancers on humanity.

Watching the news, believing the worst, giving up hope on a global scale are diseases in the heart of mankind. There is always a way to thrive. Spontaneous healing is possible. The more that people refuse to buy into the apathy of what is focused on and the more one reconnects to what is good, kind and noble in others, the more the synergy of mass healing can ensue.

Be an Individual

It is funny that someone becomes famous for standing apart from others in some unique way. Yet as soon as they become known, that individuality is stripped away from them in so many ways. They have to be afraid of public opinion or what their sponsors think. In a way, it strips them of a lot of the originality that was so appealing. Perhaps we do this to ourselves in many ways.

(Say each statement three times while tapping on your head and say it a fourth time while tapping on your chest.)

"I release losing my individualism; in all moments."

"I release energetically melting into the pot; in all moments."

"I release being a diluted version of myself; in all moments."

"I release the fear of standing out; in all moments."

"I release trying to blend; in all moments."

"I convert all the energy of trying to blend into being an original; in all moments."

"I release demonizing originals; in all moments."

"I release wearing originals down to a nub; in all moments."

"I release resenting originals; in all moments."

"I release copying originals at the expense of my own wonder; in all moments."

"I extract myself from all conformity; in all moments."

"I shatter all illusion of conformity; in all moments."

"I remove all that conformity has put on me; in all moments."

"I take back all that conformity has taken from me; in all moments."

"I transcend conformity; in all moments."

Taps to Repair Human Consciousness

(Say each statement three times while tapping on your head and say it a fourth time while tapping on your chest.)

"I declare myself a surrogate for humanity in doing these taps; in all moments."

"We release holding such a low bar on the expectations of humanity; in all moments."

"We shatter the glass ceiling on humanity; in all moments."

"We make silt of the resistance; in all moments."

"We rub out all the indoctrination of the human consciousness; in all moments."

"We remove all the ingrained conditioning; in all moments."

"We release the disconnect between the human consciousness and truth; in all moments."

"We repair the schism between the human consciousness and joy; in all moments."

"We repair the schism between the human consciousness and divinity; in all moments."

"We repair the schism between human consciousness and love; in all moments."

"We repair the schism between human consciousness and abundance; in all moments."

"We repair the schism between human consciousness and freedom; in all moments."

"We repair the schism between human consciousness and wholeness; in all moments."

"We infuse joy, love and abundance into the human consciousness' sound frequency; in all moments."

"We imbue joy, love and abundance into the human consciousness' light emanation; in all moments."

"We infuse freedom, health and wholeness into the human consciousness' sound frequency; in all moments."

"We imbue freedom, health and wholeness in the human consciousness' light emanation; in all moments."

"Human consciousness resonates, emanates and is interconnected with all life in empowerment; in all moments."

"We shift the whole flow of the Universe from introversion to expansion; in all moments."

Release from the Media's Grip

Anyone who believes that the media is unbiased and has the individual's best interests at heart is very much mistaken. It is time to awaken from a mass stupor and start thinking and discerning for ourselves. Please do these taps and share if you agree.

This is the dynamic work we do in the group sessions. The shifts happening in humanity's perception and awareness of society in the last year and a half is evidence of our dynamic work. It is subtle but profound. If you want to take part in changing the world, you may be prompted to participate with us. It requires no particular commitment to anyone or any agenda to share in the work we do.

(Say each statement three times while tapping on your head and say it a fourth time while tapping on your chest.)

"We declare ourselves surrogates for humanity in doing these taps; in all moments."

"We release being lied to by the media; in all moments."

"We release being diminished by the media; in all moments."

"We release being devalued individuals by the media; in all moments."

"We release being manipulated by the media; in all moments."

"We release being subjugated by the media; in all moments."

"We release having our voice squelched by the media; in all moments."

"We release having our vantage point skewed by the media; in all moments."

"We release being stripped of our power by the media; in all moments."

"We strip all illusion off the media; in all moments."

"We withdraw all our energy from the media; in all moments."

"We take back our power from the media; in all moments."

"We remove all masks, walls and armor from the media; in all moments."

"We shatter all glass ceilings that the media has put on us; in all moments."

"We remove all vivaxes between ourselves and the media; in all moments."

"We remove all tentacles between ourselves and the media; in all moments."

"We release worshipping the media; in all moments."

"We remove the claws of the media from our beingness; in all moments."

"We remove all programing and conditioning that the media has put on us; in all moments."

"We remove all engrams that the media has instilled in us; in all moments."

"We remove the reactionary state that the media has put us in; in all moments."

"We eliminate the first cause in regards to the media; in all moments."

"We send all energy matrices into the light and sound that empower the media; in all moments."

"We command all complex energy matrices that empower the media to be escorted into the light and sound; in all moments."

"We send all energy matrices into the light and sound that

diminish the individual; in all moments."

"We command all complex energy matrices that diminish the individual to be escorted into the light and sound; in all moments."

"We send all energy matrices into the light and sound that squelch truth; in all moments."

"We command all complex energy matrices that squelch truth to be escorted into the light and sound; in all moments."

"We nullify all contracts between ourselves and the media; in all moments."

"We recant all vows and agreements between ourselves and the media; in all moments."

"We remove all curses between ourselves and the media; in all moments."

"We remove all blessings between ourselves and the media; in all moments."

"We sever all strings, cords and wires between ourselves and the media; in all moments."

"We release deferring to the media; in all moments."

"We release worshipping the media; in all moments."

"We dissolve all karmic ties between ourselves and the media; in all moments."

"We take back our empowerment from the media, in all moments."

"We remove all the pain, burden and limitations that the media has put on us; in all moments."

"We remove all the pain, burden and limitations that we have put on all others due to the media; in all moments."

"We remove all the fear, futility and unworthiness that the media has put on us; in all moments."

"We remove all the fear, futility and unworthiness that we have put on all others due to the media; in all moments."

"We remove all the apathy, indifference and deceit that the media has put on us; in all moments."

"We remove all the apathy, indifference and deceit that we have put on all others due to the media; in all moments."

"We remove all the helplessness and illusion of separateness the media has put on us; in all moments."

"We remove all the helplessness and illusion of separateness we have put on all others due to the media; in all moments."

"We take back for ourselves and all others all that the media has taken from us; in all moments."

"We release resonating with the media; in all moments."

"We release emanating with the media; in all moments."

"We extract all of the media from our sound frequency; in all moments."

"We extract all of the media from our light emanation; in all moments."

"We extract all of the media from all 32 layers of our auric field; in all moments."

"We extract all of the media from our whole beingness; in all moments."

"We shift our paradigm from the media to exponential Joy, Love, Abundance, Truth, and Freedom; in all moments."

"We transcend the media; in all moments."

"We collapse and dissolve the media; in all moments."

"We convert the media to exponential Joy, Love, Abundance, Truth, and Freedom; in all moments."

"We are centered and empowered in exponential Joy, Love, Abundance, Truth, and Freedom; in all moments."

"We resonate, emanate and are interconnected with all life in exponential Joy, Love, Abundance, Truth, and Freedom; in all moments."

Being

The unequivocal distinction between thinking and knowing

The symbiotic relationship between coming and going

The melodic precision of a satisfying resound

Commanding a presence without uttering a sound.

A defining conjecture that becomes a decree

Obeying it faithfully, are we really free?

Incredible grace while being under fire

The fortitude it takes to fulfill any desire.

The dancing arrangement of atoms of air

Bantering with inconsistencies that aren't really there

Being is being either close or afar

We all belong somewhere wherever we are.

10/22/13

The Prism of Our Own Wonder

Do you see the humanity in each person, situation or expression of life? Everything and everyone have purpose, are trying to thrive, have a point of view. You know how you think within yourself? Everything and everyone else do that as well. They may not be aware of their self-talk, but it exists. They know themselves as individualized.

If you want to understand your own humanity and tap into your own sweetness, ask yourself what other forms of life are experiencing in that moment. Instead of watching the birds in the bath, feel what it must be like to be among them. Experience the needy anguish of your furry family members to be near you and how it translates differently with the dog or cat. Be present with those you meet, not in a too familiar way, but in a silent yet discernible, "I understand. I have been there too," kind of way.

Do you realize when you have offended your cat by not giving them the proper respect and attention that they deserve when they join you just as you are enthralled in something? Do you recognize when you have insulted your dog even if he does not? How many times a day do you send them away or dismiss them when they have something pressing to share like a ball, a cuddle or a nap?

Do you recognize what is entailed in the life of every human that shows up in your day? I am certain you would not want to swap burdens. What incredible strength, fortitude and resilience it takes for every single person to be present with you in this incredibly complicated society. Do you acknowledge a fraction of their journey with a smile or a word of kindness? Or do you dismiss them as inconsequential?

The society at large is a reflection of these infractions that we are all guilty of every day. By being aware of the journey of others and acknowledging it, we unfold life from this one-dimensional viewpoint to a myriad of expressions. We create ripple and movement and layers to our otherwise conventional world. Who is tired of painting this world with one broad brushstroke? Who wants to join me in pixelating every interaction with vibrancy and depth?

In this way, you are the creator. You live, move and have your experiences within the confines of a cutout world just like cutout dolls. It is generic and plain to the non-discerning eye of conformity. But you with your richness of depth and passion see the multifaceted reality of a world brimming with potential, individuals starving to share their unique point of view and be validated for it.

You can do that. We can do that. We, who are crumbling the last hint of rust-worn shackles away from our wrists. We can unhinge the impingement of our expressions and realize, not only our own wonder, but the wonder in all. It is not done by commiserating. It is done by seeing a glint of others' greatness as it hits the light of acceptance and using ourselves as a reflection so that they can see the prism of their own wonder. Perhaps this is the secret to how we start seeing our own greatness.

God Doesn't Hate You

It's no secret to many that organized religion has caused many to feel less connected to God than the opposite intention. Nothing on earth is perfect. A religion may have the best intention but there may be a disconnect between sacred doctrine and knowing the heart and intention of each member of the flock.

In past lives, many of us have been ostracized, excommunicated, martyred, soldiers in holy wars and just plain disillusioned. These experiences are so ingrained that they may interfere with feelings of worthiness in the present and our relationship with God.

Here are some taps that may assist with deep feelings of unworthiness and separation from Love. If you have a resistance to doing them, that could be a clue that they may be helpful in releasing some deep-seated emotions and beliefs.

(Say each statement three times while tapping on the head, and say it a fourth time while tapping the chest.)

"I release the belief that God hates me; in all moments."

"I release the belief that I am damned; in all moments."

"I release the belief that I am unworthy of God's Love; in all moments."

"I release the trauma of being martyred; in all moments."

"I release the guilt of cursing God; in all moments."

"I release the belief that I am separate from God; in all moments."

"I am centered in God's Love; in all moments."

Be Raw Energy

Clients usually get tired yet invigorated by their sessions. My last client was not as charged as she usually is at the end of a private remote session. She started telling me she was fatigued. She had a lot going on.

People who are givers feel like they are depleting themselves by giving. That is because they forget their infinite potential. Remember being a child and believing you could do anything? Children draw on that infinite component within themselves.

The sun feeds warmth, nutrition and energy to a whole solar

system. But it doesn't just emanate outward. It rolls on itself, bubbles and churns; it feeds its own self by its very nature. That is what children do and that is what adults get away from.

These taps came through for my client to do. The first one helped her feel better. Each tap seemed to recharge her instantly, and her energy field filled up and expanded. Here are the taps:

(Say each statement three times while tapping on your head and say it a fourth time while tapping on your chest.)

"I release shutting down myself as raw energy; in all moments."

"I open up the floodgates of myself as raw energy; in all moments."

"I emanate as the personification of raw energy; in all moments."

"I activate myself as raw energy; in all moments."

"I activate the exponentiation of myself as raw energy; in all moments."

"I release the fear of losing myself; in all moments."

"I emanate beyond the awareness of all universes; in all moments."

"I maintain the awareness of the boundaries of self; in all moments."

"I am centered and empowered in Divine Love; in all moments."

Release Being Egocentric

(Say each statement three times out loud while tapping on the top of your head at the crown chakra and say it a fourth time while tapping on your chest.)

"I release the obsession with the self; in all moments."

"I release being egocentric; in all moments."

"I release confusing being self-centered with being selfish; in all moments."

"I shift my paradigm from selfish to self-centered; in all moments."

"I release continuously feeding the ego; in all moments."

"I release the vortex of need attached to the ego; in all moments."

"I release being a succubus for attention; in all moments."

"I release the fear of non-existence without the ego; in all moments."

"I release the need to outshine others; in all moments."

"I release defining life as a competition of egos; in all moments."

"I release confusing having a big ego with being important; in all moments."

"I release confusing having a big ego with living my purpose; in all moments."

"I release using the ego to overcompensate for feeling lack; in all moments."

"I release allowing the ego to pull me out of my center; in all moments."

"I release wasting so much energy fixating on the needs of the ego; in all moments."

"I shift my paradigm from serving the ego to honoring others; in all moments."

"I shift my paradigm from the ego to Joy, Love, Abundance, Freedom, Life and Wholeness; in all moments."

"I am centered and empowered in Joy, Love, Abundance, Freedom, Life and Wholeness; in all moments."

"I resonate and emanate Joy, Love, Abundance, Freedom, Life and Wholeness; in all moments."

Stop Being Manipulated or Coerced

(Say each statement three times out loud while tapping on the top of your head at the crown chakra and say it a fourth time while tapping on your chest.)

"I release being manipulated and coerced into disease; in all moments."

"I release being manipulated and coerced into problems; in all moments."

"I release being manipulated and coerced into gossip; in all moments."

"I release being manipulated and coerced into apathy; in all moments."

"I release being manipulated and coerced into depression; in all moments."

"I release being manipulated and coerced into overcompensation; in all moments."

"I release being manipulated and coerced into poverty; in all moments."

"I release being manipulated and coerced into weakness; in all moments."

"I release being manipulated and coerced into helplessness; in all moments."

"I release being manipulated and coerced into anger; in all moments."

"I release being manipulated and coerced into greed; in all moments."

"I release being manipulated and coerced into attachment; in all moments."

"I release being manipulated and coerced into vanity; in all moments."

"I release being manipulated and coerced into lust; in all moments."

"I release being manipulated and coerced into sloth; in all moments."

"I release being manipulated and coerced into self-pity; in all moments."

"I release being manipulated and coerced into martyrdom; in all moments."

"I release being manipulated and coerced into servitude; in all moments."

"I release being manipulated and coerced into arrogance; in all moments."

"I release being manipulated and coerced into manipulation; in all moments."

"I release being manipulated and coerced into indifference; in all moments."

"I release being manipulated and coerced into cruelty; in all moments."

"I shift my paradigm from being manipulated and coerced to being empowered and free; in all moments."

"I am centered in freedom and empowerment; in all moments."

"I am satiated in freedom and empowerment; in all moments."

"I resonate and emanate freedom and empowerment; in all moments."

Centered in Love

A client came to me for help with panic attacks. She told me that she felt overwhelmed and that she thought that she was going to die. Both feelings are forms of processing experiences. Our thoughts and feelings are not who we are. They are gauges for maneuvering our way around the Universe.

Feelings and thoughts are like the fingertips of the body. They are only aspects of our essence. They are tools to guide us to a greater truth.

We did a lot of work around the issue and she had an ah-ha moment. She realized that meditation was a way to separate from the thoughts and the emotions to get a better understanding of the greater self.

Here are some taps to help:

(Say each statement three times while tapping on your head; say a fourth time while tapping on your chest.)

"I release the belief that I am my emotions; in all moments."

"I release the belief that I am my thoughts; in all moments."

"I align all aspects of myself in all moments."

"I am centered in Divine Love; in all moments."

If God is Love, then when we are giving love, we are giving God. We are being Godlike. In this way, may we all have a God complex. Maybe, when the whole world adopts this, the whole world will glow with the complexion of God.

6. SOURCE

Love in the End

Solar flares

Winter Blues

Indian Summer

Deja vu

Quiet outbursts

Putting allegations to bed

Are we guided by angels

Or just randomly led?

Each season's solstice

Swimming up creek

Finding answers to questions

Disinherited by the meek

Desiring to go further

Than your leash will allow

Finding God in all places

Even in worshiping a cow

Searching all temples
Revisiting old shrines
Is your God the real one?
Or is it mine?

Standing on a pulpit
Or shouting from the street
Find Love in all places
Shake hands when you meet

Nature or nurture
It doesn't really matter
If you feel God's love is innate
Or is won by your flatter

When your blood, brains and bones
Are put into the ground
It's the you that is left
That still hovers around

Ascends into heaven

Re-acclimates

Remembers it's been there

Revisits its fate

It does it all over

Again and again

Until you realize each moment

That we're all love in the end.

9/26/14

Come On in! The Water's Fine

I believe so many want to give to their hearts' content but they are afraid of being duped or looking foolish. I think it takes some of us who don't mind being duped who will put everything they have into giving, so others can feel comfortable jumping into the pool of giving too. Some want to dip their toe in but are afraid of what they may encounter. To them I say, "The water is fine! Dive right in!" The masses will follow.

Give your gifts, share your dreams, hug those trees, look into the intangible realms, awaken your spirit, rise to the occasion, dive into life, go with the flow and conquer your demons. They are merely shadows that crave the light too. Force-feed them love if you must. Just don't allow anything to prevent you from living as dynamically and adventurously as your nature will allow.

When you live on the cusp of insanity, it is then that you awaken to your truth. What could be more insane than living in a world of complacency where unkind acts are sanctioned with denial? This reality nullifies all bets to living in accordance with society. It's time to dust off and unfurl that freak flag. Wave it high over the heads of the indifferent.

Stillness isn't always peace but stagnant waters. Splash around a bit! Life should be choppy. Churn the waters. Kick your feet and propel humanity into its depth! Encourage others to realize that the water is fine.

Your Relationship with God

Know that in doing these taps, you will never disconnect from the beautiful, loving source of all of creation. This is to release all the bastardization of the sacred trust that has happened through the history of man speaking for God. Just like God is used in the present day to sway our political opinion, God has been used throughout history to manipulate the hearts and minds of man. That form of deception is what these taps are addressing.

(Say each statement three times out loud while tapping on the top of your head at the crown chakra and say it a fourth time while tapping on your heart chakra.)

"I release the belief that God hates me; in all moments."

"I release the belief that I am damned; in all moments."

"I release the belief that God is punishing me; in all moments."

"I release the belief that I am a sinner; in all moments."

"I release the belief that I am forsaken; in all moments."

"I release feeling abandoned by God; in all moments."

"I release the trauma of being sacrificed to God; in all moments."

"I release confusing God for the will of the ruling power; in all moments."

"I release the guilt and confusion of killing in God's name; in all moments."

"I release diminishing others and justifying it as God's will; in all moments."

"I release defiling the sanctity of God with my interpretation; in all moments."

"I release desecrating God; in all moments."

"I release the belief that God is anything but love; in all moments."

"I release confusing God with power; in all moments."

"I release the belief that God has an ego; in all moments."

"I release cursing God; in all moments."

"I release the belief that God has cursed me; in all moments."

"I release confusing God with the interpretation of God; in all moments."

"I recant all vows and agreements between myself and God; in all moments."

"I remove all curses between myself and God; in all moments."

"I remove all blessings between myself and God; in all moments."

"I sever all strings and cords between myself and God; in all moments."

"I dissolve all karmic ties between myself and God; in all moments."

"I remove all the pain, burden, limitations and engrams that God has put on me; in all moments."

"I remove all the pain, burden, limitations and engrams that I have put on all others due to God; in all moments."

"I take back all the Joy, Love, Abundance, Freedom, Health, Success, Security, Companionship, Peace, Life, Wholeness, Beauty, Enthusiasm, Contentment, Spirituality, Enlightenment, Confidence and Ability to Discern that God has taken from me; in all moments."

"I give back all the Joy, Love, Abundance, Freedom, Health, Success, Security, Companionship, Peace, Life, Wholeness, Beauty, Enthusiasm, Contentment, Spirituality, Enlightenment, Confidence and Ability to Discern that I have taken from all others due to God; in all moments."

"I infuse purity, reverence and love into my understanding of God; in all moments."

"I extract anything that is not sacred, pure love from my understanding of God; in all moments."

"I am centered and empowered in a loving God that is benevolent beyond reproach; in all moments."

"I Am that I Am; in all moments."

Love stays in love and allows all others to cleanse themselves by its presence. Love can't do this if it comes out of its sheen to be anything other than pure love.

Being Empowered in the Moment

The goal is to be totally immersed in the moment because that is where heaven, providence, nirvana or bliss is. Anything that detracts you from being empowered in the moment is a sabotage to your own spiritual empowerment. All thoughts, beliefs, different experiences on the time track or different realities in the space-time continuum can be a deterrent to being in heaven if they prevent you from embracing the moment. This is so of self-deprecation or the belief that you are not as empowered as any other average enlightened being.

(Say each statement below three times out loud while tapping on the top of your head at the crown chakra, and say it a fourth time while tapping on your chest at the heart chakra.)

"I declare myself a surrogate for average individuals in doing these taps; in all moments."

"I release the need to be average; in all moments."

"I release the fear of not being average; in all moments."

"I release the fear of being called out; in all moments."

"I release the fear of being persecuted; in all moments."

"I release forgetting who I am; in all moments."

"I release the fear of remembering who I am; in all moments."

"I release the fear of remembering my dreams; in all moments."

"I release forgetting my dreams; in all moments."

"I release the fear of my past lives; in all moments."

"I release forgetting my past lives; in all moments."

"I release the fear of losing myself in a dream; in all moments."

"I release the fear of losing myself in a past life; in all moments."

"I remove all vivaxes between myself and all other matter, energy, space, time, realities and dimensions; in all moments."

"I remove all tentacles between myself and all MEST*, realities, and dimensions; in all moments."

"I remove the claws of all other MEST, realities, and dimensions from my beingness; in all moments."

"I remove all programming and conditioning from all other MEST, realities and dimensions; in all moments."

"I remove all programming and conditioning that all other MEST, realities and dimensions have put on us; in all moments."

"I remove all engrams that all other MEST, realities and dimensions have put on us; in all moments."

"I collapse and dissolve all portals, wormholes, and passageways to all other MEST, realities and dimensions; in all moments."

"I remove the claws of all other MEST, realities and dimensions from our beingness; in all moments."

"I remove all the pain, burden and limitations that all other MEST, realities and dimensions have put on us; in all moments."

"I remove all the fear, futility and unworthiness that all other MEST, realities and dimensions have put on us; in all moments."

"I remove all the illusion of failure and separateness that all other MEST, realities and dimensions have put on us; in all moments."

"I send all energy matrices into the light and sound that cause us to be sidetracked by all other MEST, realities and dimensions; in all moments."

"I command all complex energy matrices that cause us to be sidetracked by other MEST, realities and dimensions to be escorted into the light and sound; in all moments."

"I recant all vows and agreements between ourselves and all other MEST, realities and dimensions; in all moments."

"I release being duped in thinking we're all other MEST, realities and dimensions; in all moments."

"I remove all curses between ourselves and all other MEST, realities and dimensions; in all moments."

"I remove all blessings between ourselves and all other MEST, realities and dimensions; in all moments."

"I take back all that all other MEST, realities and dimensions have taken from us; in all moments."

"I strip all illusion off of all other MEST, realities and dimensions; in all moments."

"I remove all masks, walls, and armor from all other MEST, realities and dimensions; in all moments."

"I collapse and dissolve all negative influences from all other MEST, realities and dimensions; in all moments."

"I release resonating with all other MEST, realities and dimensions; in all moments."

"I release emanating with all other MEST, realities and dimensions; in all moments."

"I extract all of all other MEST, realities and dimensions from our sound frequency; in all moments."

"I extract all of all other MEST, realities and dimensions from our light emanation; in all moments."

"I extract all of all other MEST, realities and dimensions from our whole beingness; in all moments."

"I shift our paradigm from all other MEST, realities and dimensions to being totally present in the moment; in all moments."

"I transcend all other MEST, realities and dimensions; in all moments."

"I am centered and empowered in being totally in the moment; in

all moments."

"I release the fear of pushing the envelope; in all moments."

"I shift my paradigm from being a chicken to being an eagle; in all moments."

"I release the fear of transcending the male God consciousness; in all moments."

"I release the fear of transcending the human consciousness; in all moments."

*MEST - matter, energy, space and time

One Thought of You

I indulged in one quick thought of you

Etched it in my mind

It transported me to a world

That alone I could not find

Where Love is not sectioned off in pairs

Single file, one to one

But is lavished generously and prevalent

On every single one

Sincerity is commonplace

Intimacy too

Kind intentions are transparent

In everything we do

Love is not locked away
Allotted to just one heart
It is what all eat, sleep, dream and wear
And which we're all a part

It's not cast off with ill regard
Or based upon a whim
No, love is what we walk through
Dance, and fly and swim

One thought of you takes me there
Heals my weary heart
That runs this body in this world of illusion
Where we are all separated and apart

Allow me one quick thought
That transforms me to a place
Where everyone in betrothed to love
In sanctity and grace

I can then withstand loneliness

As a temporary state

Love is not a random act

Payment, door prize or fate

Love is not contingent

On believing, hope or prayer

Love is allotted to everyone

Even if no one says they care

Meet me in a land

Devoid of guilt or blame

Where I am allowed to love you

With no hint of shame

Meet me at the altar

Where, in this world is only meant for two

But in this altered Universe

Is shared with everyone and you

I devote my time on earth

To showing others this world too

The one I so easily access

With just one thought of you.

Infinite Source of Love

It is funny how we size each other up and create a pecking order. Is it really necessary for survival anymore? We see that this one is better looking than we are or that this one is less socially savvy. We vacillate between feeling inferior and superior. This is a self-induced prison for all. It dries up the loving conduits.

If we could all look at the germ of Love within each, the part of them that is loved by their family and unconditionally supported, then it would be easier to not create the pecking order. The even more freeing component of this vantage point is that when we can see that germ of love in others, we can connect to our own loving core as well.

Once we realize our own nature, we can expound upon that to create beautiful synapses between ourselves and the core nature of everyone else. Where there were once dry riverbeds, there can again be perpetual flowing pathways to infinite love and connectedness between others. It will be so much easier for everyone to tap into their innate nature and be uplifted by an infinite source of Love.

Accelerate the Timeline for Manifesting Universal Joy, Love, and Abundance

(Say each statement three times while tapping on your head and say it the fourth time while tapping on your chest.)

"We declare ourselves surrogates for humanity in doing these taps; in all moments."

"We make space in this world for Universal Joy; in all moments."

"We remove all blockages to accepting Universal Joy; in all

moments."

"We activate the accelerated timeline for accepting Universal Joy; in all moments."

"We make space in this world for Universal Love; in all moments."

"We remove all blockages to accepting Universal Love; in all moments."

"We activate the accelerated timeline for accepting Universal Love; in all moments."

"We make space in this world for Universal Abundance; in all moments."

"We remove all blockages to accepting Universal Abundance; in all moments."

"We activate the accelerated timeline for accepting Universal Abundance; in all moments."

"We activate the accelerated timeline of accepting Universal Abundance; in all moments."

"We make space in this world for Universal Freedom; in all moments."

"We remove all blockages to embracing Universal Freedom; in all moments."

"We activate the accelerated timeline of accepting Universal Freedom; in all moments."

"We make space in this world for Universal Health; in all moments."

"We remove all blockages to realizing Universal Health; in all moments."

"We activate the accelerated timeline of realizing Universal Health; in all moments."

"We make space in this world for Universal Success in living one's purpose; in all moments."

"We remove all blockages to Universal Success in living one's purpose; in all moments."

"We activate the accelerated timeline of accepting Universal Success in living one's purpose; in all moments."

"We make space in this world for Universal Confidence; in all moments."

"We remove all blockages to owning Universal Confidence; in all moments."

"We activate the accelerated timeline of accepting the Universal Confidence; in all moments."

"We break up the stagnant energy; in all moments."

"We make space in this world for Universal Interconnectedness; in all moments."

"We remove all blockages to Universal Interconnectedness; in all moments."

"We activate the accelerated timeline of Universal Interconnectedness; in all moments."

"We make space in this world for Universal Creativity; in all moments."

"We remove all blockages to Universal Creativity; in all moments."

"We activate the accelerated timeline of Universal Creativity; in all moments."

"We make space in this world for Universal Peace; in all

moments."

"We remove all blockages to Universal Peace; in all moments."

"We activate the accelerated timeline of Universal Peace; in all moments."

"We make space in this world for Universal Life; in all moments."

"We remove all blockages to Universal Life; in all moments."

"We activate the accelerated timeline of Universal Life; in all moments."

"We make space in this world for Universal Wholeness; in all moments."

"We remove all blockages to Universal Wholeness; in all moments."

"We activate the accelerated timeline of Universal Wholeness; in all moments."

"We make space in this world for Universal Beauty; in all moments."

"We remove all blockages to Universal Beauty; in all moments."

"We activate the accelerated timeline of Universal Beauty; in all moments."

"We make space in this world for Universal Enthusiasm; in all moments."

"We remove all blockages to Universal Enthusiasm; in all moments."

"We activate the accelerated timeline of Universal Enthusiasm; in all moments."

"We make space in this world for Universal Contentment; in all moments."

"We remove all blockages to Universal Contentment; in all moments."

"We activate the accelerated timeline of Universal Contentment; in all moments."

"We make space in this world for Universal Spirituality; in all moments."

"We remove all blockages to Universal Spirituality; in all moments."

"We activate the accelerated timeline of Universal Spirituality; in all moments."

"We make space in this world for Universal Enlightenment; in all moments."

"We remove all blockages to Universal Enlightenment; in all moments."

"We activate the accelerated timeline of Universal Enlightenment; in all moments."

"We make space in this world for Universal Awareness; in all moments."

"We remove all blockages to Universal Awareness; in all moments."

"We activate the accelerated timeline of Universal Awareness; in all moments."

"We make space in this world for Universal Discernment; in all moments."

"We remove all blockages to Universal Discernment; in all moments."

"We activate the accelerated timeline of Universal Discernment; in all moments."

"We make space in this world for Universal Individual Empowerment; in all moments."

"We remove all blockages to Universal Individual Empowerment; in all moments."

"We activate the accelerated timeline of Universal Individual Empowerment; in all moments."

"We are centered and empowered in the activation of the accelerated timelines; in all moments."

"We resonate, emanate, and are interconnected with all life in the activation of the accelerated timelines; in all moments."

Love

Love is ongoing in every true way. Everyone that we have ever loved, we are still in love with them. We permeate with that love and pull others into it through the journey. It never ends. Love at first sight is a memory of what is.

As we go through the funhouse of time, love gets distorted. We are aghast when it is stretched or distorted, and saddened when we walk away from the mirror. But we are not separated from it. How can we be separated from love when it is the force that turns the cogs of our very own atoms?

When you turn away from the notion of love, it is like trying to turn off your own existence. It is not possible. This is so silly in concept, yet so painful for those who forget their own nature. The most confusing thing about love is that in its purest form, it strikes the consciousness as a stillness. The mind interprets this as a nothingness, which spins the whole experience as an absence of love.

All the forces of the Universe are converging to buoy you in time and space so you can realize how incredibly loved you are. Yet to the weary heart, it feels like emptiness. Life is one long journey to realize yourself as the true source of love that you are. The struggle is to challenge that base nature that says otherwise and refute the findings of the fickle emotions. Redefine and expand your definition of love. Turn love inside out like a reversible jacket and warm yourself with your own lining.

Think of love as the stillness of the Universe, which is reflected in nature. Love is the quietude of a new mother taking inventory of her new babe. It is tolerating a million transgressions of an annoying younger sibling. Love is honoring a pet's nap as you dutifully sit still so as not to wake them. It is the inner communication of the trees that nurture everyone so graciously while systemically being denied a voice.

There is no way not to be loved unless you gauge the definition by the flawed attempts of other humans to gain understanding. They are the ones flailing around in desperation for validation too. It is like looking for the starving to feed you. The best way to be embraced in love is to make a house of it from the sticks you have collected yourself. That way you always take ownership of your own house. And that is the greatest security there is.

Innate Truths

Each individual is powerful beyond compare.

Everyone is capable of reaching the heights of great accomplishments.

Joy in doing what you love is not work.

Everyone has gifts and talents to contribute to humanity. Society is overrated.

Everyone should be able to explore their talents and to discover their own gifts.

Our thoughts and feelings are palpable to others.

Our words and thoughts are tuning forks to bring one in alignment with what we say.

Everyone carries great responsibility in what they bring to others.

It is a form of mass enslavement to agree to negative scenarios.

We have been conditioned to hold ourselves in a lower state of consciousness by thoughts, words and actions.

It has become socially acceptable to agree with mass enslavement.

Those who try to free humanity with their words, actions and beliefs are demonized by those who are conditioned to the mass slavery.

We are not linear beings that live a stick figure life. We are exponential starbursts that have forgotten our dimensions.

Our energy gets mangled by being exponential but living as a linear being. It is no different than a starburst being pulled out of its orbit to tow a straight line.

All groups, including family, society, governments and religions, reinforce mass enslavement by forcing the individual into a linear stance rendering them separate from their empowerment.

If man was left alone to his own wits in understanding his relationship with Source, he would more easily embrace his innate worth and have a better awareness of himself as a spiritual being. In nature, he would understand his nature.

All groups serve the purpose of the group. In doing so, they forgo the needs of the many.

All groups are beholden to individuals to sustain them. That makes individuals more powerful than any group.

Religions worship the concept of God. God did not make man in his image. Man made God in MAN's image. That is why God is depicted as needing adulation, worship or obedience. These are things man demands of others, not God.

The Dark Ages never ended. Man has just been savvier in his ignorance.

We are on a precipice of enlightenment as all individuals witness the limitations of greed and group control.

Man is in the process of relinquishing the need for power to his craving of creativity and truth.

Our imagination and creativity feed the realms of God.

The apathetic state we have created on earth bleeds through the heavens.

A wonderful life in heaven is not owed to us simply by existing.

The welfare state that we so fear is an apathetic state that we are immersed in with individuals being unable to nurture their natural gifts. This energetic welfare state dries up as all souls awaken to their creativity, imagination, empowerment and benevolence.

We feed higher states of consciousness or heaven with our creativity and kindness.

What we do in deed and thought contributes or depletes all of heaven.

Truth and love resonate at similar frequencies. The reason there is not more love in the world is because there is so little truth.

Our governing parties do not depict our collective state of consciousness. They depict the lowest common denominator of mankind.

To see a spike in the negativity in the dynamics of governing parties reflects the negativity in society. Governments are a microcosm of what the worst of man can expect from each other.

World peace is not a form of socialism. It is realized by every individual sharing their gifts to such an extent that they are too busy to judge, belittle or take from their fellow man.

Children should be allowed to give instead of conditioned to take.

The apathetic state that we have lived in is humanity reaching a glass ceiling at the third dimension.

We are living at the fifth dimension but have taken our own issues with us as a comfort until we get accustomed to the new reality of the fifth dimension.

The reason why healing, peace, individual empowerment and greater awareness is possible is because the limitations of the third dimension are no longer there.

More and more freedom and truth will be realized as people relinquish their old state of consciousness.

Fascination with the past or dreaming of the future are two ways of preventing one from experiencing the expansiveness of the moment.

Dreams are the higher self communicating great truth to the small fraction of the brain that we use.

We are all portals for any intention that we are able to pour our passion into. We can make this portal so big that all of humanity can pass through it.

All truth that has been collected through the ages pales compared to one's ability to tap into direct knowing in connection to their higher self.

Life Is a Classroom

Remember the trepidation on your first day of a new school year? Remember the fear in meeting a new teacher? Or the belief that you were going to fail a test but then you aced it?

Your problems, or the things that you are going through, are just another lesson to ace. The people that are bothering you are just your teachers. When things get overwhelming, it is just you moving to another level.

This life is a classroom. You have passed everything so far and so the illusion of failing is just that: something we tell ourselves until we see the lesson from another vantage point. Everything here is an opportunity for growth, wisdom and advantage. Now, put on your backpack and go!

Taps to Empowerment and Love

(Say each statement three times while tapping on your head and say it a fourth time while tapping on your chest.)

"I release needing permission; in all moments."

"I release asking for permission; in all moments."

"I release the need to search; in all moments."

"I release the fear of ending the search; in all moments."

"I release confusing ending the search with being separated from my consciousness; in all moments."

"I release being driven to find God; in all moments."

"I release kowtowing to authority; in all moments."

"I release distancing myself from the Ancient Ones; in all moments."

"I release trapping myself in unworthiness; in all moments."

"I remove all filters of fear; in all moments."

"I remove all filters of isolation; in all moments."

"I remove all filters of ego; in all moments."

"I remove all filters of differentiation; in all moments."

"I release the fear of trusting; in all moments."

"I release confusing new consciousness for old consciousness; in all moments."

"I remove all engrams of old consciousness; in all moments."

"I release confusing expanding my love with bleeding out; in all moments."

"I release the fear of bleeding out; in all moments."

"I remove all linear filters; in all moments."

"I connect to all hearts; in all moments."

"I dissolve all fear filters with my love; in all moments."

"I dissolve all ego filters with my love; in all moments."

"I beckon all Souls back to love with my love; in all moments."

"I send all energy matrices into the light that are not love; in all moments."

"I command all complex energy matrices that are not love to be escorted into the light by my guides; in all moments."

"I send all energy matrices into the sound that are not love; in all moments."

"I command all complex energy matrices that are not love to be escorted into the sound by my guides; in all moments."

Choosing Love over Power

Life is a school ground for souls to have their lessons. The purpose is to acquire every kind of experience necessary so one walks willingly into the heart of love. Those of us with an understanding of this know that we have abused power in the past. It is how we have learned that we don't ever want to abuse power again. It ingrained in us that deep drive for inner peace.

We then know that it is a loving act of grace to accept others' need to have a turn at abusing power. There are so many here now on earth who are doing all they can to fill that inner void with plays of power. In the very long run, it will make them more compassionate souls. They will eventually mature and that need, along with the void, will dry up. It is a necessary step in the unfolding of soul.

The rest of us need not be surprised at the lengths others are driven to feel validated and important. We know at the core they are motivated by deficiency and pain. What we can do is take up the slack and love all to compensate for what our leaders are unable to do. The more that we all love in all situations, the more we can encourage all to self-regulate and take the high ground. The more we all pour incredible love into the world, the more we can bring along all of the fledgling souls who are still struggling. Maybe it has never been done before because it has never been tried.

The more we give the exploits of power our attention or feel like the effect of them, the more we will be feeding them with high-octane fuel. Prove this to yourself by taking your attention off of worldly affairs and watch others try to pull you back into them. It is a disservice to us all to give our sacred attention to the squabbles of the spiritually immature. The more we focus on the Love, the more that love will be our mainstay.

The Reversed Alchemy of Turning Love to Fluid State

Love is like water in that it can be transformed to liquid, solid or gas. We have kept love in a solid state for way too long. Giving a gift or giving your love to just one person at a time is keeping love in a solid state. It is easier to control and doesn't spill on others but the person who is handling the love feels special and in charge.

This is what some religions have done with love. They keep it to acts of devotion and staying within the confines of their faith. They use stringent doctrine to gauge love. That is a very solid love. The reason prayer has been so important is that it converts love to a liquid or gaseous state but within the confines of a religion. It is still a very stringent form of love.

A liquid state of love is shared in doing kindness for others and having that love spill over onto others who are privy to the interaction. It is being loving to your family, but not only to your family. It is also being loving to other forms of life and all individuals. Love is fluid in the lives of some.

Gaseous love is living life with a deep reverence and gratitude. Gratitude is formless and can be breathed into the body with no conscious intention or need to try. The person is so immersed in love that gratitude just permeates their very atoms. They have achieved the alchemy of turning love into a gaseous state. And all those around them can partake in the graciousness of their abilities. This is a love that can rejuvenate the world.

The more we all transform love into a fluidity and then something others partake of through osmosis, the more we transform the very ether of life. This is how we uplift consciousness. We do this by putting no conditions on love or whom or what we love. The more we make love available to all, the more love will permeate and uplift all of life.

The New Alchemy

So many people are under the assumption that life is supposed to be easy. That there was a time when life was so simple and everything was handed to you. That was an illusion created by the materialistic generations of the modern era. It is something that needs to be addressed because it is isolating people in a false belief that life is something that doesn't take effort.

When in history was it easy? When people were foraging for food all day and hunting to survive? When people were migrating to new lands and figuring out a whole set of rules with their different environments? Was life easy during the centuries of the Crusades or the lifetimes of modern warfare? There have always been many variables to factor in to create a safe and secure environment.

When was love easy? People believe that they are just supposed to find the love of their life and live happily ever after with a white picket fence and the perfect school district. When was love ever perfect? Was it the centuries of arranged marriages where love was more about a bounty and a daughter was a selling point? Was it the lifetimes when people were together out of convenience to keep a land, name, or kingdom safe from outsiders and a marriage was a way to secure alliances? Were these the ideal times?

Why is it so important for women to feel young and beautiful? Was it because of all the lifetimes that their family's wealth depended on their beauty for a bargaining chip? Or their ability to attract a man to take care of them was literally a life or death situation? Or the times they got abandoned or rejected because they were too old to hunt for themselves? Without a male to provide for them, they were left behind by their tribe.

Do you know why it is considered so important to wait to have sex before marriage? It has little to do with God's law. It is a manmade law. Man did not want to have the neighboring tribe impregnate his daughters. He would then, in a sense, be giving his inheritance to the enemy in the form of his grandchildren. To a man's fragile ego and sense of ownership, this would be the highest insult.

He injected this mandate into his perception of Source and it has played out through history. All that is left of the original reason is the bigotry and judgment we see play out today. It is true that we are all a reflection of God--but the highest of man not the lowest common denominator. Man, projecting his pettiness onto a loving Source, has distorted the perception of God and twisted so many to a manmade will. God is love. God loves love. It is man who is jealous, petty and judgmental.

These are all primal issues that have played out in our psyche and have been stored in our DNA. They play out in our irrational fears and beliefs that everyone else has it better than we do and that no one understands the depths of our loneliness and despair. The truth of the matter is that our loneliness and disappointments in life are our commonality. They are what we all have as a common factor to transcend. Doing so brings the succor to being here.

The illusion that life is easier for everyone else is a misconception that creates further isolation. When there is a tragedy, everyone comes together because they understand everyone else is suffering as well and they can put their needs aside for the benefit of others. It is what gets them through in a time of crisis. Well, we are all in a time of crisis right now. Now is the time to pull together in that commonality for all of humanity.

We are on the precipice of receiving a new responsibility as a species. It is to accept the life conditions as they come and turn that life into something beautiful and wondrous from the raw materials that we have. The raw materials are our fortitude, resilience, unique abilities, passion, awareness and kindness. These are the building blocks of an incredible life of expansion and wonder.

What we do with our personal toolbox is up to us. We are the alchemists in the field study of awakening. Our depth, love and ingenuity will get us beyond the setback of a limited understanding of our own omnipotence. This has been deliberately erased from our tutelage.

If we can erase all the conditioning, if we can attune to the higher senses of our gut feelings and promptings of the heart, we can be guided to mass awakening. Our gut feelings and the prompting of the heart are our north star when given a mangled map to our true home. But like the North Star, our subtle senses will guide us to our destination. When we are kind, aware and present with integrity and truth, we glide more easily through the lands of illusion. Godspeed in us all finding our course.

Free Yourself by Sharing Your Gifts

Most people have it backwards. They wait until everything in their life is in balance before they will think about living their purpose. Most times that doesn't happen, and that is why so many people are disappointed in life and feel unfulfilled. But when people live their purpose, every area of their life falls into balance.

Look about you and pick up the sticks and blessings about you. Collect them in your arms and carry them to your sacred chamber. Piece them together and craft them into a fine instrument. Sand them and work them until they are smooth of all that does not represent your heart.

Use this instrument as your implement to fulfill your purpose. You are not worthless. You have merely scattered your wealth amongst the heavens and have waited for it wash back on the shores of your little self. They have. Now is the time to recollect, reinvent, and rename yourself.

You are not unworthy in any way. You hold the key to the multitudes embracing their own wonderment. They watch you from afar in the distant land of their own wonderment. They watch you like a moving light fleck on the moon and wonder if it is real. Are you real? Show them.

Show them your heart, soul and pure intention. Show them the pain from which you have emerged. Show them the umbilical cord to the shame that you cut when you recognize your true self. Teach them how to sever from the pain themselves.

Instruct them to tie the cord in two spaces to cut off the food supply to negativity. Tie off the self from this world of angst. Tie off the anguish from the self-pity. Wait for the throbbing pulse to weaken between these two parts. Cut yourself free.

Be sovereign in the Love. Beyond reproach. Let no one take you from the peace. You are sustained and immersed in the omniscience of a new dawn. You are the you, you always knew that you were. Forgetting the limitations that you had once adopted, you are free my friend in integrity and Light. You are free.

Transcending

Any group that says that it is the way to absolute truth is putting a cap on truth. It may be the purest way to truth and that can be absolutely right, but at some point, the individual has to break away from the rocket and maintain orbit of their own accord. To prevent this natural progression from occurring is defeating the whole purpose of the rocket.

The rocket itself can't maintain the orbit that the individual has been catapulted to. The sheer bulk of its words and guidelines are enough to ground the individual. One can stay in the hull of the rocket out of fear of crashing and burning, or one can do that task that all its training has led it to and trust in the process of transcending. It is done alone and unencumbered by doctrine.

This is the true test of mastership. It is not about loyalty or allegiance to the process but a willingness to soar to new heights in new realms. It is about encouraging others in their individuality to detach from all fear and to surrender all adornments, to be enlightened and sustained in the reality of unconditional, perpetual, pristine, divine love.

By being loving and kind in the world, we are acting as the breath of God.

Gaia Speaks

The cold strikes the human sky

Huddled in dwellings the natives ask why

Buried in arrogance and piles of snow

Believing there's nothing they don't possibly know

As a species they desecrate all natural gifts

Indifference accumulates in heavy white drifts

Cycles of weather come and go

Indolence the only fruit man's willing to sow

So many lessons left on the table

Humanity crippled by the willing and able

"Power" let out one last haughty laugh

Willing to sacrifice the last fatted calf

It will run this world to the ground

Frack it to ashes, a lifeless mound

Till Gaia steps in with an even brow

To balance the scales in the "here and now"

Dispensing truth that was once called treason

Gifting many with the ability to reason

Restoring justice back to the land

As a handful stand by who understand

There's no need to hoard what's in the ground

When abundance and blessings are all around

God: The Ultimate Search Engine

There's no need to take an eye for an eye

Leaving society glazed over, unable to cry

Abundance for all! The original decree

Is restored to every man, animal, species and tree

Taking for taking's sake is finally disarmed

Greed, glitz and gluttony stripped of its charm

Abusive power has become the enemy at large

As it finally sinks in, it's no longer in charge

In this ruthless weather, one stark truth ensues

The restoration of humanity exists in the empowerment of you

Thinking you are unworthy, unable to cope

Is telling everyone to give up all hope

Get off your ass, shake off the crumbs

Pound feeling back into your parts that went numb

You're not on the sidelines of some spectator sport

You are here to get messy, get involved, give support

The small you, you thought you were, was part of the lie

You can see through the illusion if you give it a try

Everyone is a superhero with their own special power

When you don't share your gifts, you just grow mean and sour

Embrace all your talents, hone all your crafts

The weather will break, when you get this! Alas...

One more truth that you really need to see

Gaia speaks to your heart through this message from me.

2/26/15

Prayers Needed!

I realized another layer to why prayer requests bother me so much. They represent a mentality that is either thinking too small or too selfishly. They represent the taker mentality. I know that sounds harsh but there are real issues that need to be addressed. The more that people are concerned with their own little lives, the less that these issues are addressed.

Again, I know this sounds harsh, but it represents my vantage point and understanding. The world is skewed by the taking mentality. The majority want to get their share. The greed and selfishness that are systemic in a world still primed for war show up in every single one of us as selfish intentions.

Our own lack of awareness, caring, and giving to others is an atom in the systemic greed that has created the apathy, indifference and imbalance in the world today. What we think, feel, say or do is reflected in what is thought, felt, said and done in the world at large. So when people are focused on their own needs, it is a distraction from the needs of so many suffering all around the world with nowhere to turn and no one to assist them.

I took a lot of criticism when I mentioned this issue before. People ruthlessly defended their right to ask for prayers for themselves, their dear ones, a friend of a friend or a distant cousin of a friend of a friend. Some of the requests were simply a cry for love. That is easy to do. I pour love into every being all over the world regularly as part of my contemplation practice. But to suck in attention instead of acknowledging one's own genius and sharing is unforgivable. The world is in dire need of the outflowing of your gifts.

You know how the best way to learn something is to teach it. Well, the best way to be healed from something is to heal others. Sending your prayers out to others who are in need more than you, beyond asking for help, or for whom it has never occurred that assistance is possible, is where love and prayers do the most good.

So please, if you are inclined to pray for others, or if you want to shift the world's paradigm from taking to giving, or if you are also frustrated when others ask for prayers to deal with their own spiritual lessons, please lend your prayers to any of the following issues. We will augment their effectiveness with a group consciousness and I will add my own healing abilities as an enhancer. I feel these souls and go to them as much as possible. Your prayers will truly help them.

Please pray for:

- All who live in poverty, hunger and ignorance
- Woman around the world who have few human rights
- All who are locked up and forgotten in prisons, basements or their own lives
- All who are neglected, forsaken, judged, diminished, controlled or who have given up hope
- Everyone who is being raped, tortured, or humiliated right now or ever
- All animals and people born in indifference and don't know what love is
- People who are so depraved that the only goal is to kill as many people a possible
- Everyone whose home, family, way of life is destroyed, even humans
- All those who are sucking poison down their lungs or gills with no other option
- All those who perpetuate a vindictive God
- All those who are targeted by a vindictive God
- All those who are sentenced to a life of apathy by a lack of choices
- All those sentenced to a life of entitlement which, for many, is a gilded form of ignorance
- All those who are dangling the strings of power and control over the masses
- All of the rest who are unwittingly dangled by strings
- Those who choose power over love
- Those who are afraid to speak their truth
- Those who are conditioned to fail
- All who are not recognized for their gifts and wisdom, including all trees
- Those who have contempt or indifference for a better world

- Those who refuse to share their genius out of false humility or fear
- Those who never think of anyone beyond their own walls.

This is the shortlist of those who are in dire need of prayer and love. All the taps and the techniques I give out are meant to help all these groups as well. They are always in my peripheral awareness. Perhaps doing the taps and reading my posts will make room for them in your peripheral awareness too.

All are worthy of love. By lessening the gap between the loved and the unloved, we can raise the quality of love for all. Our issues, losses, experiences and plights are mostly opportunities to strengthen our fortitude in this spiritual adventure. Those on the list are doing just that to a greater capacity. If nothing else, they deserve our love and respect for their fortitude.

You Are Who You Are

Either you know yourself to be a divine spark of God with freedom of choice or a breathing piece of matter that's a victim of circumstance. Decide who you are. If you are a victim of circumstance, then everyone else is a victim of circumstance as well. We are all made of the same stuff. But if you see the greatness in others, you must recognize greatness in yourself. If you then recognize greatness in yourself by default, you must take ownership of it.

You must then acquaint yourself with all the amenities that being a divine spark of God affords you. Because being a victim in an empowered state of awareness is just too much of a transgression to reasonably tolerate. This is what so many of us are grappling with right now. We are learning the blueprints and instruction manuals of this empowered self.

To shrivel up and cower on a wind glider or soar into the setting sun sniveling on one's knees is too ridiculous for any soul to wrestle with. Stand up and operate the equipment that you were equipped with. Don't you dare allow anyone to pull you around on a string or tow you to serve their own agenda. Operate under your own accord. Anything else is unworthy of the greatness of your capabilities.

A New Way to Pray

Instead of keeping a mental note of who is in need and who wants this and who needs that, why not assume all are worthy because they are! Why not just adopt the strategy that all would appreciate some extra love and support? Why not just send out our loving intention to all in a perpetual prayer of loving intention for every single being in the Universe?

Maybe the souls that need it most don't have any friends to reach out to, are in so much pain that they don't even know how to articulate it, are in such a state of apathy that they are paralyzed in their own despair, or are in an animal, plant, or mineral form. Maybe these souls could use loving prayers just as much as our friends who are having a crisis and being stretched in the moment.

Sending out loving intention to all eliminates the need for scrutiny, judgment or any other micromanagement that the ego or the mind would do. It keeps one in a perpetual state of loving prayer and it elevates humanity by having so many living conduits to the ultimate source pouring omniscient love into every corner of the Universe.

As for one's self, it is a healthy habit of keeping one centered, non-judgmental, always immersed in a loving flow and always contributing. Maybe being in a state of a perpetual outflowing of love is our natural state. Maybe the reason the world is so stressed is because so many have come out of this state. Maybe it is time for everyone to forget all their conditioning and just return to the love. Maybe by adopting this stance, we return to a synergy that returns the world to an uplifting place for all.

We Are the Paradigm Shift

We are here to Awaken, Inspire, Encourage, Teach, Heal, Lead, Love and Nurture each other. The days of falling into place are gone! We are here to blur the lines, push the envelope, cut to the chase, make snap decisions, hug a tree or two, jump off the precipice without a net and live our purpose in our incredible bliss.

We are meant to dive head first into the universal heart of humanity, forgo holding back, relinquish saving ourselves, forget what's in it for us. We are one. We are amazing. We are strongest when we free fall together in a perpetual blaze of Joy, Love, Abundance, Freedom and Wholeness for all.

It is no longer your bank account that defines you, a silly sequence of numbers guarded in a box built of power. It is your heart; it is your passion; it is your ability to connect with humanity through the illusion of separateness. It is about reaching through the clouds of indifference to touch the heart of someone who is still struggling with the fever of being alone. It is giving them a gentle, loving nudge to awaken them from the fitful nightmare. It is staying present with them for a minute as they wake up and get their bearings.

This is what we do for each other. This is what I do in sharing whatever gifts I have. It is with such a fervor to console everyone who is wondering why. It is for every soul who is struggling alone or shivering in a sheath of indifference. It is our love that warms them. We don't have to make others hear us to be heard. We need to merely whisper into the wind and we soothe the souls who hunger to feel the acceptance that we offer unencumbered with motive.

We are the paradigm shift. We have changed gears from being imprisoned by the mind to being awakened to the heart. We are the shift we are experiencing. Embrace your dynamic ability to empower the universe with your single voice. You are at the helm of an incredible upgrade in humanity. The more you embrace your dynamic self, the more you quicken its step. It is so.

GLOSSARY OF TERMS

There are some very complicated metaphysical concepts that do not need to be so difficult to understand. Anything that is fathomable in the Universe should be able to be simplified so a child can understand them. For instance, there are no words that explain the energy pull between two things. That would be the word vivaxes. As we become more enlightened, we will need more and more words to explain our ever expanding relationship with energy.

Claws: Sometimes and in some instances, one will feel psychically gripped by an issue. The best way to depict the feeling of this is with the word claws.

Engrams: Engrams are the way that past issues are stored in our energy field. Think of how a groove in a vinyl record plays a song repeatedly when a needle is inserted in the groove. An engram is a groove in your energy field that plays a behavior repeatedly.

Enlightenment: The formula process of meeting all of the negativity within you and stripping it away so one is no longer at the mercy of the ego and sees one more as a reflection of the higher realms than in reactionary mode.

Light Bodies: We seem like solid energy. But we are really made of layers of energy consisting of different vibrations. Our physical body is the coarsest. Then the emotions create a layer of vibration around that. People know that layer as the astral level of vibration. Then there is the level that contains the memory of every past experience. This layer is called the causal plane and the records are called the akashic records. After that layer of vibration is the mental realm. This is the same layer as the ego and it is why it is difficult to see beyond the mental realm because the ego tries to prevent it. Above that level, the duality of the lower vibrations is dropped and then energy beyond that is one of such purity, it registers as a neutrality. That is why feeling good is not the highest expression of love, but loving neutrality or detachment is a more spiritual state. The ego will convey this as bliss but in its true state, it is neither positive nor negative.

Light Emanation: We are not solid matter. In energy, we are a light emanation and a sound frequency woven together to give the illusion of matter.

Matrix (pl. matrices): Stagnant energy can exist in cloud form. We walk through it all the time during the day. It can affect our moods. If we walk through energy and it identifies with our vibration, it may collect in us as individuals and seem like an intrusion.

Complex Energy Matrix: When an energy matrix intrudes upon your energy system and identifies itself with a personality. It may convince you and it that it is an aspect of you or that it is a totally different individual that has taken you over in some way. It is merely stagnant energy that needs to be dissipated. No melodrama necessary. Just release it with the taps

Portal: An energetic gateway.

Psychic Stream of Energy: A compilation of a similar vibration of thoughts and emotions that creates a cloud like energy that can affect those who are subjected to it.

Sound Frequency: One of the two aspects of ourselves, the other one being Light emanation. All energy is either Light or Sound. Knowing ourselves as Sound Frequencies and Light Emanations is breaking ourselves down to our true state devoid of ego and ego limitations. It is as a Sound Frequency or Light Emanation that we are capable of traveling in all realms and knowing ourselves as Omniscient, Omnipotent and Omnipresent. It is also a means of communicating with Source or God in its native tongue.

Strings: When two energy sources touch, a string of connecting energy is formed between them. If attention is kept on this string, it can become reinforced with obsessive or repetitive thoughts. These strings need to be broken if one is going to be free of the object of the taps.

Tentacle: Energy that reaches out and attaches to someone perhaps to take from them or feed off their energy.

Vivaxis: An energy pull between two or more people, places or things.

Vortex: A vortex is an energy pull similar to a gravitational pull between two components. For example, there is a vortex between the sun and all the planets and there is a vortex between the earth and moon.

Wei chi: The "skin" on the surface of your energy field that provides a natural barrier to energies interrupting your natural function. It gets pierced and broken during trauma and then it is more difficult for an energy to hold its electromagnetic charge. Someone whose wei chi is in tact may have a natural magnetism.

www.jenuinehealing.com/sft-dictionary/

ABOUT THE AUTHOR

Jen Ward is an Ascended Master. This entails being a Reiki Master, gifted healer, inspirational speaker, author of many books and an innovator of a healing modality for self-empowerment. She offers a simple but dynamic protocol to assist individuals in clearing up all their energy imbalances (karma) with every person, experience, belief system and the Universe. She enables all those struggling, to cross the bridge of self-discovery, with her encouragement and instruction. Her passion is to empower the world by encouraging all individuals in their own miraculous healing adventure.

Jen is considered a sangoma, a traditional African shaman who channels ancestors, and clears energy by emoting sounds and vocalizations. An interesting prerequisite to being a sangoma is to have survived being on the brink of death. When it was first revealed that Jen was a sangoma, she had not yet fulfilled the rigorous prerequisites necessary. However, in April 2008, through a series of traumas, she returned to civilization meeting all the requirements. She passed through the transforming process of enlightenment. She returned to the world of humanity a devout soul inspired to serve.

Jen currently works diligently in the physical world and in the worlds of energy to assist all souls to reach greater heights of awareness and empowerment. Those who believe they have "arrived," may be the most entrenched in the mental realms. They can painlessly free themselves without relinquishing the comfort of their current belief system. All that needs to be released will fall away naturally. "Fear, in all its subtle forms of denial and judgment, will naturally fall away."

Many people report receiving healing assistance from Jen or protection in the dream state and even more subtle realms. Jen is passionate to shatter the mentality of sitting at the feet of another. She shares truth and wisdom graciously and abundantly. Jen makes the practice of doling out truth in increments to set up the dynamic of personality worship obsolete. Her passion is to assist the world over the brink of all perceived limitations, beyond the mind's scope, into the realms of enlightenment.

OTHER BOOKS BY JEN WARD

Enlightenment Unveiled: Expound into Empowerment. This book contains case studies to help you peel away the layers to your own empowerment using the tapping technique.

Grow Where You Are Planted: Quotes for an Enlightened "Jeneration." Inspirational quotes that are seeds to shift your consciousness into greater awareness.

Perpetual Calendar: Daily Exercises to Maintain Balance and Harmony in Your Health, Relationships and the Entire World. 369 days of powerful taps to use as a daily grounding practice for those who find meditation difficult.

Children of the Universe. Poetry to Elevate the Reader to the 5th Dimension. Passionate prose to lead the reader lovingly into expanded consciousness.

Letters of Accord: Assigning Words to Unspoken Truth. Truths that the ancient ones want you to know to redirect your life and humanity back into empowerment.

The Do What You Love Diet: Finally, Finally, Finally, Feel Good in Your Own Skin. Revolutionary approach to regaining fitness by tackling primal imbalances in relationship to food.

Emerging from the Mist: Awakening the Balance of Female Empowerment in the World. Release all the issues that prevent someone from embracing their female empowerment.

Affinity for All Life: Valuing Your Relationship with All Species. This book is a means to strengthen and affirm your relationship with the animal kingdom.

The Wisdom of the Trees. If one is struggling for purpose, they can find love, and truth by tuning into the Wisdom of the Trees.

Chronicles of Truth. Truth has been buried away for way too long. Here is a means to discover the truth that lies dormant within yourself.

Healing Your Relationships. This book is a means to open up communications and responsiveness to others so that clarity and respect can flourish again in society.

How to Awaken Your Inner Dragon: Visualizations to Empower Yourself and the World. Tap into the best possible version of you and the world.

Collecting Everyday Miracles: Commit to Being Empowered. This book is a thought provoking means to recreate the moment of conception with everyday miracles. It is through gratitude and awareness. This is what this book fosters.

The SFT Lexicon: Spiritual Freedom Technique. Tap into the powerful ability of the mind to self-heal.

Past Lives, Dreams and Inspiration. People are starving for truth. Unfortunately, they have been conditioned to dismiss their dreams and all remnants of past lives in discovering their own trajectory connection to truth. This book gives life to the expansiveness of self-discovery through one's past lives and dream experiences. There is no greater form of inspiration than discovering one's own depth.

2018 A Turning Point: Shift from Primal Mode to Enlightenment. If in 2018 you sensed a shift in the world, if you sensed an internal struggle happening on the world's behalf, if you are fascinated with truths that are hidden from the masses, or if you have some programming left that you would like to eliminate, this book is for you.

All of Jen's books can be found on her website at www.jenuinehealing.com.

Jen Ward

www.ingramcontent.com/pod-product-compliance
Lightning Source LLC
Chambersburg PA
CBHW032146080426
42735CB00008B/606